Free Will

BLACKWELL READINGS IN PHILOSOPHY

Series Editor: Steven M. Cahn

Blackwell Readings in Philosophy are concise, chronologically arranged collections of primary readings from classical and contemporary sources. They represent core positions and important developments with respect to key philosophical concepts. Edited and introduced by leading philosophers, these volumes provide valuable resources for teachers and students of philosophy, and for all those interested in gaining a solid understanding of central topics in philosophy.

Free Will

Edited by

Robert Kane

BLACKWELL Publishers

Copyright © Blackwell Publishers Ltd 2002
Editorial matter and organization copyright © Robert Hilary Kane 2002

First published 2002

2 4 6 8 10 9 7 5 3 1

Blackwell Publishers Inc.
350 Main Street
Malden, Massachusetts 02148
USA

Blackwell Publishers Ltd
108 Cowley Road
Oxford OX4 1JF
UK

Library of Congress Cataloging-in-Publication Data

Free will / edited by Robert Kane.
    p. cm. — (Blackwell readings in philosophy; 3)
    Includes bibliographical references and index.
    ISBN 0-631-22101-8 (alk. paper) — ISBN 0-631-22102-6 (pbk.: alk. paper)
    1. Free will and determinism. I. Kane, Robert, 1938 – II. Series.
    BJ1461 . F75 2001
    123'.5—dc21
                                   2001037591

British Library Cataloguing in Publication Data
A CIP catalogue record for this book is available from the British Library.

Typeset in 10/12.5pt Palatino
by Kolam Information Services Pvt. Ltd, Pondicherry, India

This book is printed on acid-free paper.

To Russell Hilary Kane, in memoriam

Contents

viii   *Contents*

Acknowledgments

The authors and publishers gratefully acknowledge the following for permission to reproduce copyright material:

Chisholm, Roderick., "Human Freedom and the Self" from the Lindley Lecture, 1964. Copyright by the Department of Philosophy, University of Kansas, reprinted by permission of the author and the University of Kansas.

Dennett, Daniel, "I Could Not Have Done Otherwise – So What?" *The Journal of Philosophy* LXXXI, 10 (October, 1984): 553–67, 10 page edited version.

Edwards, Paul, "Hard and Soft Determinism" from *Determinism and Freedom in the Age of Modern Science* (ed. Sidney Hook). Copyright 1958 by New York University Press and Professor Ernest B Hook.

Fischer, John Martin., "Frankfurt-style Examples: Responsibility and Semi-compatibilism" from "Recent Work on Moral Responsibility" *Ethics* 110 (October) 1999. Reprinted by permission of the author and The University of Chicago Press.

Frankfurt, Harry G., "Freedom of the Will and the Concept of a Person" *The Journal of Philosophy* LXVIII, 1 (January 14, 1971): 5–20.

Ginet, Carl, "Freedom, Responsibility and Agency" from *The Journal of Ethics* 1:1 (1997): 374–380, with kind permission of Kluwer Academic Publishers, Dordrecht.

Hasker, William, "God, Time, Knowledge and Free Will: The Historical Matrix" from *God, Time and Knowledge*. Copyright William Hasker (Cornell University Press, Ithaca, 1989).

Hodgson, David, "Chess, Life and Superlife" *The Journal of Consciousness Studies* vol. 6, no. 8–9 (1999), reprinted with permission from David Hodgson's article "Hume's Mistake".

Inwagen, Peter van, "The Incompatibility of Free Will and Determinism" from *An Essay on Free Will*. Copyright Peter van Inwagen (Oxford University Press, New York and Oxford, 1983).

Inwagen, Peter van, "The Mystery of Metaphysical Freedom" (excerpted) from *Metaphysics: The Big Questions* (ed. Peter van Inwagen and Dean Zimmerman) (Blackwell Publishers, Oxford, 1998).

Kane, Robert, "Free Will: New Directions for an Ancient Problem" new article: parts adapted from "Free Will: Ancient Dispute, New Themes" from *Reason and Responsibility* (ed. Joel Feinberg and Russell Chafer-Landau) (Wadsworth Publishers, 2001, courtesy Thomson Learning).

Nielsen, Kai, "The Compatibility of Freedom and Determinism" from *Reason and Practice*. Copyright Kai Nielsen (Harper and Row Publishers, New York, 1971).

O'Connor, Timothy, "The Agent as Cause" from *Metaphysics: The Big Questions* (ed. Peter van Inwagen and Dean Zimmerman) (Blackwell Publishers, Oxford, 1998).

Pereboom, Derk., "The Explanatory Irrelevance of Alternative Possibilities" from "Alternative Possibilities and Causal Histories" *Philosophical Perspectives* 14 (2000), reprinted by permission of Blackwell Publishers, Oxford.

Skinner, B.F., "Walden Two: Freedom and the Behavioral Sciences" from *Walden 2* by B. F. Skinner © 1977, reprinted by permission of Pearson Educational, Inc., Upper Saddle River, NJ 07458.

St Augustine, "Divine Foreknowledge, Evil and the Free Choice of the Will" from *On the Free Choice of the Will* (trans. A Benjamin and L Hackstaff) © 1964, reprinted by permission of Pearson Education, Inc., Upper Saddle River, NJ. 07458.

Watson, Gary, "Responsibility and the Limits of Evil: Variations on a Strawsonian Theme," pp. 256–86 (edited extract from p. 256–61 and 265–74) in Ferdinand Schoeman (ed.) *Responsibility, Character and Emotions* (Cambridge University Press, Cambridge, UK, 1988).

Wolff, Susan "Sanity and the Metaphysics of Responsibility" (15 pages) from Ferdinand Schoeman (ed.) *Responsibility, Character and Emotions* (Cambridge University Press, Cambridge, UK, 1988).

The publishers apologize for any errors or omissions in the above list and would be grateful to be notified of any corrections that should be incorporated in the next edition or reprint of this book.

Introduction

Robert Kane

"There is a disputation that will continue till mankind is raised from the dead, between the necessitarians and the partisans of free will." These are the words of twelfth-century Persian poet, Jalalu'ddin Rumi.[1] The problem of free will and necessity (or determinism), of which Rumi speaks, has puzzled the greatest minds for centuries – including well-known philosophers, literary figures, theologians, scientists, legal theorists and psychologists – as well as many ordinary people. It has affected and been affected by both religion and science.

In his classic poem, *Paradise Lost*, John Milton describes the angels debating how some of them could have sinned of their own free wills given that God had made them intelligent and happy.[2] Why would they have done it? And why were they responsible for it rather than God, since God had made them the way they were and had complete foreknowledge of what they would do? While puzzling over such questions, even the angels, Milton tells us, were "in Endless Mazes lost" (not a comforting thought for us humans). On the scientific front, issues about free will lead us to ask about the nature of the physical universe and our place in it (are we determined by physical laws and movements of the atoms?), about human psychology and the springs of action (can our actions be predicted by those who know our psychology?), about social conditioning, moral responsibility, crime and punishment, right and wrong, good and evil, and much more.

To dive into these questions, the best way to begin is with two pivotal notions of freedom and responsibility.

Freedom

Nothing could be more important than freedom to the modern world. All over the globe, the trend (often against resistance) is toward societies that are more free. But why do we want freedom? The simple, and not totally adequate, answer is that to be more free is to have the capacity and opportunity to satisfy more of our desires. In a free society we can walk into a store and buy almost anything we want. We can choose what movies to see, what music to listen to, whom to vote for.

But these are what you might call *surface* freedoms. What is meant by *free will* runs deeper than these everyday freedoms. To see how, suppose we had maximal freedom to make such choices to satisfy our desires and yet the choices we actually made were manipulated by others, by the powers that be. In such a world we would have a great deal of everyday freedom to do whatever we wanted, yet our free *will* would be severely limited. We would be free to *act* or choose *what* we willed, but would not have the ultimate say about what it is that we willed. Someone else would be pulling the strings, not by coercing us against our wishes, but by manipulating us into having the wishes they wanted us to have.

You may be thinking that, to some extent, we do live in such a world, where we are free to make numerous choices, but are manipulated into making many choices we do make by advertising, television, public relations, spin doctors, salespersons, marketers, and sometimes even by friends, parents, relatives, rivals, or enemies. One indication of how important free will is to us is that people generally feel revulsion at such manipulation and feel demeaned by it when they find out they have been subjected to it. You may think you are your own person because you have chosen in accord with your wishes, but then find out that these wishes were manipulated by others who wanted you to choose in exactly the way you did. Such situations are demeaning because we realize we were not our own persons; and having free will is about being your own person.

The problem is brought out in a striking way by twentieth-century utopian novels, such as Aldous Huxley's *Brave New World* and B. F. Skinner's *Walden Two*.[3] In the fictional societies described in these famous works, people can have and do what they will or choose, but only to the extent that they have been conditioned by behavioral engineers or neurochemists to will or choose what they can have and do. In *Brave New World*, the lower-echelon workers are under the influence of powerful drugs so that they do not dream of things they cannot have. They are quite content to play miniature golf all weekend. They can do what they want, though their wants are meager and controlled by drugs.

The citizens of Skinner's *Walden Two* have a richer existence than the workers of *Brave New World*. Yet their desires and purposes are also covertly controlled, in this case by behavioral engineers. Walden Two-ers live collectively in a kind of rural commune; and because they share duties of farming and raising children, they have plenty of leisure. They pursue arts, sciences, and crafts, engage in musical performances, and enjoy what appears to be a pleasant existence. In the selection from *Walden Two* in this volume, the fictional founder of this society, a fellow named Frazier, forthrightly says that their pleasant existence is brought about by the fact that, in his community, persons can do whatever they want or choose because they have been behaviorally conditioned since childhood to want and choose only what they can have and do.

Thus Frazier can say that Walden Two "is the freest place on earth," since persons there have maximal freedoms of choice and action – they can choose and do anything they want. And in a way he is right. For there is no *coercion* in Walden Two and no *punishment* because no one has to be forced to do anything against his or her will. No one harasses the citizens and no one has to harass them. Yet one might argue, as one of Frazier's critics argues in the novel (he is a philosopher named Castle visiting Walden Two) that all this *surface* freedom is bought at the expense of a *deeper* freedom of the will, since the citizens of Walden Two can have and do anything they want only because they have been conditioned not to want anything they cannot have. But Frazier is unfazed by this criticism. Admitting that this deeper freedom does not exist in Walden Two, Frazier argues in our selection that this is no real loss. Echoing the novel's author, B. F. Skinner (a foremost defender of behaviorism in psychology), Frazier thinks this so-called deeper freedom of the will is an illusion in the first place. We do not and cannot have it anyway, inside *or* outside Walden Two.

In our ordinary lives, Frazier and Skinner are saying, we are just as much the products of upbringing and social conditioning as the citizens of Walden Two, though we may delude ourselves into thinking otherwise. Along with many scientists, Skinner believed the idea that we could be original creators of our own wills – causes of ourselves, so to speak – is an impossible ideal. If we trace the psychological springs of our actions back to childhood, we find that we were less free then, not more. Thus the gauntlet is thrown down by Frazier and Skinner and other modern thinkers. Free will is an illusion. So settle for the only freedom you can have, which is the freedom to do what you want without coercion, punishment, constraint, or oppression.

Responsibility

Reflecting thus on the idea of freedom is one way to understand the free will problem. Another way is by reflecting on the notion of responsibility. Free will in the sense just described is also intimately related to notions of accountability, blameworthiness, and praiseworthiness for actions. Suppose a young man is on trial for an assault and robbery in which his victim was beaten to death. Let us say we attend his trial on a daily basis. At first, our thoughts of the young man are filled with anger and resentment. But as we listen daily to how he came to have the mean character and perverse motives he did have – a sordid story of parental neglect, child abuse, sexual abuse, bad role models – some of our resentment against the young man is shifted over to the parents and others who abused and mistreated him. We begin to feel angry with them as well as him. (Note how natural this reaction is.) Yet we aren't quite ready to shift all of the blame away from the young man himself. We wonder whether some residual responsibility may not belong to him. Our questions become: to what extent is *he* responsible for becoming the sort of person he now is? Was it *all* a question of bad parenting, societal neglect, social conditioning, and the like, or did he have any role to play in it?

These are crucial questions about free will and they are questions about what may be called his ultimate responsibility. We know that parenting and society, genetic makeup and upbringing, have an influence on what we become and what we are. But were these influences entirely *determining* or did they "leave anything over" for us to be responsible for? That is what we want to know about the young man. The question of whether he is merely a victim of his bad circumstances or has some residual responsibility for being what he is – the question, that is, of whether he became the person he is *of his own free will* – seems to depend on whether these other factors were or were not *entirely* determining.[4]

Free Will and Determinism

The problem of free will arises when by reflections such as these people are led to wonder whether their actions and characters are determined by factors over which they have no control, and hence whether there is some kind of conflict between free will and determinism. This is why doctrines of *determinism* or *necessity* have been so important in the history of debates about free will. Whenever such doctrines appear in history, they indicate that humans have reached a higher stage of self-consciousness in which they begin to wonder about the sources of their behavior and about their place as actors in the universe.[5] The possible determining factors that provoke such reflections may include fate or God, the laws of physics, heredity and environment, unconscious motives, psychological or social conditioning, behavioral engineers, hidden controllers, and others. But they invariably lead us to question whether we are really our own persons, creators of our own wills, responsible for ourselves. Philosophy begins in wonder, said the ancient philosopher Aristotle, and no source of wonder cuts deeper into our self-image than this one about free will. No person wants to be a pawn in some unknown chess game.

Determinist or necessitarian threats to free will have taken many historical forms – fatalistic, logical, theological, physical, biological, psychological, social – but there is a core idea running through all doctrines of determinism which shows why they pose a threat to free will. Any event is *determined*, according to this core notion, just in case it *must* be the case, that given the determining conditions (e.g., the decrees of fate, the foreordaining acts of God, antecedent physical causes plus laws of nature), the (determined) event will occur. In more familiar terms, the occurrence of the determined event is *inevitable* or *necessary*, given the determining conditions. Historical doctrines of determinism refer to different kinds of determining conditions, but they all imply that every event (or at least every human choice and action) is determined in this sense.

To see where the conflict lies, turn now to free will. We believe we have free will when we view ourselves as agents capable of influencing the world in various ways. Open alternatives seem to lie before us. We reason and deliberate among them and choose. We feel (1) it is "up to us" what we choose and how we act; and this means we could have chosen or acted otherwise. For, as Aristotle said, "when acting is 'up to us,' so is not acting."[6] This "up-to-usness" also suggests that (2) the sources of our actions lie in us and not outside us in something beyond our control. Given these conditions, one can see why determinism would be a threat to free will. If one or another form of determinism were true, it seems that it would *not* be (1) "up to us" what we chose from an array of alternative possibilities, since only one alternative would be possible; and so we could not have done otherwise. And it seems that (2) the sources or origins of our actions would not be in us but in something else (such as the decrees of fate, the foreordaining acts of God, or antecedent causes and laws of nature) outside us and beyond our control.

But while these conflicts between free will and determinism seem evident to many people, they are far from the last word on a subject as difficult as this one. Many philosophers and scientists, especially in modern times, have argued that, despite appearances to the contrary, determinism poses no real threat to free will, or at least to any kind of freedom or free will "worth wanting," as Daniel Dennett has put it.[7] So the question of whether determinism is true is not the only question of concern in free will debates. One must also consider whether determinism (in any or all of its forms) really does conflict with free will. Many modern thinkers, as we shall see in this volume, deny that there is such a conflict and claim that free will is *compatible* with determinism. They do not deny that being controlled or manipulated by other persons (such as Skinnerian controllers) would take away freedom, but they deny that mere determination by heredity or environment or the laws of physics (without control or manipulation by other persons) is objectionable in the same way. As a result, modern debates about free will must focus on two questions, not one – the *determinist question*: "are all events (including all human actions) determined?" and the *compatibility question*: "is free will compatible (or incompatible) with determinism?" Answers to these questions give rise to two of the major divisions in modern free will debates, between *determinists* and *indeterminists*, on the one hand, and between *compatibilists* and *incompatibilists*, on the other. There are further questions that matter about free will, as we shall see, but these two are the questions one must begin with in order to understand the free will problem. Let us look at them in turn.

The Determinist Question

Many people wonder why worries about determinism persist at all today, when universal determinism is no longer accepted even in the physical sciences, which were once the stronghold of determinism. In the eighteenth century, a great physicist, the Marquis de Laplace, could confidently predict that a superintelligent being knowing all the physical facts about the world at one moment, and applying Newton's laws of motion, could know everything that is going to happen in the future down to the minutest detail.[8] This Laplacean or Newtonian vision of universal determinism can no longer be taken for granted today. Modern quantum physics, we are told, has introduced indeterminism into the physical world. Much of the behavior of elementary particles, it is said, from quantum jumps in atoms to radioactive decay, is not precisely predictable and can be explained only by statistical, not deterministic, laws. We are also told that the uncertainty and indeterminacy of the quantum world, according to the standard view of it, is not due to our limitations as knowers, but to the unusual nature of the physical particles themselves, which have both wave-like and particle-like properties. No superintelligence (not even God perhaps) could know the exact positions and momenta of all the particles of the universe at a given moment, because the particles do not *have* exact positions and momenta at the same time (the Heisenberg uncertainty principle); and hence their future behavior is not precisely predictable or determined.

One might think these indeterministic developments in modern physics would have disposed of philosophical worries about free will. Why be concerned that free will conflicts with determinism, if determinism is not true? Yet worries about free will have not gone away in the twentieth century. In fact, they have become more pressing than ever today, despite these developments in physics – as the readings in this volume demonstrate. How are we to account for this? First, there is continuing controversy about the meaning of quantum physics itself, whether it really is indeterministic or really is the last word on physical reality. The new world of quantum reality is as mysterious as free will itself. But, second, even if it is granted that elementary particles are not always precisely determined, what implications would this have for *human behavior*? Contemporary determinists often point out that while quantum indeterminacy is significant for elementary particles, its indeterministic effects are usually insignificant in large physical systems such as the human brain and body.[9] Physical systems involving many particles and higher energies tend to be regular and predictable in their behavior, according to quantum physics itself. Thus, these determinists argue that we can continue to regard *human behavior* as determined "for all practical purposes" or "near-determined," whatever the truth should be about elementary particles. And this is all that matters in free will debates.

A third consideration complicates matters even further. Suppose for the sake of argument that quantum jumps or other undetermined events in the brain or body *did* sometimes have large-scale undetermined effects on human behavior. How would this help with free will? Suppose a choice was the result of a quantum jump or other undetermined event in a person's brain. Would this be a free choice? Such undetermined effects in the brain or body would happen by chance and would be unpredictable and uncontrollable – like an unanticipated occurrence of a thought or the jerking of an arm which one could not predict or control – quite the opposite of what we take free and responsible actions to be.[10] It seems that such events would occur spontaneously and would be more of a nuisance, or a curse, like epilepsy, than an enhancement of our freedom. A dilemma emerges out of such reflections. If free will is not compatible with determinism, it does not appear to be compatible with indeterminism or chance either. Would the discovery of indeterminism in nature make us more free – or less?

To these considerations, we can add a fourth and final reason why indeterministic developments in twentieth-century physics have not resolved the free will issue. While determinism has been in retreat in the physical sciences in the twentieth century, developments in sciences other than physics – in biology, neuroscience, psychology, psychiatry, social and behavioral sciences – seem to have been moving in the opposite direction. They have convinced many persons that more of their behavior is determined by causes unknown to us and beyond our control than previously believed. These scientific developments are many, but they surely include a greatly enhanced knowledge of the influence of genetics and heredity on human behavior. (Note the controversy caused by the recent mapping of the human genetic code which naturally arouses fears of future control of behavior by genetic manipulation.) Other relevant scientific developments include greater awareness of biochemical influences on the brain; the susceptibility of human moods and behavior to drugs; the advent of psychoanalysis and other theories of unconscious motivation; the development of computers and intelligent machines that mimic aspects of human thinking in deterministic ways (like Deep Blue, the chess master computer); comparative studies of animal and human behavior suggesting that much of our motivation and behavior is a product of our evolutionary history; and pervasive influences of psychological, social, and cultural conditioning upon upbringing and subsequent behavior.

It is difficult not to be influenced by these scientific developments which we encounter in the newspapers every day. But do they establish that we lack free will? Not necessarily. They make clear that there are numerous influences on our behavior that we do not control. But the question is whether these influences are completely determining or whether they leave some "leeway" for us to have an influence on what sorts of persons we become and how we live. Are we all entirely victims of our circumstances, like the young man on trial, or do we have any say in the matter? We have to work with traits we have inherited; we have to cope with numerous influences in our social and cultural environments that become ever more invasive. But do we have to accept the claim of Frazier and Skinner that in our ordinary lives we are no better off than the citizens of Walden Two, because we are also completely determined by our psychological and social conditioning, though we are less aware of it?

For many people today, this issue may seem to be settled against free will, so pervasive is the influence of science on our thinking. But it is far from settled; and we will find that the readings in this volume take different sides on it.

The Compatibility Question

These continuing worries about determinism make the second pivotal question about free will (the "compatibility question") even more important. Is free will compatible (or incompatible) with determinism? The free will problem arose because people assumed there was some kind of conflict between free will and determinism. But if the conflict is not real, if free will and determinism really are compatible, then worries about determinism would have been misplaced. The centuries-old problem of free will would not only be solved, it would be "dissolved." For the supposed conflict that gave rise to it in the first place would be illusory.

This *compatibilist* solution to the free will problem has been popular since the seventeenth century and continues to be popular among philosophers and scientists today because (among other things) it provides a simple way of reconciling our ordinary experience of being free with scientific views of human beings in the natural and social sciences. If compatibilists are right, we can have both freedom and determinism. Still, most ordinary persons tend to resist the idea that free will and determinism are compatible, at least initially. They tend to agree with Immanuel Kant, who called compatibilism "a wretched subterfuge" or William James, who called it a "quagmire of evasion." Yet the continuing popularity of compatibilism and the difficulties of making sense of an indeterminist free will show why the compatibility question is so important. One can no longer simply assume that free will and determinism conflict. Arguments must be given to show *why* they conflict, if they do.

Arguments for the incompatibility of free will and determinism are considered in several readings of this volume. To understand them, recall the two central features of free will mentioned earlier. We feel we have free will when (1) it is "up to us" what we do from an array of open or alternative possibilities, and (2) the sources or origins of our actions lie in us and not in anyone or anything else beyond our control. Arguments for the incompatibility of free will and determinism usually proceed from one or both of these conditions; and most modern arguments focus on condition (1) – the requirement that it is up to us what we do only if we had *alternative possibilities* or *could have done otherwise*. The most widely discussed argument for incompatibilism of this kind in contemporary philosophy is presented in one of the readings of this volume, "The Incompatibility of Freedom and Determinism" by Peter van Inwagen. The argument is usually called the "consequence argument" and is stated informally by van Inwagen as follows:

> If determinism is true, then our acts are the consequences of the laws of nature and events in the remote past. But it is not up to us what went on before we were born; and neither is it up to us what the laws of nature are. Therefore the consequences of these things (including our own acts) are not up to us.[11]

To say it is not "up to us" what "went on before we were born," or "what the laws of nature are," is to say that there is nothing we *can now do* to change the past or alter the laws of nature (it is beyond our control), which seems true enough. But if determinism is true, the past before we were born and the laws entail our present actions. So it seems that there is nothing we can now do to make our present actions other than they are. We cannot do otherwise and hence lack alternative possibilities. And if free will requires alternative possibilities, we cannot have free will.

   This argument has considerable force, though it turns out to be more complicated than first appearances suggest. In his reading selection, van Inwagen develops the argument more formally and attempts to answer objections to it by compatibilists. Critics of the consequence argument usually focus attention on what it means to say that an agent "could have done otherwise," or generally what it means to say that someone "can" or has the *power* or *ability* to do anything at all. Such claims are trickier than they first appear to be. Suppose Molly has just graduated from law school and is trying to decide whether to join a large law firm in Chicago or a smaller firm in Omaha. The large firm offers more opportunities, but it is also more competitive; and she is wary of living in such a big city. After adding up all the pros and cons, she decides finally that the Chicago offer is better career-wise and she chooses it. What does it mean to say that her choice was *free* because she "could have chosen otherwise" – she could have chosen to join the firm in Omaha?

   Compatibilists argue that this could not mean that she might have chosen Omaha, given all the *same* beliefs, desires and other *reasons* or *motives* that led her to choose Chicago. Nor could it mean that she may have chosen Omaha at the end of the very same *deliberation* that led her to prefer Chicago and choose it. That wouldn't make sense, they argue. It would have been irrational for her to choose Omaha given exactly the same reasons and deliberation that led her to favor Chicago. To say she could have chosen otherwise must mean something else – something like: *if* she had had *different* beliefs or desires, or had reasoned differently, or if other thoughts had entered her mind, then she *would* (or might) have done otherwise and chosen Omaha instead. But this means that saying she could have done otherwise, and hence that her choice was free, means only that she would have done otherwise, if things had been different – if *the past had been different in some way*. And this hypothetical claim does not conflict with determinism, for it may have been determined that the past was not in fact different. The hypothetical claim does not require (what seems impossible) that she could have "changed the past" or "altered the laws of nature," as the consequence argument supposes. It merely means that if the past had been different she would have done otherwise.

This is the response made to the consequence argument by *classical compatibilists*, and it is defended in another reading of this volume by Kai Nielsen, "The Compatibility of Freedom and Determinism." Nielsen and other classical compatibilists (who include many well-known philosophers such as Thomas Hobbes, David Hume, and John Stuart Mill) argue that we are "free" when there is an *absence of constraints* or *impediments* preventing us from doing what we want to do (we are not tied down, no one is holding a gun to our head, we are not paralyzed, and so on). Classical compatibilists, such as Nielsen, admit that freedom does indeed imply that our actions must be "up to us" in the sense that we "could have done otherwise." But saying we could have done otherwise, they insist, means only that no constraints or impediments would have prevented us from doing otherwise, *if* we had wanted to. Putting it in another way, it means we had the *capacity* and *opportunity* to do otherwise, and would have done so if our desires or other motives had been different. Once we realize that "could have done otherwise" has this *hypothetical* or *conditional* meaning, Nielsen argues, we will not be tempted to think that freedom of action or free will (i.e., freedom of choice) is incompatible with determinism for the reasons given in the previous paragraph.

Classical compatibilism of this sort has been an extremely popular view among philosophers and scientists in the twentieth century. It is defended in this volume not only by Nielsen, but also by Skinner (whose view of freedom is similar to Nielsen's). But many other thinkers find classical compatibilism unsatisfying. In our readings it is criticized by *incompatibilists*, including van Inwagen and also Roderick Chisholm in another reading ("Human Freedom and the Self") who challenge the hypothetical or conditional analyses of "could have done otherwise" favoured by classical compatibilists like Nielsen and Skinner. The readings of Nielsen and Skinner, on one side, and van Inwagen and Chisholm, on the other, provide a overview of the pros and cons of the classical compatibilism as a solution to the free will problem.

Moral Responsibility and Alternative Possibilities

But classical compatibilists are not the only critics of incompatibilism and the consequence argument. Other modern compatibilists, such as Daniel Dennett, prefer a more radical attack on all arguments for the incompatibility of free will and determinism. In another reading in this volume, "I Could Not Have Done Otherwise – So What?," Dennett questions whether the power to do otherwise really is required for free will and moral responsibility in the first place, as incompatibilists such as van Inwagen and Chisholm suppose. Dennett asks us to consider the case of Martin Luther. When Luther broke with the Church in Rome, initiating the Protestant Reformation, he made the famous statement "Here I stand, I can do no other." Suppose, says Dennett, that Luther was literally right about himself at that moment. Given his character and motives at the time, he literally could not have done otherwise. Does this mean Luther was not acting of his own free will or was not responsible for his act at that moment? Not at all, says Dennett. "We simply do not exempt someone from blame or praise for an act because we think he could do no other" or because his act is determined by his character. In saying "I can do no other," Luther was not renouncing free will or moral responsibility, according to Dennett; he was taking full responsibility for acting of his own free will. It was the most responsible act of his life. Dennett concludes that neither free will nor moral responsibility require "could have done otherwise"; and he offers other subtle arguments in support of the same conclusion. If he is right, arguments for incompatibilism, such as the consequence argument, could not get off the ground. Those who incline to incompatibilism or find the consequence argument compelling must therefore answer his arguments.

Another kind of argument for the claim that free will and moral responsibility do not require alternative possibilities or the power to do otherwise is discussed in two further readings that follow Dennett's – by John Martin Fischer and Derk Pereboom. These readings consider some challenging examples originally introduced into free will debates by Harry Frankfurt, that have come to be known as "Frankfurt-style examples."[12] These intriguing examples were introduced by Frankfurt with the intent of showing that moral responsibility (and hence any free will that entails moral responsibility) does not require alternative possibilities or the power to do otherwise. So these examples, if correct, would also undermine the consequence argument and other arguments for incompatibilism.

Frankfurt's original example involved a person named Black who has control over another agent, called Jones. Black has enormous powers and can make Jones do whatever he (Black) wants by controlling Jones' brain through drugs or electronic probes. Black will not intervene, however, if Jones chooses on his own to do what Black wants. Suppose in these circumstances that Jones has a choice to make, say to vote for candidate A or candidate B. Black wants Jones to vote for A and will prevent him from voting for B. But Black waits to see what Jones will do on his own and will not intervene unless he has to, that is, unless Jones is going to choose B. As it turns out, Jones chooses A on his own, so Black does not intervene. Frankfurt argues that it is reasonable to suppose in such a case that Jones could be morally responsible for his choice, since Jones acted entirely on his own and Black stayed out of the picture, playing no role in the actual choice. Yet Jones literally could not have done otherwise because Black would not have let him vote for B if he had given any indication of doing so. So it appears, Frankfurt argues, that persons can be morally responsible for what they have done even if they could not have done otherwise.

Examples of this kind have played a significant role in contemporary debates about free will. In the two readings on them in this volume, Fischer and Pereboom take different stances. Fischer ("Frankfurt-style Examples, Responsibility and Semi-compatibilism") provides an informative survey of recent debates about Frankfurt-style examples, considering new and ingenious versions of them. Fischer believes such examples do show that moral responsibility does not require alternative possibilities and is therefore compatible with determinism. But he distinguishes between *freedom* and *moral responsibility*. While Fischer thinks moral responsibility does not require alternative possibilities (because of Frankfurt-style examples) and so is compatible with determinism, he does think freedom requires alternative possibilities and so is not compatible with determinism (because of the consequence argument). This unusual (have-it-both-ways) view is called "semi-compatibilism" by Fischer.

Pereboom (in "The Explanatory Irrelevance of Alternative Possibilities") agrees that Frankfurt-style examples show that moral responsibility does not require alternative possibilities. But he thinks that traditional Frankfurt-style examples and the newer versions of such examples discussed by Fischer do not succeed in showing this. They are subject to serious objections. So he offers an original Frankfurt-style example of this own, which he thinks clinches the case.[13] These readings by Fischer and Pereboom, taken together with the readings of van Inwagen and Dennett, provide an instructive introduction to contemporary debates about the relations between moral responsibility, alternative possibilities, determinism, and free will.

Hierarchical Motivation, Sanity, and Reactive Attitudes: New Compatibilist Theories

We have seen that influential philosophers such as Dennett and Frankfurt do not believe that free will and moral responsibility require alternative possibilities or the power to do otherwise. But it seems legitimate to ask these thinkers what they believe free will and moral responsibility *do* require if they do *not* require alternative possibilities. We seem to have strong intuitions that free will and responsibility entail the power to do otherwise. If someone denies these intuitions, they will have to do more than offer striking counterexamples about Luther or Frankfurt-style examples. They must also give us plausible alternative accounts of free will and responsibility of their own that do not require alternative possibilities or the absence of determinism.

Frankfurt tries to do just that in a further reading, "Freedom of the Will and the Concept of a Person," which follows the Pereboom essay. In this influential paper, Frankfurt is concerned with the more general question of what makes something a *person* or a *self*; and he thinks this question is related to free will. Frankfurt argues that persons, unlike similar animals, have a capacity for *reflective self-evaluation* that is manifested in the formation of *second-order desires* – desires to have or not have various first-order desires. For example, an alcoholic may have a desire to drink. But he may also desire not to have the desire to drink because he does not want to destroy his marriage and family. A drug addict may desire a drug, but may also desire to be rid of that debilitating desire. These desires to have or not to have *other* desires are "second-order" desires. Second-order desires that certain first-order desires be effective (or not be effective) in action are called by Frankfurt "second-order volitions."

Animals have first-order desires, Frankfurt says, but only *persons* are capable of reflective self-evaluation whereby they can rise above their first-order desires and want to have different desires – or want to be different than they are. Since free will requires such a capacity for reflective self-evaluation, it is a capacity that only persons can have. Our *wills* (first-order desires) are *free*, according to Frankfurt, when they are in conformity with certain of our second-order desires (second-order volitions), so that we have the wills (first-order) we want (second-order) to have. The alcoholic and drug addict do not have free wills in this sense. While they may desire not to act on the desire to drink or take the drug, they can't help themselves and so they drink or take the drug anyway. Their first-order desires are not in conformity with their second-order volitions. They do not have the wills they want to have.

Frankfurt's view is called a "hierarchical theory" of motivation and free will for obvious reasons. (Desires or motives do not have to stop at the second-order on such a view. There may be third and higher-order desires or motives as well.) According to hierarchical theorists like Frankfurt, classical compatibilism (the view defended by Nielsen and Skinner) is deficient because it gives us only a theory of freedom of *action* (being able to do what we will), but not a theory of freedom of *will* (being able to will what we will, so to speak). (This is Frankfurt's version of the distinction between surface freedom and deeper freedom that we encountered in *Walden Two*.) But hierarchical theories, like Frankfurt's, remain *compatibilist* about free will and determinism since they define free will in terms of a conformity between desires at different levels without requiring that desires at any level, including higher-order desires, be *undetermined*. As Frankfurt puts this, it does not matter how we came to have the wills we want to have – whether by a deterministic process of social conditioning or not. What matters is that we do have the wills we want to have and the power to realize them in action. That is what makes us free. It does not even matter if we could not do otherwise, according to Frankfurt, as long as we are not conflicted in our desires like the addict or alcoholic, so that we are wholeheartedly committed to what we are doing and no constraints or impediments stand in the way of our doing what we want.

In the reading that follows Frankfurt's, Susan Wolf ("Sanity and the Metaphysics of Responsibility") critically examines Frankfurt's hierarchical theory of free will along with several other influential compatibilist accounts of freedom and responsibility put forward by Gary Watson and Charles Taylor. Wolf refers to Frankfurt's view and these other views as "Deep Self" theories (they are also sometimes called "Real Self" theories). According to Deep Self theories, one has free will when one acts from one's *deep* or *real* or *authentic* self, whether that real or authentic self is defined in terms of one's higher-order motives (Frankfurt), or one's values (Watson) or the strong valuations (Taylor) one is most committed to. Wolf thinks there is some truth to Deep Self theories, but she also argues that they fall short of giving us a fully adequate account of freedom and responsibility. She tries to illustrate this by developing the striking example of JoJo, "the favorite son of Jo the First, an evil and sadistic dictator of a small underdeveloped country." Wolf's discussion of JoJo and similar examples leads her to argue that something more than acting from one's Deep Self must be required for free will; and this in turn leads her to consider the role of sanity and insanity and the role of appreciating right from wrong in free and responsible action.

In the reading following Wolf's, Gary Watson ("Responsibility and the Limits of Evil: Variations on a Strawsonian Theme") also considers issues of responsibility, sanity, morality, and punishment in relation to free will. Watson does so by focusing on the fascinating real life case of Robert Harris, the psychopathic multiple murderer who was on death row in California at the time Watson was writing. The story of Harris's family and troubled life leading up to his brutal crimes leads Watson to some deep reflections on the roots of evil and the limits of freedom. Watson also uses the Harris case to critically examine another influential modern compatibilist view to free will, the "reactive attitude" theory of P. F. Strawson. In a seminal essay, "Freedom and Resentment" (1962), Strawson argues that free will issues are about the conditions for holding persons responsible for their actions; and he argues further that responsibility is constituted by persons adopting certain *reactive attitudes* to one another – attitudes such as resentment, admiration, gratitude, indignation, guilt, blame, and the like. To be responsible, according to Strawson, is to be a "fit" subject of such attitudes. It is to be part of a "form of life" or "moral community" in which people can appropriately take such reactive attitudes to each other and thus hold each other responsible. This is what we do when we admire other people or resent or blame them for their behavior. Strawson then notes that we would not give up this form of life or moral community if we found that determinism was true because we could not give up such a form of life and remain human. Thus, he thinks we do not have to imagine that our actions are undetermined to continue taking the reactive attitudes seriously and holding others responsible.

Watson is attracted to Strawson's influential "reactive attitude" view (which Watson calls an "expressive theory" of responsibility). But in this reading, Watson poses questions about how we are to determine whether someone is inside or outside the "moral community" so that they *are* fit subjects for the reactive attitudes in Strawson's sense. Robert Harris rejected the moral community and would not respond to its attitudes, placing himself entirely outside of it. (Even his fellow prisoners on death row feared and hated him.) Was he morally responsible for his actions – a fit subject for resentment and blame? If so, why? If not, why not? These are the questions Watson sensitively explores in his article.

The Intelligibility Question: Incompatibilist or Libertarian Views of Free Will

Dennett, Frankfurt, Wolf, and Watson attempt to give accounts of free will and responsibility according to which they are compatible with determinism. Intriguing and challenging as these theories are, many people continue to resist compatibilism. They find it hard to rid themselves of the intuition that there is some sort of conflict between free will and determinism, whether this incompatibility is captured by the consequence argument or in some other way. Such *incompatibilists* try to hold on to the traditional idea that "true" free will is not compatible with determinism, and that compatibilist theories are not giving us the whole story. We now turn to views of this incompatibilist kind.

Incompatibilists about free will and determinism who *also* believe that free will exists (and thus deny that determinism is true) are referred to as *libertarians* in modern writings on free will. Libertarians are believers in a traditional incompatibilist free will and hence deny that all human choices or actions are determined. Libertarianism in this sense is not to be confused with the political doctrine of libertarianism. The two do share a name – from the Latin *liber*, meaning "free" – and an interest in freedom. But libertarians about free will are not necessarily committed to all the views about limited government held by political libertarians. Libertarians about free will may in fact hold different political views – conservative, liberal, libertarian, or whatever – so long as they share a commitment to the ideal of persons having responsibility for their actions and their lives in an ultimate sense that is incompatible with determinism. There will be no confusion about these terms, if one keeps in mind that libertarianism *about free will,* as the term is used throughout this volume, is solely defined by the following three theses: (1) free will is not compatible with determinism (incompatibilism), (2) free will exists (in an incompatibilist sense), and so (3) determinism is false.

Contemporary libertarians in this sense must not only answer the determinist and compatibility questions by denying that determinism is true and arguing that free will and determinism are incompatible. These tasks are hard enough. But they must also address another and even more daunting question at the heart of modern free will debates that we have not yet considered. This is the *intelligibility question*: can we make sense of a freedom or free will that is incompatible with determinism? Is such a (libertarian) freedom intelligible, or is it, as many critics contend, mysterious or incoherent? The culprit in this case is not determinism, but *indeterminism*. Recall the dilemma mentioned earlier: if free will is not compatible with determinism, it does not seem to be compatible with indeterminism either. (You might say that the compatibility question is about the first half of this dilemma, while the intelligibility question is about the second half.) Undetermined events would seem to be a matter of chance. But chance events are not under the control of anything. How then could they be free or responsible actions?

We encountered this problem briefly in the earlier discussion of physics and free will. Suppose a choice was the result of a quantum jump or other undetermined event in your brain. Would it be a free choice? It would seem rather to be a matter of chance, like the sudden occurrence of a thought or the uncontrolled jerking of an arm. Why was one choice made rather than the other? One could not say why, if it resulted from chance. It would have just "happened." Reflections such as these lead to claims that undetermined choices or actions would be "arbitrary," "capricious," "random," "irrational," "uncontrolled," "inexplicable," or merely matters of "luck" or "chance" – so that undetermined *free* choice makes no sense.

Such is the challenge of the intelligibility question. It is spelled out in a striking way in another reading of this volume by Peter van Inwagen ("The Mystery of Metaphysical Freedom"). By invoking examples of free choice in humans, angels, and God, van Inwagen shows how puzzling undetermined or chance choices would be; and he concludes that an undetermined free will (or "metaphysical freedom" as he calls it) remains an insoluble mystery. It may seem puzzling that, in his first reading for this volume, van Inwagen defended the incompatibility of free will and determinism by way of the consequence argument, while in this second reading, he questions whether an indeterminist freedom can be made intelligible. But while van Inwagen's view is unusual, it is not inconsistent. He believes that no one to date has been able to give an intelligible account of libertarian free will (or "metaphysical freedom"); and he has doubts about the possibility of doing so. Yet van Inwagen also feels the consequence argument is undeniably sound, so he thinks we must continue to believe in an undetermined free will even if we do not know how to make sense of it. We must believe metaphysical freedom exists, but how it exists is a mystery. Some great philosophers of the past have held similar views. For example, Immanuel Kant held that we must believe in an undetermined free will because it is presupposed by our practical reasoning and our moral life. But Kant also believed that science and theoretical reason could not explain how an undetermined free will was possible. We had to believe it on faith.

A libertarian free will that requires indeterminism is certainly difficult to understand, but not everyone is ready to concede that it is completely mysterious or unintelligible. Several other readings in this volume accept the challenge of trying to make sense of libertarian free will and thereby answering the intelligibility question. The first of these readings was briefly mentioned earlier – Roderick Chisholm's "Human Freedom and the Self." In this influential paper, Chisholm argues that the free will issue seems insoluble as long as we think the only options are that free actions are determined or undetermined (by prior events). There is a third option, he thinks, besides determinism or indeterminism, namely *self-determination* or *agent-causation*. Free actions may be determined or caused, but they are caused by selves or agents and not by prior events. The additional causal factor – an agent- or "immanent" cause – is not in turn caused by prior events because it is not itself an event and therefore not of the right type to be caused. The free agent, Chisholm says, must be a "prime mover unmoved." In his reading, he tries to show how such a view could be made intelligible.

A theory like Chisholm's is usually called an *agent-cause* or *agent-causal* theory of free will. (The expressions are hyphenated to highlight the fact that the agent causation in question is of a special "nonevent" or "non-occurrent" kind that cannot be spelled out wholly in terms of causation by prior physical and psychological events.) Agent-cause theories, like Chisholm's, have their critics. Yet many people agree with Chisholm that some appeal to a special kind of causation, such as agent-causation, is the only way to make sense of a libertarian or indeterminist free will. They reason that if free actions are undetermined by events, then something else must determine them if they are not to occur by chance. Another agent-causal libertarian who believes this is Timothy O'Connor. In his reading ("The Agent as Cause"), O'Connor defends an alternative agent-cause theory that tries to improve upon and answer some of the objections to traditional agent-cause theories like Chisholm's. O'Connor also addresses another issue closely related to the free will issue –

namely, the mind–body problem. Many people think that agent-causation (and hence libertarian free will generally) would require a dualism of mind and body such as Descartes held, because agent-causation is supposed to involve a special causal relation that is irreducible to natural causes. O'Connor discusses this issue, arguing that one does not have to be a Cartesian dualist about mind and body to hold an agent-causal libertarian view.

Not everyone agrees that appeals to special kinds of agency or causation, such as agent-causation – or noumenal selves or Cartesian egos – are the only way to make sense of libertarian free will. Many libertarians themselves find appeals to special forms of agency or causation, such as agent-causation, problematic and suspicious; and they would like to do without them. So agent-causal theories are not the only kind of libertarian theory in contemporary philosophy. There are others; and the two most important libertarian alternatives – *simple indeterminism* and *causal indeterminism* – are discussed in two other readings following O'Connor's.

A "simple indeterminist" libertarian view is defended by Carl Ginet (in "Freedom, Responsibility and Agency"). Ginet's view depends upon a distinction between *reasons explanations* and *causal explanations* of action. Reasons explanations of actions are answers to the question "*Why* did he or she do that (raise a hand, speak angrily, go to the store)?" which cite *reasons* or *motives* of the agent, such as beliefs, wants, desires, preferences, intentions, and other psychological attitudes. (He raised his hand because he *wanted* to get your attention; she spoke angrily because she *believed* you had insulted her.) It is often assumed that the wants, beliefs, and other reasons in such explanations explain because the wants and beliefs cause the actions. But Ginet denies that reasons explanations are a species of causal explanation. If actions can be explained without being *caused* by reasons, as he argues they can be, then actions can be explained without being *determined* by reasons as well. Ginet contends that such a "simple indeterminist" account of reasons and action, together with a suitable account of the nature of action, will suffice to account for free will. And he criticizes agent-cause theories such as those of Chisholm and O'Connor for adding a special kind of agency or causation that he thinks is problematic and superfluous.

In the reading following Ginet's, Robert Kane ("Free Will: New Directions for an Old Problem") defends a third possible libertarian approach to free will, often called "causal indeterminism."[14] Kane agrees with Ginet in rejecting agent-causal theories, like those of Chisholm and O'Connor. But he also does not think that libertarians have to deny that reasons cause actions or deny (as does Ginet) that reasons explanations are a species of causal explanations in order to make sense of incompatibilist free will. What matters is that the relevant causal relations between reasons and actions need not always be deterministic (they may sometimes be nondeterministic or probabilistic). In other words, "undetermined" need not mean "uncaused"; and reasons, like other kinds of causes, may "incline without necessitating." Kane attempts to show that such a causal indeterminist view can make sense of free will and go some way toward reconciling it with modern images of human beings in the natural and social sciences without appealing to special forms of agency or causation. Kane also offers in this reading an alternative approach to the compatibility question, arguing that there is another way to argue for the incompatibility of free will and determinism that relies on a notion of ultimate responsibility rather than merely on alternative possibilities.

The attempt to reconcile incompatibilist or libertarian free will with science is also a theme of the reading by David Hodgson ("Chess, Life and Superlife"). Hodgson tries to show how a libertarian account of choice might be compatible with physical causation as understood by quantum physics by considering some analogies with different kinds of games. Hodgson begins with the familiar game of chess, moves on to the less familiar, but intriguing, "Game of Life" developed by modern mathematicians and computer scientists, and finally considers his own alternative game of "Superlife." If our actual universe is like the Superlife universe, Hodgson argues, as it well might be, we can see how free will could be a part of it.

Hard Determinism and Successor Theories: Definitions of the Standard Positions

As the preceding sections indicate, the main division in contemporary debates about free will is between the *compatibilists*, on one side, who believe free will is compatible with determinism, and *libertarians*, on the other, who continue to believe in a traditional free will that is not compatible with determinism. Most people who think about free will tend to come down on one or another of these two sides in the debate. But compatibilism and libertarianism by no means exhaust the possible positions. Another significant position in free will debates is *hard determinism*. Hard determinists agree with libertarians that free will is incompatible with determinism. But (unlike libertarians), hard determinists are convinced that human behavior is for all intents and purposes determined, so that we do *not* have free will in the incompatibilist sense required for genuine moral responsibility. The expression "hard determinism" originated with the American philosopher and psychologist William James at the beginning of the twentieth century, who distinguished hard determinism from *soft determinism*.[15] Both hard and soft determinists affirm that all human behavior is determined. But soft determinists are *compatibilists* who insist that determinism does not undermine any free will or responsibility worth having, while hard determinists are *incompatibilists* who take a harder line: since determinism is true (alas!), free will does not exist in a sense required for genuine responsibility, accountability, blameworthiness, or desert.

The hard determinist position is defended in this volume by Paul Edwards ("Hard and Soft Determinism"). Few thinkers historically have been willing to embrace hard determinism unqualifiedly, since it would require wholesale changes in the way we think about human relations and attitudes. But Edwards believes that hard determinism is a more coherent view than soft determinism (which he believes, in partial agreement with James, to be something of an "evasion"). In my comments on the Edwards reading I also discuss some other recent defenses of positions on free will that are not exactly hard determinist, but are similar to hard determinism in rejecting *both* compatibilist *and* libertarian accounts of free will. Like Edwards, advocates of these contemporary "successor views" to hard determinism, as they might be called, reject compatibilism because they are convinced that (1) free will is not compatible with determinism. Yet most also reject libertarianism because they believe that (2) libertarian free will is impossible *whether determinism is true or not*. In other words, these successor views to hard determinism accept *both* sides of the dilemma: free will is not compatible with determinism and it is not compatible with indeterminism either. So hard determinism and successor views to it like these constitute a "third rail" in current free will debates – since they are alternatives to both compatibilist and libertarian views.

With this in mind, we might now summarize the standard positions on free will commonly referred to throughout this volume. These designations of standard positions can sometimes be confusing, but you will understand most of what is said about them if you keep the following in mind:

Compatibilists hold that free will is compatible with determinism.
Soft determinists are compatibilists who also hold that determinism is true.

Incompatibilists hold that free will is not compatible with (conflicts with) determinism.

Libertarians are incompatibilists who also believe that free will exists (so that determinism must be false).

Hard determinists are incompatibilists who also hold that determinism is true so that free will does not exist. (Advocates of *successor views* to hard determinism are incompatibilists who also hold (along with hard determinists) that incompatibilist free will does not exist. But most hold this because they believe incompatibilist free will is impossible *whether* determinism is true or not.)

Religion and Free Will: Theological Determinism

For many people, the deepest philosophical questions about free will have a religious source. They arise from the thought that an all-knowing and all-powerful God must have known in advance and foreordained (or "predestined") everything we do. Recall the angels debating in John Milton's classic poem, *Paradise Lost*, how they could have *freely* chosen to serve or reject God, if God had made them what they were and had complete foreknowledge of what they would do. The same problem applies to humans. Many theologians throughout the centuries (in various theistic traditions, Jewish, Christian, Muslim, and others) have believed that God's power, knowledge, and providence would be unacceptably compromised if one did not affirm that all events in the universe, including all human choices and actions, were foreordained and foreknown by God. But many other thinkers argued, with equal force, that if God did in fact foreordain or foreknow all human choices and actions, then no one could have chosen or acted differently. How then could humans be free and responsible for their actions in a sense that would justify divine rewards and punishments? Wouldn't the ultimate responsibility for good and bad deeds – and hence responsibility for evil – go back to God? And how could we square that with the idea that God is all-good and could not be the source of the world's evils?

These are not merely questions for religious believers. Many have turned away from belief in God because of an inability to answer such questions. Why does God allow so much evil in the world? A common answer was that God is not the source of evil. Rather it comes from the free choices and actions of humans and angels who reject God. But if God foreknew what these free creatures would do when they were created and made them the way they are, why is the responsibility not God's after all? The most profound and influential attempt to address these questions in the ancient world was by St. Augustine of Hippo (354–430). In the reading selection in this volume from his classic work, *On the Free Choice of the Will* (391), Augustine argues that God's complete foreknowledge of what we would do does not take away our free will; so that we alone, and not God, are ultimately responsible for our good or bad deeds.

In the reading that follows Augustine's, William Hasker ("God, Time, Knowledge and Freedom: The Historical Matrix") critically examines the most important solutions to the problem of divine foreknowledge and human freedom in the history of philosophy, including the views of Augustine, Boethius, Thomas Aquinas, William of Ockham, and others. Hasker's essay also provides an instructive summary of the various solutions to this problem of foreknowledge and free will that are still being debated today by theologians and philosophers and thus a useful overview of the religious dimensions of the free will problem.

An Overview of the Readings

The readings of this volume are organized for convenience into five parts. Part I provides an introduction to the free will problem and its four readings represent each of the major standard positions. Skinner's "Walden Two: Human Freedom and the Behavioral Sciences" introduces the problem of free will as I have described it earlier in this introduction. Nielsen's "The Compatibility of Freedom and Determinism" (along with the Skinner selection) represents the classical *compatibilist* position on free will. Chisholm's "Human Freedom and the Self" is a statement of the *libertarian* position in its most common "agent-causal" form. Finally, Edwards' "Hard and Soft Determinism" is a defense of the traditional *hard determinist* position.

Part II addresses arguments for and against the incompatibility of free will and determinism. Van Inwagen's "The Incompatibility of Free Will and Determinism" defends the consequence argument. Dennett's "I Could Not Have Done Otherwise – So What?" addresses crucial issues upon which the consequence argument depends concerning whether free will and moral responsibility require alternative possibilities. The readings by Fischer and Pereboom on Frankfurt-style examples pursue these issues about freedom, moral responsibility and alternative possibilities further from different perspectives.

Part III provides an overview of new *compatibilist* theories of free will that are meant to be improvements of the classical compatibilism represented by the Nielsen essay. Frankfurt's "Freedom of the Will and the Concept of a Person" defends a "hierarchical theory" of motivation and free will. Wolf's "Sanity and the Metaphysics of Responsibility" discusses "Deep Self" or "real self" theories and Watson's "Responsibility and the Limits of Evil" examines the "reactive attitude" theory of P. F. Strawson in the light of the striking case of Robert Harris, the psychopathic killer on death row.

Part IV provides an overview of recent *incompatibilist* or *libertarian* theories of free will that attempt to address the intelligibility question: can one reconcile free will with indeterminism and thereby make sense of a free will that is incompatible with determinism? Van Inwagen's "The Mystery of Metaphysical Freedom" states this intelligibility problem in a challenging way and argues that no solution is currently available for it. The readings of O'Connor, Ginet, and Kane discuss three ways in which contemporary libertarians have attempted to address the intelligibility question – by appeal to agent-causation, simple indeterminism, and causal indeterminism. Hodgson's "Chess, Life and Superlife" attempts to show how free will might be reconciled with physical indeterminism by considering analogies with various kinds of games.

Finally, Part V considers the religious dimensions of the free will problem. St. Augustine's "Divine Foreknowledge, Evil, and the Free Choice of the Will" is a classic defense of the idea that God's power and knowledge can be reconciled with human freedom, while William Hasker's "God, Time, Knowledge and Freedom: The Historical Matrix" provides an overview of past and present debates about divine foreknowledge and human freedom.

Notes

1 Rumi (1956), p. 77. Throughout this volume, references will be made to works by author and date. The Bibliography at the end of the volume contains the complete references.
2 Milton, *Paradise Lost* (1955): prologue.
3 Huxley, *Brave New World* (1989). Skinner, *Walden Two* (1962).
4 This is why we are naturally inclined to ask in cases like this whether someone else in exactly the same circumstances might have acted differently.
5 In my book, *The Significance of Free Will* (1996), chapter 6, I discuss at greater length how this higher stage of self-consciousness arises and what it means concerning issues about the meaning of life as well as free will.
6 Aristotle (1915), 1113b6.
7 See Dennett, *Elbow Room* (1984), chapter 1.

8 Laplace, *A Philosophical Essay on Probabilities* (1951).
9 Determinists who make this claim include Honderich (1988, 1973) and Weatherford (1991), among many others.
10 This complaint is made by many contemporary philosophers and scientists, including some in this volume. See the readings by Nielsen and Dennett, for example.
11 van Inwagen, *An Essay on Free Will* (1983), p. 56.
12 Frankfurt, "Alternative Possibilities and Moral Responsibility" (1969).
13 It should be noted that, while Pereboom agrees with Fischer that moral responsibility does not require alternative possibilities, he does not conclude, as does Fischer, that *therefore* moral responsibility is compatible with determinism. For Pereboom thinks there is another way to show that moral responsibility (and free will) are incompatible with determinism without invoking alternative possibilities. Thus he rejects Fischer's semicompatibilism and argues that incompatibilism about both moral responsibility and free will can be maintained despite Frankfurt-style examples. Moreover, since Pereboom also believes that libertarian free will does not exist either, he claims we lack free will in the deeper sense required for ultimate responsibility. He calls this view "hard incompatibilism." I say more about such a view and others like it in the "Comments and Questions" that follow the reading by Paul Edwards in this volume, "Hard and Soft Determinism."
14 O'Connor also calls this view "causal indeterminism" in his paper. Ginet calls it the "indeterministic causation" view. This view is also sometimes called "event-causal" libertarianism to distinguish it from "agent-causal" libertarianism.
15 James, "The Dilemma of Determinism" (in James, 1956).

Part I:

The Free Will Problem: Standard Positions: Compatibilism, Libertarianism, Hard and Soft Determinism

1

Walden Two: Freedom and the Behavioral Sciences

B. F. Skinner

Editor's Introduction

B. F. Skinner was one of the most influential behavioral psychologists of the twentieth century. He argued that the behavior of humans and other animals was most effectively influenced by reward rather than punishment. By rewarding certain behaviors (associating them with pleasant stimuli or the removal of unpleasant stimuli) one could reinforce or increase their frequency. Such principles of "operant conditioning," as Skinner called his methods, were first applied experimentally to pigeons. (He taught pigeons to play table tennis, among other things, by such methods.) But Skinner also believed an effective science of human behavior could be constructed upon such principles and argued for such a science of human behavior throughout his long career.

The passages reprinted here are from Skinner's well-known utopian novel *Walden Two*, published in 1948. Walden Two is a rural community situated in a lush valley in which the principles of Skinner's behavioral psychology are put into practice. The citizens live in apartment buildings that are something like dormitories or co-ops; they eat in communal dining halls and farm the land organically to support themselves. (Henry David Thoreau's *Walden* was very much on Skinner's mind when he wrote *Walden Two*. Self-reliance and attunement with nature are everywhere in evidence, but not for an individual alone as in Thoreau's Walden, rather for a whole community.) Children are reared by the community of Walden Two in accordance with the principles of operant conditioning to be model citizens, by reward rather than punishment. Thus there is no need for punishment in Walden Two and no need for coercion or forcing people to do things against their will. People are free to do whatever they want – because they have been behaviorally conditioned to want what they can do. But Skinner thinks that is a small price to pay for such freedom and happiness. They have to work on average only four hours a day because everyone contributes; and they have a great deal of choice about what work they will do on any given day. If one chooses a nasty job, like cleaning latrines, one only has to work an hour that day; if one chooses an easy job, like sitting in the entrance booth to greet visitors while reading a book, one might have to work eight hours. There is thus plenty of leisure in Walden Two which is given over to the pursuit of the arts and sciences. All in all, it is portrayed as a very pleasant place.

The novel revolves around a visit to Walden Two by a professor of psychology at a local college, named Burris (who is the narrator of the novel). Burris takes along with him four of his psychology students, two young men and two young women, and a colleague of his at the college, a professor of philosophy, named Castle. The visitors are shown around Walden Two by a fellow named Frazier, who is a psychologist and founder of Walden Two. Frazier is an obvious mouthpiece for Skinner. He defends Walden Two and the beliefs on which it is based against the objections of the visitors, especially those of Castle. In the passage reprinted here Castle suggests that Walden Two is a "fascist state" completely controlled by behavioral engineers. Frazier argues to the contrary that Walden Two is the "freest place on earth." Most of the citizens don't even know Frazier founded the place. He has no more privileges or power than any other citizen.

This lively debate between Frazier and Castle raises many important questions about free will. It is worth noting that, at the end of the novel, the psychology professor Burris and two of the students decide to stay in Walden Two. Castle, with his "outdated" philosophical views, leaves in disgust. (His very name suggests a medieval view of things.) And two of the students decide to leave because they will not give up their "middle-class" way of life.

B. F. Skinner Selections from *Walden Two*

"Mr. Castle," said Frazier very earnestly, "let me ask you a question. I warn you, it will be the most terrifying question of your life. *What would you do if you found yourself in possession of an effective science of behavior?* Suppose you suddenly found it possible to control the behavior of men as you wished. What would you do?"

"That's an assumption?"

"Take it as one if you like. *I* take it as a fact. And apparently you accept it as a fact too. I can hardly be as despotic as you claim unless I hold the key to an extensive practical control."

"What would I do?" said Castle thoughtfully. "I think I would dump your science of behavior in the ocean."

"And deny men all the help you could otherwise give them?"

"And give them the freedom they would otherwise lose forever!"

"How could you give them freedom?"

"By refusing to control them!"

"But you would only be leaving the control in other hands."

"Whose?"

"The charlatan, the demagogue, the salesman, the ward heeler, the bully, the cheat, the educator, the priest – all who are now in possession of the techniques of behavioral engineering."

"A pretty good share of the control would remain in the hands of the individual himself."

"That's an assumption, too, and it's your only hope. It's your only possible chance to avoid the implications of a science of behavior. If man is free, then a technology of behavior is impossible. But I'm asking you to consider the other case."

"Then my answer is that your assumption is contrary to fact and any further consideration idle."

"And your accusations –?"

"– were in terms of intention, not of possible achievement."

Frazier sighed dramatically.

"It's a little late to be proving that a behavioral technology is well advanced. How can you deny it? Many of its methods and techniques are really as old as the hills. Look at their frightful misuse in the hands of the Nazis! And what about the techniques of the psychological clinic? What about education? Or religion? Or practical politics? Or advertising and salesmanship? Bring them all together and you have a sort of rule-of-thumb technology of vast power. No, Mr. Castle, the science is there for the asking. But its techniques and methods are in the wrong hands – they are used for personal aggrandizement in a competitive world or, in the case of the psychologist and educator, for futilely corrective purposes. My question is, have you the courage to take up and wield the science of behavior for the good of mankind? You answer that you would dump it in the ocean!"

"I'd want to take it out of the hands of the politicians and advertisers and salesmen, too."

"And the psychologists and educators? You see, Mr. Castle, you can't have that kind of cake. The fact is, we not only *can* control human behavior, we *must*. But who's to do it, and what's to be done?"

"So long as a trace of personal freedom survives, I'll stick to my position," said Castle, very much out of countenance.

"Isn't it time we talked about freedom?" I said. "We parted a day or so ago on an agreement to let the question of freedom ring. It's time to answer, don't you think?"

"My answer is simple enough," said Frazier. "I deny that freedom exists at all. I must deny it – or my program would be absurd. You can't have a science about a subject matter which hops capriciously about. Perhaps we can never *prove* that man isn't free; it's an assumption. But the increasing success of a science of behavior makes it more and more plausible."

"On the contrary, a simple personal experience makes it untenable," said Castle. "The experience of freedom. I *know* that I'm free."

"It must be quite consoling," said Frazier.

"And what's more – you do, too," said Castle hotly. "When you deny your own freedom for the sake of playing with a science of behavior, you're acting in plain bad faith. That's the only way I can explain it." He tried to recover himself and shrugged his shoulders. "At least you'll grant that you *feel* free."

"The 'feeling of freedom' should deceive no one," said Frazier. "Give me a concrete case."

"Well, right now," Castle said. He picked up a book of matches. "I'm free to hold or drop these matches."

"You will, of course, do one or the other," said Frazier. "Linguistically or logically there seem to be two possibilities, but I submit that there's only one in fact. The determining forces may be subtle but they are inexorable. I suggest that as an orderly person you will probably hold – ah! you drop them! Well, you see, that's all part of your behavior with respect to me. You couldn't resist the temptation to prove me wrong. It was all lawful. You had no choice. The deciding factor entered rather late, and naturally you couldn't foresee the result when you first held them up. There was no strong likelihood that you would act in either direction, and so you said you were free."

"That's entirely too glib," said Castle. "It's easy to argue lawfulness after the fact. But let's see you predict what I will do in advance. Then I'll agree there's law."

"I didn't say that behavior is always predictable, any more than the weather is always predictable. There are often too many factors to be taken into account. We can't measure them all accurately, and we couldn't perform the mathematical operations needed to make a prediction if we had the measurements. The legality is usually an assumption – but none the less important in judging the issue at hand."

"Take a case where there's no choice, then," said Castle. "Certainly a man in jail isn't free in the sense in which I am free now."

"Good! That's an excellent start. Let us classify the kinds of determiners of human behavior. One class, as you suggest, is physical restraint – handcuffs, iron bars, forcible coercion. These are ways in which we shape human behavior according to our wishes. They're crude, and they sacrifice the affection of the controllee, but they often work. Now, what other ways are there of limiting freedom?"

Frazier had adopted a professorial tone and Castle refused to answer.

"The threat of force would be one," I said.

"Right. And here again we shan't encourage any loyalty on the part of the controllee. He has perhaps a shade more of the feeling of freedom, since he can always 'choose to act and accept the consequences,' but he doesn't feel exactly free. He knows his behavior is being coerced. Now what else?"

I had no answer.

"Force or the threat of force – I see no other possibility," said Castle after a moment.

"Precisely," said Frazier.

"But certainly a large part of my behavior has no connection with force at all. There's my freedom!" said Castle.

"I wasn't agreeing that there was no other possibility – merely that *you* could see no other. Not being a good behaviorist – or a good Christian, for that matter – you have no feeling for a tremendous power of a different sort."

"What's that?"

"I shall have to be technical," said Frazier. "But only for a moment. It's what the science of behavior calls 'reinforcement theory.' The things that can happen to us fall into three classes. To some things we are indifferent. Other things we like – we want them to happen, and we take steps to make them happen again. Still other things we don't like – we don't want them to happen and we take steps to get rid of them or keep them from happening again.

"*Now*," Frazier continued earnestly, "if it's in our power to create any of the situations which a person likes or to remove any situation he doesn't like, we can control his behavior. When he behaves as we want him to behave, we simply create a situation he likes, or remove one he doesn't like. As a result, the probability that he will behave that way again goes up, which is what we want. Technically it's called 'positive reinforcement.'

"The old school made the amazing mistake of supposing that the reverse was true, that by removing a situation a person likes or setting up one he doesn't like – in other words by punishing him – it was possible to *reduce* the probability that he would behave in a given way again. That simply doesn't hold. It has been established beyond question. What is emerging at this critical stage in the evolution of society is a behavioral and cultural technology based on positive reinforcement alone. We are gradually discovering – at an untold cost in human suffering – that in the long run punishment doesn't reduce the probability that an act will occur. We have been so preoccupied with the contrary that we always take 'force' to mean punishment. We don't say we're using force when we send shiploads of food into a starving country, though we're displaying quite as much *power* as if we were sending troops and guns."

"I'm certainly not an advocate of force," said Castle. "But I can't agree that it's not effective."[...]

"Now, early forms of government are naturally based on punishment. It's the obvious technique when the physically strong control the weak. But we're in the throes of a great change to positive reinforcement – from a competitive society in which one man's reward is another man's punishment, to a cooperative society in which no one gains at the expense of anyone else.

"The change is slow and painful because the immediate, temporary effect of punishment overshadows the eventual advantage of positive reinforcement. We've all seen countless instances of the temporary effect of force, but clear evidence of the effect of not using force is rare. That's why I insist that Jesus, who was apparently the first to discover the power of refusing to punish, must have hit upon the principle by accident. He certainly had none of the experimental evidence which is available to us today, and I can't conceive that it was possible, no matter what the man's genius, to have discovered the principle from casual observation."

"A touch of revelation, perhaps?" said Castle.

"No, accident. Jesus discovered one principle because it had immediate consequences, and he got another thrown in for good measure."

I began to see light.

"You mean the principle of 'love your enemies'?" I said.

"Exactly! To 'do good to those who despitefully use you' has two unrelated consequences. You gain the peace of mind we talked about the other day. Let the stronger man push you around – at least you avoid the torture of your own rage. *That's* the immediate consequence. What an astonishing discovery it must have been to find that in the long run you could *control the stronger man* in the same way!"

"It's generous of you to give so much credit to your early colleague," said Castle, "but why are we still in the throes of so much misery? Twenty centuries should have been enough for one piece of behavioral engineering."

"The conditions which made the principle difficult to discover made it difficult to teach. The history of the Christian Church doesn't reveal many cases of doing good to one's enemies. To inoffensive heathens, perhaps, but not enemies. One must look outside the field of organized religion to find the principle in practice at all. Church governments are devotees of *power*, both temporal and bogus."

"But what has all this got to do with freedom?" I said hastily.

Frazier took time to reorganize his behavior. He looked steadily toward the window, against which the rain was beating heavily.

"Now that we *know* how positive reinforcement works and why negative doesn't," he said at last, "we can be more deliberate, and hence more successful, in our cultural design. We can achieve a sort of control under which the controlled, though they are following a code much more scrupulously than was ever the case under the old system, nevertheless *feel free*. They are doing what they want to do, not what they are forced to do. That's the source of the tremendous power of positive reinforcement – there's no restraint and no revolt. By a careful cultural design, we control not the final behavior, but the *inclination* to behave – the motives, the desires, the wishes.

"The curious thing is that in that case the *question of freedom never arises*. Mr. Castle was free to drop the matchbook in the sense that nothing was preventing him. If it had been securely bound to his hand he wouldn't have been free. Nor would he have been quite free if I'd covered him with a gun and threatened to shoot him if he let it fall. The question of freedom arises when there is restraint – either physical or psychological.

"But restraint is only one sort of control, and absence of restraint isn't freedom. It's not control that's lacking when one feels 'free,' but the objectionable control of force. Mr. Castle felt free to hold or drop the matches in the sense that he felt no restraint – no threat of punishment in taking either course of action. He neglected to examine his positive reasons for holding or letting go, in spite of the fact that these were more compelling in this instance than any threat of force.

"We have no vocabulary of freedom in dealing with what we want to do," Frazier went on. "The question never arises. When men strike for freedom, they strike against jails and the police, or the threat of them – against oppression. They never strike against forces which make them want to act the way they do. Yet, it seems to be understood that governments will operate only through force or the threat of force, and that all other principles of control will be left to education, religion, and commerce. If this continues to be the case, we may as well give up. A government can never create a free people with the techniques now allotted to it.

"The question is: Can men live in freedom and peace? And the answer is: Yes, if we can build a social structure which will satisfy the needs of everyone and in which everyone will want to observe the supporting code. But so far this has been achieved only in Walden Two. Your ruthless accusations to the contrary, Mr. Castle, this is the freest place on earth. And it is free precisely because we make no use of force or the threat of force. Every bit of our research, from the nursery through the psychological management of our adult membership, is directed toward that end – to exploit every alternative to forcible control. By skillful planning, by a wise choice of techniques we *increase* the feeling of freedom.

"It's not planning which infringes upon freedom, but planning which uses force. A sense of freedom was practically unknown in the planned society of Nazi Germany, because the planners made a fantastic use of force and the threat of force.

"No, Mr. Castle, when a science of behavior has once been achieved, there's no alternative to a planned society. We can't leave mankind to an accidental or biased control. But by using the principle of positive reinforcement – carefully avoiding force or the threat of force – we can preserve a personal sense of freedom."

Frazier threw himself back upon the bed and stared at the ceiling.

Comments and Questions on B. F. Skinner: "Walden Two: Freedom and the Behavioral Sciences"

1.   Frazier claims that Walden Two is the "freest place on earth" while Castle thinks it lacks any freedom whatsoever. To Castle, it is a thor-

oughly fascist or totalitarian state. They seem to be operating with different notions of freedom. How would you define what each of them means by freedom? Who do you side with in this debate – Frazier or Castle? Which one is right about the freedom of Walden Two? Or are both of them right, or both wrong?

2.   If we had a science of human behavior at our disposal, says Frazier, and we knew what the good life was, why shouldn't we use that science to make the good life available to all and make people happy? But what is "the good life," asks Castle at another point in the novel, and who is to decide what the good life is for other people? Isn't this issue of knowing the good life the missing link in Frazier's program of behavioral control? Frazier responds: "Of course, I know nothing about your course in ethics, but the philosopher in search of a rational basis for deciding what is good has always reminded me of the centipede trying to decide how to walk. Simply go ahead and walk! We all know what's good, until we stop to think about it." Frazier goes on to say that "the good life" consists of five things: (a) good health, (b) a minimum amount of unpleasant labor, (c) a chance to exercise one's talents and abilities, (d) intimate and satisfying personal relations and (e) plenty of leisure (and Walden Two affords all of them). He concludes: "And that's all, Mr. Castle – absolutely all. I can't give you a rational justification for any of it. I can't reduce it to any principle of 'the greatest good.' This *is* the Good Life. We know it. It's a fact, not a theory. It has an experimental justification, not a rational one." That experimental justification is Walden Two itself which is a kind of scientific experiment showing us what the good life can be like. Is this an adequate answer to Castle's question about what the good life is and who is to decide what it is? It is difficult to deny that we all want a good measure of the five things Frazier mentions as ingredients of the good life. So has he adequately defined the Good Life? And how, if at all, is this question about the Good Life – and who decides what it is – connected to the issue of free will?

3.   It is an interesting exercise to compare Skinner's *Walden Two* to other famous dystopian works of the twentieth century such as Aldous Huxley's *Brave New World* (1932) and George Orwell's *1984*. Interestingly enough, Orwell was writing *1984* in 1948, the same year as *Walden Two*. Orwell simply inverted the last two digits of that date to get 1984. Skinner would argue that Huxley's Brave New World and the society of Orwell's 1984 really are fascist or totalitarian states in the worst sense of those terms. *Brave New World* depicts a hierarchical society in which elites rule over lower-echelon workers who are controlled by drugs. By contrast, Walden Two is an egalitarian society in which everyone has a rich and

lively personal life. Orwell's 1984 society is a police state in which all thought and behavior is monitored by the powers that be and misbehavior is severely punished. By contrast, there is no punishment in Walden Two and no coercion. Thus the objectionable features of *Brave New World* and *1984* are not to be found in Walden Two, Skinner would argue. So one can't object to Walden Two as one might object to these other utopian societies. Is Skinner right about this? A suggested exercise is to read all three novels and test your answer further.

Suggested Reading

Skinner's views are further developed in a philosophical work, *Beyond Freedom and Dignity* (1971). Bruce Waller's *Freedom Without Responsibility* (1990) is an interesting defense of some of Skinner's ideas about free will and responsibility by a philosopher. Aldous Huxley's *Brave New World* ([1932] 1989) and George Orwell's *1984* (1949) are well-known dystopian novels that can be usefully compared to (and contrasted with) *Walden Two*.

2

The Compatibility of Freedom and Determinism

Kai Nielsen

Editor's Introduction

Kai Nielsen is Professor of Philosophy at the University of Calgary. He is past President of the Canadian Philosophical Association and past editor of the *Canadian Journal of Philosophy*. In the selections reprinted here from his book *Reason and Practice* (1971), Nielsen defends a classical *compatibilist* view of free will, according to which freedom in every worthwhile sense is compatible with determinism. The common belief that free will and determinism conflict, he argues, arises from a variety of misconceptions which he attempts to expose in this reading. The classical compatibilist view that Nielsen defends in this selection was held by many important figures in the history of modern philosophy, as he notes, including Thomas Hobbes, David Hume, and John Stuart Mill; and it has been a very popular view among philosophers and scientists in the twentieth century, including G. E. Moore, Moritz Schlick, and A. J. Ayer. Nielsen not only asserts that freedom is compatible with determinism. Like many other classical compatibilists, he also believes that determinism is true. So his view represents *soft determinism* as well as compatibilism.

I

[...]
What I now wish to consider is what I take to be the most significant question we can ask about determinism and human conduct: Is determinism compatible with our central beliefs concerning the freedom of conduct

and moral responsibility? It was because they thought that such beliefs were plainly incompatible that Dostoevsky and James were so nagged by determinism. With such philosophers as Thomas Hobbes, David Hume, John Stuart Mill, Moritz Schlick, and A. J. Ayer – all staunch defenders of the compatibility thesis – there is a vast shift not only in argument but also in attitude. There is no *Angst* over the ubiquitousness of causal laws. There is no feeling that life would be meaningless and man would be a prisoner of his past if determinism were true. Holbach is wrong. Even if determinism is true, freedom is not an illusion. The belief that it is an illusion is a philosophical confusion resting on a failure to pay sufficiently close attention either to the actual role of our concept of freedom in our lives or to the actual nature of determinism. It is such a twin failure that generates the conflicts we have been investigating.

The crucial point to note initially is that Mill and Schlick, as much as Holbach and Darrow, are thoroughgoing determinists. But they are determinists who do not believe that freedom and determinism are incompatible. James dismissed this position contemptuously with the label "soft determinism". For him "soft determinism" had an emotive force similar to "soft on Communism". But while a summer bachelor is no bachelor at all, a soft determinist is just as much a determinist as a hard determinist. I shall continue to use the label "soft determinism" – although I shall not use it in any derogatory sense – to refer to the view that maintains that determinism and human freedom are logically compatible. (Sometimes in the literature they are called "compatibilists".) A view such as Holbach's or Darrow's, which Schlick says rests on "a whole series of confusions," I shall call "hard determinism". (Sometimes in the literature "hard determinists" are called "incompatibilists", for they believe freedom and determinism are incompatible.) But both hard and soft determinists agree that every event or state, including every human action or attitude, has a cause; that is, for anything whatsoever there are sufficient conditions for its occurrence.

The at least *prima facie* surprising thing is that these soft determinists still believe in the freedom of conduct and believe that human beings are – at least sometimes, anyway – responsible moral agents capable of acting in specific situations in ways other than those in which they in fact acted. Let us see how the soft determinist argument unfolds.

II

Morality, soft determinists argue, has or should have no interest in the determinism/indeterminism controversy. Morality is indeed vitally interested in the freedom of conduct, for it only makes sense to say that men ought to do one thing rather than another on the assumption that sometimes they can do other than what they in fact do. If no man can do other than what he does in fact do, then all talk of what men ought to do or what is right and wrong is indeed senseless. But to be interested in the freedom of conduct, as morality properly is, is not at all to be interested in some mysterious and no doubt illusory "freedom of the will". "Freedom" has its opposite, "compulsion" or "coercion". A man is free if he does not act under compulsion. He is free when he is able to do what he wants to do or when his acts and actions are in accordance with his own choices and decisions, and when what he wants to do or what he chooses is not determined by some person, force, or some disposition, such as kleptomania, which has gained ascendency over him. He is, by contrast, unfree to the extent that he is unable to achieve what he wants to achieve and to act in accordance with choices based on his own rational deliberation because of either outside influence or psychological malaise. "Freedom" does not mean some scarcely intelligible state of affairs, "exemption or partial exemption from causal law" or "breach of causal continuity". To be free is to have the ability and opportunity to do what one wants to do and to act in accordance with one's own rational deliberations, without constraint and compulsion. It is something which, of course, admits of degrees.

Mill, Schlick, and Ayer argue that an anthropomorphic view of our language tricks us into thinking that man cannot be free if determinism is true. People tend to think that if determinism is true, events are in the power of other events and a person's acts or actions cannot alter the course of events. What will happen in the future is already fixed by immutable causal laws. But such views rest on unrealistic, anthropomorphic thinking. They are scarcely a part of a tough-minded deterministic world perspective.

Similar anthropomorphic transformations are made with "necessity" and the little word "cause". And this, too, leads to needless befuddlement by causing us to misunderstand the actual workings of our language. It is, for example, terribly easy for the unwary to confuse causal and logical necessitation. But there is a very considerable difference in the meaning of "must" in "If you cut off his head, he must die" and "If it is a square, it must have four sides". In the latter case – an example of logical necessitation – "having four sides" follows by virtue of the meaning of the term "square". The "must" refers to this logical relationship. In the former case, it holds in virtue of something in the world. People also infer mistakenly that the event or effect is somehow contained in the cause. But this mystification is hardly intelligible.

There is also, as Schlick points out, a persistent confusion between laws of nature and legal laws. The word "law" has very different meanings in such cases. Legal laws *prescribe* a certain course of action. Many of them are intended to constrain or coerce you into acting in a certain way. But laws of nature are not prescriptions to act in a certain way. They do not constrain you; rather, they are statements of regularities, of *de facto* invariable sequences that are parts of the world. In talking of such natural laws we often bring in an uncritical use of "force", as if the earth were being pushed and pulled around by the sun. Putting the matter this way makes one feel as if one is always being compelled or constrained, when in reality one is not. Without the anthropomorphic embellishment, it becomes evident that a determinist commits himself, when he asserts that *A* causes *B*, to the view that *whenever* an event or act of type *A* occurs, an event or act of type *B* will occur. The part about compulsion or constraint is metaphorical. It is because of the metaphor, and not because of the fact, that we come to think that there is an antithesis between causality and freedom. It is the *manner* here and not the *matter* that causes the trouble.

Demythologized and correctly conceived, causal necessity as applied to human actions is, Mill argues, simply this: Given the motives that are present to an individual's mind, and given the character and disposition of the individual, the manner in which he will act can be "unerringly inferred." That is to say, if we knew the person thoroughly, and knew all the inducements acting upon him, we could predict or retrodict his conduct with as much certainty as we can predict any physical event. This, Mill argues, is a bit of common sense and is in reality not in conflict with our operative concept of human freedom, for even if we say that all human acts are in principle predictable, this is not to say that people are acting under compulsion or constraint, for to say that their actions are predictable is not to say or even to give one to understand that they are being manipulated by anything or anybody. Being under some sort of compulsion or constraint is what limits our freedom.

III

The natural reaction to such a belief is this: If "causal necessity" means anything, it means that no human being could, *categorically* could, do anything other in exactly similar circumstances than what he in fact does. If determinism is true, we must believe that for every event and for every action there are sufficient conditions, and when these conditions obtain, the action must occur. Since this is so, aren't all our actions in reality under constraint and thus, after all, not really free?

Soft determinists try to show that such an objection is a snarl of conceptual confusions, and that once we untangle them we will not take this incompatibilist line. A. J. Ayer makes one of the clearest and most forceful defenses of this view. His argument will be followed here, with a few supplementations from Mill.

The conceptual facts we need to clarify are these: If the word "freedom" is to have a meaning, it must be contrasted with something, for otherwise it is quite unintelligible. If I tell you I have just bought a wok, but I cannot contrast a wok with any *conceivable* thing that I would *deny* is a wok or not assert is a wok, then I have not been able to convey to you the meaning of "wok". In fact, if it is not so contrastable, it is indeed meaningless. The same thing obtains for any descriptive term. Thus, "freedom", if it is to be intelligible, must be contrastable with something. There must at least be some *conceivable* situations in which it is correct to use the word and some *conceivable* situations in which it would not be correct. Yet it is plainly not an unintelligible sound, but a word with a use in our discourse. So we must look for its nonvacuous contrast. It is here where the soft determinists' initial point is critical. "Freedom" is to be contrasted with "constraint" or "compulsion" rather than with "determinism", for if we try to contrast it with "determinism", it is far from clear that we get an intelligible contrast. It is not clear what sort of an action we would count as a "causeless action". But if we contrast "freedom" and "constraint", the contrast is clear. So we should say that a man's action is not free when it is constrained or when he is compelled to do what he does.

Suppose I say, "There is to be no smoking in the classroom." By this act I put the people in the room under constraint. I limit their freedom. But suppose Fearless Fosdick lights up anyway and I say, "Put it out, Mister, if you want to stay in the class." I in effect compel him, or at least attempt to compel him, to put it out. Being compelled or constrained to do something may very well entail that the act has a cause. But plainly the *converse* does not hold. As Ayer puts it, "From the fact that my action is causally determined it does not necessarily follow that I am constrained to do it." This is an important point to make, for to say this is in effect to claim that it does not necessarily follow from the fact that my actions are determined that I am not free. But, as I have said, if instead we take "freedom" and "being causally determined" as our contrastable terms, we get no clear contrast. On the other hand, even in a deterministic world we have with our above distinction between "freedom" and "compulsion" or "constraint" preserved the needed contrast. [...]

A kleptomaniac cannot correctly be said to be a free agent, in respect to his stealing, because even if he does go through what appears to be deliberations about whether to steal or not to steal, such deliberations are irrelevant to his actual behavior in the respect of whether he will or will not steal. Whatever he resolved to do, he would steal all the same.

This case is important because it clearly shows the difference between the man – the kleptomaniac – who is not free with respect to his stealing and an ordinary thief who is. The ordinary thief goes through a process of deciding whether or not to steal, and his decision decisively effects his behavior. If he actually resolved to refrain from stealing, he could carry out his resolution. But this is not so with the kleptomaniac. Thus, this observable difference between the ordinary thief and the kleptomaniac, quite independently of the issue of determinism, enables us to ascertain that the former is freer than the latter. [...]

IV

Yet, in spite of these evident contrasts, we are still haunted, when we are in the grip of a philosophical perplexity about freedom and determinism, by the question, or muddle felt as a question: Do not all causes equally necessitate? Is it not arbitrary "to say that a person is free when he is necessitated in one fashion but not when he is necessitated in another"?

Soft determinists reply that if "necessitate" merely means "cause", then of course "All causes equally necessitate" is equivalent to "All causes equally cause" – and that is hardly news. But "All causes equally constrain or compel" is not true. If one event is the cause of another, we are stating that the event said to be the effect would not have occurred if it had not been for the occurrence of the event said to be the cause. But this states nothing about compulsion or constraint. There is indeed an invariable concomitance between the two classes of events; but there is no compulsion in any but a metaphorical sense. Such invariable concomitance gives a necessary but not sufficient condition for causation. It is difficult and perhaps even impossible to say what constitutes a sufficient condition. But given the frequent situations in which we speak of one thing causing another without asserting or implying a compulsion or constraint, they plainly are not further necessary conditions. (When I watch a wren in the park my behavior has causes sufficient for its occurrence, but I was neither compelled, constrained, nor forced to watch the wren.) Whatever more we need beyond invariable concomitance for causation, compulsion isn't one of the elements.

Even in a deterministic world we can do other than what we in fact do, since all "cans" are constitutionally iffy. That is to say, they are all hypothetical. This dark saying needs explanation. Consider what we actually mean by saying, "I could have done otherwise." It means, soft determinists argue, "I should have acted otherwise if I had chosen" or "I would have done otherwise if I had wanted to". And "I can do X" means "If I want to I shall do X" or "If I choose to do X I will do X".

In general, soft determinists argue, we say a man is free rather than unfree when the following conditions hold:

1. He could have done otherwise if he had chosen to.
2. His actions are voluntary in the sense that the kleptomaniac's stealing is not.
3. Nobody compelled him to choose as he did.

Now it should be noted that these conditions are frequently fulfilled or satisfied. Thus, "freedom" has a definite contrast and application. Basically it contrasts with constraint. Since this is so, we can say when it is true or probably true to assert that a man is free, and when it is false or probably false to say that he is free. Given the truth of this, it is evident that a man can act as a free and responsible moral agent even though his actions are determined. If we are not talking about some obscure notion of "free will" but about what Schlick calls the "freedom of conduct", freedom is after all compatible with determinism.

Comments and Questions on Kai Nielsen's "The Compatibility of Freedom and Determinism"

1. Nielsen says: "Even if determinism is true, freedom is not an illusion. The belief that it is an illusion is a philosophical confusion resting on a failure to pay sufficiently close attention either to the actual role of the concept of freedom in our lives or to the actual nature of determinism." What is it, according to Nielsen, about "the actual role of the concept of freedom in our lives" that we fail to attend to when we mistakenly think that it conflicts with determinism? What is it about "the actual nature of determinism" that we fail to attend to when we mistakenly think it conflicts with freedom? Is Nielsen right about all this?
2. Nielsen says we ordinarily think that kleptomaniacs who steal compulsively are not acting freely or of their own free will, whereas ordinary thieves who are not kleptomaniacs are acting freely and should be held

responsible for their acts. But the difference between the two, he thinks, is not that one of them is determined and the other is not, since both may be determined. What then *does* he think the difference is between the kleptomaniac and the ordinary thief if it is not a matter of one of them being determined and the other not? Do you agree with Nielsen's treatment of the case of the kleptomaniac? Does it show that what we ordinarily mean by freedom and responsibility is compatible with determinism, as he claims?

Suggested Reading

For other twentieth-century defenses of a classical compatibilist and soft determinist positions like Nielsen's, see Moritz Schlick, "When is a Man Responsible?" (1966) and A. J. Ayer, "Freedom and Necessity" (1954). For criticisms of classical compatibilism, see the next reading in this volume by Roderick Chisholm ("Human Freedom and the Self"). Other critics of classical compatibilism are J. L. Austin, "Ifs and Cans" (1961) and Keith Lehrer," 'Can's Without 'If's" (1968).

3

Human Freedom and the Self

Roderick Chisholm

Editor's Introduction

Roderick Chisholm was Professor of Philosophy at Brown University and former President of the American Philosophical Association. In this selection, he gives a now classic statement of the *libertarian* position on free will, according to which human beings have a freedom of the will that is *incompatible* with determinism. The puzzle that Chisholm addresses in this influential paper is that free will not only appears to conflict with a deterministic view of human action; it also appears to conflict with an indeterministic view of human action. Free actions cannot be (deterministically) caused, but neither can they be uncaused, or happen merely by chance. The only way out for Chisholm is to assume that there is a third option: free actions *are* caused, but *"not* by other events or states of affairs, but by the agent, whatever he may be." The special *agent-causation* he describes, which cannot be reduced to causation by events, is also called "immanent causation" by Chisholm. One must postulate such a thing, he thinks, to account for a *self-determination* that is not reducible to either determinism or indeterminism – and thus to solve the free will problem.

A staff moves a stone, and is moved by a hand, which is moved by a man.
Aristotle, Physics, 256a

1.   The metaphysical problem of human freedom might be summarized in the following way: Human beings are responsible agents; but this fact appears to conflict with a deterministic view of human action (the view that every event that is involved in an act is caused by some other event);

and it *also* appears to conflict with an indeterministic view of human action (the view that the act, or some event that is essential to the act, is not caused at all). To solve the problem, I believe, we must make somewhat far-reaching assumptions about the self or the agent – about the man who performs the act.

Perhaps it is needless to remark that, in all likelihood, it is impossible to say anything significant about this ancient problem that has not been said before.[1]

2.   Let us consider some deed, or misdeed, that may be attributed to a responsible agent: one man, say, shot another. If the man *was* responsible for what he did, then, I would urge, what was to happen at the time of the shooting was something that was entirely up to the man himself. There was a moment at which it was true, both that he could have fired the shot and also that he could have refrained from firing it. And if this is so, then, even though he did fire it, he could have done something else instead. (He didn't find himself firing the shot "against his will," as we say.) I think we can say, more generally, then, that if a man is responsible for a certain event or a certain state of affairs (in our example, the shooting of another man), then that event or state of affairs was brought about by some act of his, and the act was something that was in his power either to perform or not to perform.

But now if the act which he *did* perform was an act that was also in his power *not* to perform, then it could not have been caused or determined by any event that was not itself within his power either to bring about or not to bring about. For example, if what we say he did was really something that was brought about by a second man, one who forced his hand upon the trigger, say, or who, by means of hypnosis, compelled him to perform the act, then since the act was caused by the *second* man it was nothing that was within the power of the *first* man to prevent. And precisely the same thing is true, I think, if instead of referring to a second man who compelled the first one, we speak instead of the *desires* and *beliefs* which the first man happens to have had. For if what we say he did was really something that was brought about by his own beliefs and desires, if these beliefs and desires in the particular situation in which he happened to have found himself caused him to do just what it was that we say he did do, then since *they* caused it, *he* was unable to do anything other than just what it was that he did do. It makes no difference whether the cause of the deed was internal or external; if the cause was some state or event for which the man himself was not responsible, then he was not responsible for what we have been mistakenly calling his act.

If a flood caused the poorly constructed dam to break, then, given the flood and the constitution of the dam, the break, we may say, *had* to occur and nothing could have happened in its place. And if the flood of desire caused the weak-willed man to give in, then he, too, had to do just what it was that he did do and he was no more responsible than was the dam for the results that followed. (It is true, of course, that if the man is responsible for the beliefs and desires that he happens to have, then he may also be responsible for the things they lead him to do. But the question now becomes: *is* he responsible for the beliefs and desires he happens to have? If he is, then there was a time when they were within his power either to acquire or not to acquire, and we are left, therefore, with our general point.)

One may object: But surely if there were such a thing as a man who is really *good*, then he would be responsible for things that he would do; yet, he would be unable to do anything other than just what it is that he does do, since, being good, he will always choose to do what is best. The answer, I think, is suggested by a comment that Thomas Reid makes on an ancient author. The author had said of Cato, "He was good because he could not be otherwise," and Reid observes: "But this saying, if understood literally and strictly, is not the praise of Cato, but of his constitution, which was no more the work of Cato, than his existence."[2] If Cato was himself responsible for the good things that he did, then Cato, as Reid suggests, was such that, although he had the power to do what was not good, he exercised his power only for that which was good.

All of this, if it is true, may give a certain amount of comfort to those who are tender-minded. But we should remind them that it also conflicts with a familiar view about the nature of God – with the view that St Thomas Aquinas expresses by saying that "every movement both of the will and of nature proceeds from God as the Prime Mover."[3] If the act of the sinner *did* proceed from God as the Prime Mover, then God was in the position of the second agent we just discussed – the man who forced the trigger finger, or the hypnotist – and the sinner, so-called, was *not* responsible for what he did. (This may be a bold assertion, in view of the history of western theology, but I must say that I have never encountered a single good reason for denying it.)

There is one standard objection to all of this and we should consider it briefly.

3.   The objection takes the form of a stratagem – one designed to show that determinism (and divine providence) is consistent with human

responsibility. The stratagem is one that was used by Jonathan Edwards and by many philosophers in the present century, most notably, G. E. Moore.[4]

One proceeds as follows: The expression

(a) He could have done otherwise,

it is argued, means no more nor less than

(b) If he had chosen to do otherwise, then he would have done otherwise.

(In place of "chosen," one might say "tried," "set out," "decided," "undertaken," or "willed.") The truth of statement (b), it is then pointed out, is consistent with determinism (and with divine providence); for even if all of the man's actions were causally determined, the man could still be such that, *if* he had chosen otherwise, then he would have done otherwise. What the murderer saw, let us suppose, along with his beliefs and desires, *caused* him to fire the shot; yet he was such that *if*, just then, he had chosen or decided *not* to fire the shot, then he would not have fired it. All of this is certainly possible. Similarly, we could say, of the dam, that the flood caused it to break and also that the dam was such that, *if* there had been no flood or any similar pressure, then the dam would have remained intact. And therefore, the argument proceeds, if (b) is consistent with determinism, and if (a) and (b) say the same thing, then (a) is also consistent with determinism; hence we can say that the agent *could* have done otherwise even though he was caused to do what he did do; and therefore determinism and moral responsibility are compatible.

Is the argument sound? The conclusion follows from the premises, but the catch, I think, lies in the first premise – the one saying that statement (a) tells us no more nor less than what statement (b) tells us. For (b), it would seem, could be true while (a) is false. That is to say, our man might be such that, if he had chosen to do otherwise, then he would have done otherwise, and yet *also* such that he could not have done otherwise. Suppose, after all, that our murderer could not have *chosen*, or could not have *decided*, to do otherwise. Then the fact that he happens also to be a man such that, if he had chosen not to shoot he would not have shot, would make no difference. For if he could *not* have chosen *not* to shoot, then he could not have done anything other than just what it was that he did do. In a word: from our statement (b) above ("If he had chosen to do otherwise, then he would have done otherwise"), we cannot make an inference to (a) above ("He could have done otherwise") unless we can *also* assert:

(c) He could have chosen to do otherwise.

And therefore, if we must reject this third statement (c), then, even though we may be justified in asserting (b), we are not justified in asserting (a). If the man could not have chosen to do otherwise, then he would not have done otherwise – *even if* he was such that, if he *had* chosen to do otherwise, then he would have done otherwise.

The stratagem in question, then, seems to me not to work, and I would say, therefore, that the ascription of responsibility conflicts with a deterministic view of action.

4.   Perhaps there is less need to argue that the ascription of responsibility also conflicts with an indeterministic view of action – with the view that the act, or some event that is essential to the act, is not caused at all. If the act – the firing of the shot – was not caused at all, if it was fortuitous or capricious, happening so to speak out of the blue, then, presumably, no one – and nothing – was responsible for the act. Our conception of action, therefore, should be neither deterministic nor indeterministic. Is there any other possibility?

5.   We must not say that every event involved in the act is caused by some other event; and we must not say that the act is something that is not caused at all. The possibility that remains, therefore, is this: We should say that at least one of the events that are involved in the act is caused, not by any other events, but by something else instead. And this something else can only be the agent – the man. If there is an event that is caused, not by other events, but by the man, then there are some events involved in the act that are not caused by other events. But if the event in question is caused by the man then it *is* caused and we are not committed to saying that there is something involved in the act that is not caused at all.

But this, of course, is a large consequence, implying something of considerable importance about the nature of the agent or the man.

6.   If we consider only inanimate natural objects, we may say that causation, if it occurs, is a relation between *events* or *states of affairs*. The dam's breaking was an event that was caused by a set of other events – the dam being weak, the flood being strong, and so on. But if a man is

responsible for a particular deed, then, if what I have said is true, there is some event, or set of events, that is caused, *not* by other events or states of affairs, but by the agent, whatever he may be.

I shall borrow a pair of medieval terms, using them, perhaps, in a way that is slightly different from that for which they were originally intended. I shall say that when one event or state of affairs (or set of events or states of affairs) causes some other event or state of affairs, then we have an instance of *transeunt* causation. And I shall say that when an *agent*, as distinguished from an event, causes an event or state of affairs, then we have an instance of *immanent* causation.

The nature of what is intended by the expression "immanent caus-ation" may be illustrated by this sentence from Aristotle's *Physics*. "Thus, a staff moves a stone, and is moved by a hand, which is moved by a man" (Book VII, Chap. 5, 256a, 6–8). If the man was responsible, then we have in this illustration a number of instances of causation – most of them transeunt but at least one of them immanent. What the staff did to the stone was an instance of transeunt causation, and thus we may describe it as a relation between events: "the motion of the staff caused the motion of the stone." And similarly for what the hand did to the staff: "the motion of the hand caused the motion of the staff." And, as we know from physiology, there are still other events which caused the motion of the hand. Hence we need not introduce the agent at this particular point, as Aristotle does – we *need* not, though we *may*. We *may* say that the hand was moved by the man, but we may *also* say that the motion of the hand was caused by the motion of certain muscles; and we may say that the motion of the muscles was caused by certain events that took place within the brain. But some event, and presumably one of those that took place within the brain, was caused by the agent and not by any other events.

There are, of course, objections to this way of putting the matter; I shall consider the two that seem to me to be most important.

7.   One may object, firstly: "If the *man* does anything, then, as Aris-totle's remark suggests, what he does is to move the *hand*. But he certainly does not *do* anything to his brain – he may not even know that he *has* a brain. And if he doesn't do anything to the brain, and if the motion of the hand was caused by something that happened within the brain, then there is no point in appealing to 'immanent causation' as being some-thing incompatible with 'transeunt causation' – for the whole thing, after all, is a matter of causal relations among events or states of affairs."

The answer to this objection, I think, is this: It is true that the agent does not *do* anything with his brain, or to his brain, in the sense in which he *does* something with his hand and does something to the staff. But from this it does not follow that the agent was not the immanent cause of something that happened within his brain.

We should note a useful distinction that has been proposed by Professor A. I. Melden – namely, the distinction between "making something A happen" and "doing A."[5] If I reach for the staff and pick it up, then one of the things that I *do* is just that – reach for the staff and pick it up. And if it is something that I do, then there is a very clear sense in which it may be said to be something that I know that I do. If you ask me, "Are you doing something, or trying to do something, with the staff?", I will have no difficulty in finding an answer. But in doing something with the staff, I also make various things happen which are not in this same sense things that I do: I will make various air-particles move; I will free a number of blades of grass from the pressure that had been upon them; and I may cause a shadow to move from one place to another. If these are merely things that I make happen, as distinguished from things that I do, then I may know nothing whatever about them; I may not have the slightest idea that, in moving the staff, I am bringing about any such thing as the motion of air-particles, shadows, and blades of grass.

We may say, in answer to the first objection, therefore, that it is true that our agent does nothing to his brain or with his brain; but from this it does not follow that the agent is not the immanent cause of some event within his brain; for the brain event may be something which, like the motion of the air-particles, he made happen in picking up the staff. The only difference between the two cases is this: in each case, he made something happen when he picked up the staff; but in the one case – the motion of the air-particles or of the shadows – it was the motion of the staff that caused the event to happen; and in the other case – the event that took place in the brain – it was this event that caused the motion of the staff.

The point is, in a word, that whenever a man does something A, then (by "immanent causation") he makes a certain cerebral event happen, and this cerebral event (by "transeunt causation") makes A happen.

8.   The second objection is more difficult and concerns the very concept of "immanent causation," or causation by an agent, as this concept is to be interpreted here. The concept is subject to a difficulty which has long been associated with that of the prime mover unmoved. We have said that there must be some event A, presumably some cerebral event,

which is caused not by any other event, but by the agent. Since A was not caused by any other event, then the agent himself cannot be said to have undergone any change or produced any other event (such as "an act of will" or the like) which brought A about. But if, when the agent made A happen, there was no event involved other than A itself, no event which could be described as *making* A happen, what did the agent's causation consist of? What, for example, is the difference between A's just happening, and the agent's *causing* A to happen? We cannot attribute the difference to any event that took place within the agent. And so far as the event A itself is concerned, there would seem to be no discernible difference. Thus Aristotle said that the activity of the prime mover is nothing in addition to the motion that it produces, and Suarez said that "the action is in reality nothing but the effect as it flows from the agent."[6] Must we conclude, then, that there is no more to the man's action in causing event A than there is to the event A's happening by itself? Here we would seem to have a distinction without a difference – in which case we have failed to find a *via media* between a deterministic and an indeterministic view of action.

The only answer, I think, can be this: that the difference between the man's causing A, on the one hand, and the event A just happening, on the other, lies in the fact that, in the first case but not the second, the event A *was* caused and was caused by the man. There was a brain event A; the agent did, in fact, cause the brain event; but there was nothing that he did to cause it.

This answer may not entirely satisfy and it will be likely to provoke the following question: "But what are you really *adding* to the assertion that A happened when you utter the words 'The agent *caused* A to happen'?" As soon as we have put the question this way, we see, I think, that whatever difficulty we may have encountered is one that may be traced to the concept of causation generally – whether "immanent" or "transeunt." The problem, in other words, is not a problem that is peculiar to our conception of human action. It is a problem that must be faced by anyone who makes use of the concept of causation at all; and therefore, I would say, it is a problem for everyone but the complete indeterminist.

For the problem, as we put it, referring just to "immanent causation," or causation by an agent, was this: "What is the difference between saying, of an event A, that A just happened and saying that someone caused A to happen?" The analogous problem, which holds for "transeunt causation," or causation by an event, is this: "What is the difference between saying, of two events A and B, that B happened and then A happened, and saying that B's happening was the *cause* of A's happening?" And the only answer that one can give is this – that in the one case the agent was the cause of A's happening and in the other case event B was the cause of A's happening. The nature of transeunt causation is no more clear than is that of immanent causation.

9.   But we may plausibly say – and there is a respectable philosophical tradition to which we may appeal – that the notion of immanent causation, or causation by an agent, is in fact more clear than that of transeunt causation, or causation by an event; and that it is only by understanding our own causal efficacy, as agents, that we can grasp the concept of *cause* at all. Hume may be said to have shown that we do not derive the concept of *cause* from what we perceive of external things. How, then, do we derive it? The most plausible suggestion, it seems to me, is that of Reid, once again: namely that "the conception of an efficient cause may very probably be derived from the experience we have had ... of our own power to produce certain effects."[7] If we did not understand the concept of immanent causation, we would not understand that of transeunt causation.

10.   It may have been noted that I have avoided the term "free will" in all of this. For even if there is such a faculty as "the will," which somehow sets our acts agoing, the question of freedom, as John Locke said, is not the question *"whether the will be free"*; it is the question *"whether a man be free."*[8] For if there is a "will," as a moving faculty, the question is whether the man is free to will to do these things that he does will to do – and also whether the man is free *not* to will any of those things that he does will to do, and, again, whether he is free to will any of those things that he does not will to do. Jonathan Edwards tried to restrict himself to the question – "Is the man free to do what it is that he wills?" – but the answer to the question will not tell us whether the man is responsible for what it is that he *does* will to do. Using still another pair of medieval terms, we may say that the metaphysical problem of freedom does not concern the *actus imperatus*, it does not concern the question whether we are free to accomplish whatever it is that we will or set out to do; it concerns the *actus elicitus*, the question whether we are free to will or to set out to do those things that we do will or set out to do.

11.   If we are responsible, and if what I have been trying to say is true, then we have a prerogative which some would attribute only to God: each of us, when we act, is a prime mover unmoved. In doing what we

do, we cause certain events to happen, and nothing – or no one – causes us to cause those events to happen.

12.   If we are thus prime movers unmoved and if our actions, or those for which we are responsible, are not causally determined, then they are not causally determined by our *desires*. And this means that the relation between what we want or what we desire, on the one hand, and what it is that we do, on the other, is not as simple as most philosophers would have it.

We may distinguish between what we might call the "Hobbist approach" and what we might call the "Kantian approach" to this question. The Hobbist approach is the one that is generally accepted at the present time, but the Kantian approach, I believe, is the one that is true. According to Hobbism, if we *know*, of some man, what his beliefs and desires happen to be and how strong they are, if we know what he feels certain of, what he desires more than anything else, and if we know the state of his body and what stimuli he is being subjected to, then we may *deduce*, logically, just what it is that he will do – or, more accurately, just what it is that he will try, set out, or undertake to do. Thus Professor Melden has said that "the connection between wanting and doing is logical."[9] But according to the Kantian approach to our problem, and this is the one that I would take, there is no such logical connection between wanting and doing, nor need there even be a causal connection. No set of statements about a man's desires, beliefs, and stimulus situation at any time implies any statement telling us what the man will try, set out, or undertake to do at that time. As Reid put it, though we may "reason from men's motives to their actions and, in many cases, with great probability," we can never do so "with absolute certainty."[10]

This means that, in one very strict sense of the terms, there can be no science of man. If we think of science as a matter of finding out what laws happen to hold, and if the statement of a law tells us what kinds of events are caused by what other kinds of events, then there will be human actions which we cannot explain by subsuming them under any laws. We cannot say, "It is causally necessary that, given such and such desires and beliefs, and being subject to such and such stimuli, the agent will do so and so." For at times the agent, if he chooses, may rise above his desires and do something else instead.

But all of this is consistent with saying that, perhaps more often than not, our desires do exist under conditions such that those conditions necessitate us to act. And we may also say, with Leibniz, that at other times our desires may "incline without necessitating."[...]

Notes

1 The general position to be presented here is suggested in the following writings, among others: Aristotle, *Eudemian Ethics*, book II, ch. 6; *Nicomachean Ethics*, book III, chs 1–5; Thomas Reid, *Essays on the Active Powers of Man*; C. A. Campbell, "Is 'Free Will' a Pseudo-Problem?" *Mind*, n.s. 60 (1951), pp. 441–65; Roderick M. Chisholm, "Responsibility and Avoidability," and Richard Taylor, "Determination and the Theory of Agency," in Sidney Hook, ed., *Determinism and Freedom in the Age of Modern Science* (New York: New York University Press, 1958).
2 Thomas Reid, *Essays on the Active Powers of the Human Mind* (Cambridge, Mass.: MIT Press, 1969; first published 1788), p. 261.
3 *Summa Theologia*, First Part of the Second Part, Question VI: "On the Voluntary and Involuntary."
4 Jonathan Edwards, *Freedom of the Will* (New Haven, Conn.: Yale University Press, 1957); G. E. Moore, *Ethics* (Home University Library, 1912), ch. 6.
5 A. I. Melden, *Free Action* (Oxford: Blackwell, 1961), especially ch. 3. Mr Melden's own views, however, are quite the contrary of those proposed here.
6 Aristotle, *Physics*, book III, ch. 3; Suarez, *Disputations Metaphysicae*, Disputation 18, Section 10.
7 Reid, *Essays on the Active Powers*, p. 39.
8 John Locke, *Essay Concerning Human Understanding*, book II, ch. 21.
9 Melden, *Free Action*, p. 166.
10 Reid, *Essays on the Active Powers*, p. 291.

Comments and Questions on Roderick Chisholm's "Human Freedom and the Self"

1. The following objection is often made against Chisholm's notion of agent- or immanent causation. We do ordinarily recognize that *things* or *substances*, such as agents, can cause events or happenings. We say for example that the rock broke the window or the cat caused the lamp to fall from the table. But these claims are usually elliptical ways of saying that certain events or states of affairs involving the things or substances caused the events. Thus it was the rock's-being-thrown-at-the-window and the rock's-being-heavy which caused the window to break; and it was the cat's-jumping-up-on-the-table that caused the lamp to fall. But these hyphenated expressions describe *events* or *states* of affairs involving the rock and the cat that caused the window to break and the lamp to fall. They are simply cases of ordinary causation by events or occurrences. Why can't we say the same thing about the free actions of human agents? If I opened the door it was because I *saw* my friend coming up the walk, I

wanted to greet him, so I *pulled* on the door handle till the door opened. Once again these are events or states involving me that caused the door to open and constituted my opening the door. Why should human agency be treated differently than other causation by things or substances? Why assume that agent-causation cannot also be spelled out in terms of event causation? Some of the relevant events and states may be psychological (perceptions, thoughts, wants, beliefs, etc.), but psychological events or states are still states or events? How might Chisholm, or a defender of his agent-causal view, respond to this objection?

2.   In section 3 of the reading, Chisholm criticizes hypothetical or conditional interpretations of "could have done otherwise" like those put forward by Nielsen in the preceding selection and by other classical compatibilists such as G. E. Moore, whom Chisholm mentions. What exactly is Chisholm's criticism of such analyses and do you think it succeeds?

3.   It has been objected by many philosophers that Chisholm's notion of agent- or immanent causation – or the agent as a "prime mover un-moved" – is mysterious and obscure because he does not explain in detail how it is supposed to work. Chisholm actually tries to defend himself against such a charge in the reading. How does he do so and do you think he succeeds?

Suggested Reading

For further defenses of agent-causal libertarianism similar to Chisholm's but different in details, see Timothy O'Connor's essay in this volume, "The Agent as Cause." Also see the essays by O'Connor, Randolph Clarke, and William Rowe in *Agents, Causes and Events: Essays on Free Will and Determinism* (1995), edited by O'Connor, and O'Connor's *Persons and Causes* (2000). William Rowe's *Thomas Reid on Morality and Freedom* (1991) discusses the agent-causal view of the eighteenth-century philosopher Thomas Reid, and defends an agent-causal theory similar to Reid's. John Thorp, *Free Will* (1980), and Randolph Clarke, "Agent Causation and Event Causation in the Production of Free Action" (1996), also defend different kinds of agent-causal views. For criticisms of agent-causal views like Chisholm's and these others, see the readings later in this volume by Peter van Inwagen ("The Mystery of Metaphysical Freedom"), Carl Ginet, and Robert Kane. Other critics of agent-causation include Ted Honderich, *How Free Are You?* (1993), Susan Wolf, *Freedom Within Reason* (1990), John Bishop, *Natural Agency* (1989), and Bernard Berofsky, *Freedom from Necessity* (1987).

4

Hard and Soft Determinism

Paul Edwards

Editor's Introduction

Paul Edwards was a Professor of Philosophy at New York University and was general editor of the *Encyclopedia of Philosophy* (1967). In the article reprinted here, he offers a clear and forceful defense of the *hard determinist* position on free will. He notes that the compatibilist and soft determinist positions of such philosophers as Hobbes, Hume, and Mill (defended in an earlier reading by Nielsen) have been very popular in the twentieth century. Yet Edwards thinks that for all its virtues, soft determinism is not a finally adequate view. He thinks that William James' charge that soft determinism is a "quagmire of evasion" was a little too nasty, but not entirely wrong. Free will is not compatible with determinism, as soft determinists claim, according to Edwards: and since he is also convinced that human actions are determined, he thinks that hard determinism is the only viable option.

In his eassy "The Dilemma of Determinism," William James makes a distinction that will serve as a point of departure for my remarks. He there distinguishes between the philosophers he calls "hard" determinists and those he labels "soft" determinists. The former, the hard determinists, James tells us, "did not shrink from such words as fatality, bondage of the will, necessitation and the like." He quotes a famous stanza from Omar Khayyám as representing this kind of determinism:

> With earth's first clay they did the last man knead,
> And there of the last harvest sowed the seed.
> And the first morning of creation wrote
> What the last dawn of reckoning shall read. [...]

James mentioned no names other than Omar Khayyám. But there is little doubt that among the hard determinists he would have included Jonathan Edwards, Anthony Collins, Holbach, Priestley, Robert Owen, Schopenhauer, Freud, and also, if he had come a little earlier, Clarence Darrow.

James of course rejected both hard and soft determinism, but for hard determinism he had a certain respect: the kind of respect one sometimes has for an honest, straightforward adversary. For soft determinism, on the other hand, he had nothing but contempt, calling it a "quagmire of evasion." "Nowadays," he writes, "we have a soft determinism which abhors harsh words, and repudiating fatality, necessity and even predetermination, says that its real name is 'freedom.'" From his subsequent observations it is clear that he would include among the evasionists not only neo-Hegelians like Green and Bradley but also Hobbes and Hume and Mill....

The theory James calls soft determinism, especially the Hume-Mill-Schlick variety of it, has been extremely fashionable during the last twenty-five years, while hardly anybody can be found today who has anything good to say for hard determinism. In opposition to this contemporary trend, I should like to strike a blow on behalf of hard determinism in my talk today. I shall also try to bring out exactly what is really at issue between hard and soft determinism. I think the nature of this dispute has frequently been misconceived chiefly because many writers, including James, have a very inaccurate notion of what is maintained by actual hard determinists, as distinct from the bogey men they set up in order to score an easy victory.

To begin with, it is necessary to spell more fully the main contentions of the soft determinists. Since it is the dominant form of soft determinism at the present time, I shall confine myself to the Hume-Mill-Schlick theory. According to this theory there is in the first place no contradiction whatsoever between determinism and the proposition that human beings are sometimes free agents. When we call an action "free" we never in any ordinary situation mean that it was uncaused; and this emphatically includes the kind of action about which we pass moral judgments. By calling an action "free" we mean that the agent was not compelled or constrained to perform it. Sometimes people act in a certain way because of threats or because they have been drugged or because of a posthypnotic suggestion or because of an irrational overpowering urge such as the one that makes a kleptomaniac steal something he does not really need. On such occasions human beings are not free agents. But on other occasions they act in certain ways because of their own rational desires, because of their own unimpeded efforts, because they have chosen to act in these ways. On these occasions they are free agents although their actions are just as much caused as actions that are not deemed free. In distinguishing between free and unfree actions we do not try to mark the presence and absence of causes but attempt to indicate the *kind* of causes that are present.

Secondly there is no antithesis between determinism and moral responsibility. When we judge a person morally responsible for a certain action, we do indeed presuppose that he was a free agent at the time of the action. But the freedom presupposed is not the contracausal freedom about which indeterminists go into such ecstatic raptures. It is nothing more than the freedom already mentioned – the ability to act according to one's choices or desires. Since determinism is compatible with freedom in this sense, it is also compatible with moral responsibility. In other words, the world is after all wonderful: we can be determinists and yet go on punishing our enemies and our children, and we can go on blaming ourselves, all without a bad intellectual conscience.

Mill, who was probably the greatest moralizer among the soft determinists, recognized with particular satisfaction the influence or alleged influence of one class of human desires. Not only, for example, does such lowly desire as my desire to get a new car influence my conduct. It is equally true, or so at least Mill believed, that my desire to become a more virtuous person does on occasion influence my actions. By suitable training and efforts my desire to change my character may in fact bring about the desired changes. If Mill were alive today he might point to contemporary psychiatry as an illustration of his point. Let us suppose that I have an intense desire to become famous, but that I also have an intense desire to become a happier and more lovable person who, among other things, does not greatly care about fame. Let us suppose, furthermore, that I know of a therapy that can transform fame-seeking and unlovable into lovable and fame-indifferent character structures. If, now, I have enough money, energy, and courage, and if a few other conditions are fulfilled, my desire may actually lead to a major change in my character. Since we can, therefore, at least to some extent, form our own character, determinism according to Mill is compatible not only with judgments of moral responsibility about this or that particular *action* flowing from an unimpeded desire, but also, within limits, with moral judgements about the *character* of human beings.

I think that several of Mill's observations were well worth making and that James's verdict on his theory as a "quagmire of evasion" is far too derogatory. I think hard determinists have occasionally written in such a way as to suggest that they deny the causal efficacy of human desires and efforts. [...]

But when all is said and done, there remains a good deal of truth in James's charge that soft determinism is an evasion. For a careful reading of their works shows that none of the hard determinists really denied that human desires, efforts, and choices make a difference in the course of events. Any remarks to the contrary are at most temporary lapses. This, then, is hardly the point at issue. If it is not the point at issue, what is? Let me at this stage imagine a hard determinist replying to a champion of the Hume-Mill theory: "You are right," he would say, "in maintaining that some of our actions are caused by our desires and choices. But you do not pursue the subject far enough. You arbitrarily stop at the desires and volitions. We must not stop there. We must go on to ask where *they* come from; and if determinism is true there can be no doubt about the answer to this question. Ultimately our desires and our whole character are derived from our inherited equipment and the environmental influences to which we were subjected at the beginning of our lives. It is clear that we had no hand in shaping either of these." A hard determinist could quote a number of eminent supporters. "Our volitions and our desires," wrote Holbach in his little book *Good Sense*, "are never in our power. You think yourself free, because you do what you will; but are you free to will or not to will; to desire or not to desire?" And Schopenhauer expressed the same thought in the following epigram: "A man can surely do what he wills to do, but he cannot determine what he wills."

Let me turn once more to the topic of character transformation by means of psychiatry to bring out this point with full force. Let us suppose that both *A* and *B* are compulsive and suffer intensely from their neuroses. Let us assume that there is a therapy that could help them, which could materially change their character structure, but that it takes a great deal of energy and courage to undertake the treatment. Let us suppose that *A* has the necessary energy and courage while *B* lacks it. *A* undergoes the therapy and changes in the desired way. *B* just gets more and more compulsive and more and more miserable. Now, it is true that *A* helped form his own later character. But his starting point, his desire to change, his energy and courage, were already there. They may or may not have been the result of previous efforts on his own part. But there must have been a first effort, and the effort at that time was the result of factors that were not of his making.

The fact that a person's character is ultimately the product of factors over which he had no control is not denied by the soft determinists, though many of them don't like to be reminded of it when they are in a moralizing mood. Since the hard determinists admit that our desires and choices do on occasion influence the course of our lives, there is thus no disagreement between the soft and the hard determinists about the empirical facts. However, some hard determinists infer from some of these facts that human beings are never morally responsible for their actions. The soft determinists, as already stated, do not draw any such inference. In the remainder of my paper I shall try to show just what it is that hard determinists are inferring and why, in my opinion, they are justified in their conclusion.

I shall begin by adopting for my purposes a distinction introduced by C. A. Campbell in his extremely valuable article "Is Free Will a Pseudo-Problem?"[1] in which he distinguishes between two conceptions of moral responsibility. Different persons, he says, require different conditions to be fulfilled before holding human beings morally responsible for what they do. First, there is what Campbell calls the ordinary unreflective person, who is rather ignorant and who is not greatly concerned with the theories of science, philosophy, and religion. If the unreflective person is sure that the agent to be judged was acting under coercion or constraint, he will not hold him responsible. If, however, he is sure that the action was performed in accordance with the agent's unimpeded rational desire, if he is sure that the action would not have taken place but for the agent's decision, then the unreflective person will consider ascription of moral responsibility justified. The fact that the agent did not ultimately make his own character will either not occur to him, or else it will not be considered a sufficient ground for withholding a judgment of moral responsibility.

In addition to such unreflective persons, continues Campbell, there are others who have reached "a tolerably advanced level of reflection."

> Such a person will doubtless be acquainted with the claims advanced in some quarters that causal law operates universally; or/and with the theories of some philosophies that the universe is throughout the expression of a single supreme principle; or/and with the doctrines of some theologians that the world is created, sustained and governed by an Omniscient and Omnipotent Being.

Such a person will tend to require the fulfillment of a further condition before holding anybody morally responsible. He will require not only that the agent was not coerced or constrained but also – and this is taken to be an additional condition – that he "could have chosen otherwise than he actually did." I should prefer to put this somewhat differently, but it will not affect the main conclusion drawn by Campbell, with which I agree. The reflective person, I should prefer to express it, requires not only that the agent was not coerced; he also requires that the agent *originally chose his own character* – the character that now displays itself in his choices and desires and efforts. Campbell concludes that determinism is indeed compatible with judgments of moral responsibility in the unreflective sense, but that it is incompatible with judgments of moral responsibility in the reflective sense.

Although I do not follow Campbell in rejecting determinism, I agree basically with his analysis, with one other qualification. I do not think it is a question of the different senses in which the term is used by ignorant and unreflective people, on the one hand, and by those who are interested in science, religion, and philosophy, on the other. The very same persons, whether educated or uneducated, use it in certain contexts in the one sense and in other contexts in the other. Practically all human beings, no matter how much interested they are in science, religion, and philosophy, employ what Campbell calls the unreflective conception when they are dominated by violent emotions like anger, indignation, or hate, and especially when the conduct they are judging has been personally injurious to them. On the other hand, a great many people, whether they are educated or not, will employ what Campbell calls the reflective conception when they are not consumed with hate or anger – when they are judging a situation calmly and reflectively and when the fact that the agent did not ultimately shape his own character has been vividly brought to their attention. Clarence Darrow in his celebrated pleas repeatedly appealed to the jury on precisely this ground. If any of you, he would say, had been reared in an environment like that of the accused or had to suffer from his defective heredity, *you* would now be standing in the dock.[...] Darrow nearly always convinced the jury that the accused could not be held morally responsible for his acts; and certainly the majority of the jurors were relatively uneducated.[...]

Before I conclude I wish to avoid a certain misunderstanding of my remarks. From the fact that human beings do not ultimately shape their own character, I said, it *follows* that they are never morally responsible. I do not mean that by reminding people of the ultimate causes of their character one makes them more charitable and less vengeful. Maybe one does, but that is not what I mean. I mean "follow" or "imply" in the same sense as, or in a sense closely akin to, that in which the conclusion of a valid syllogism follows from the premises. The effectiveness of Darrow's pleas does not merely show, I am arguing, how powerfully he could sway the emotions of the jurors. His pleas also brought into the open one of the conditions the jurors, like others, consider necessary on reflection before they hold an agent morally responsible. Or perhaps I should say that Darrow *committed* the jurors in their reflective nature to a certain ground for the ascription of moral responsibility.[2]

Notes

1 *Mind*, 1951.
2 This paper was written in the hope of stimulating discussion of a position which has not received adequate attention in recent years. The position was stated rather bluntly and without the necessary qualifications because of limitations of time. I hope to return to the subject at greater length in the near future, and on that occasion to present a more balanced treatment which will attempt to meet criticisms made in the discussion. (*December* 1957.)

Comments and Questions on Paul Edwards's "Hard and Soft Determinism"

1.   Edwards says some nice things about soft determinism, but ultimately he rejects it. What are his reasons for thinking that soft determinism is inadequate? Do you agree with them? Why or why not?
2.   One objection that is likely to be raised to Edwards's essay is this: he seems to proceed as if the choice were between soft or hard determinism because he seems convinced that human behavior is determined. Presumably, he thinks that while quantum physics may be indeterministic, it has no relevance to human action and freedom. And like Skinner he thinks the human sciences – biological, social, and behavioral sciences – suggest that human behavior is largely determined by heredity and environment. But Edwards does not try to prove that determinism is true and this is a weakness of his argument. Could one come to conclusions similar to Edwards's without jumping to conclusions about whether determinism is true or not? Yes, and some contemporary philosophers have done so. For example, Ted Honderich (*How Free Are You?* (1993)) and Derk Pereboom (*Living Without Free Will* (2001)) hold views similar to Edwards's hard determinism while remaining noncommittal about whether determinism is true. Views of Honderich, Pereboom, and others like them might therefore be called "successor views" to classical hard determinism. A classical hard determinist like Edwards believes (1) that free will is incompatible with determinism, and (2) that (an

incompatibilist or libertarian) free will does not exist because (3) determinism is true. The successor views of Honderich and Pereboom agree with Edwards about (1) and (2), but they remain noncommittal about (3), preferring to leave the issue of determinism to the physicists. (Thus Pereboom calls his successor view "hard incompatibilism" because it is like hard determinism, but without assuming determinism.) But why do these successor views reject an incompatibilist or libertarian free will (thesis 2) if they do not commit themselves to the truth of determinism? One reason (given by Honderich) is that in place of thesis (3) (determinism is true) of the hard determinist view, one might substitute (3') that free will is not compatible with determinism *and* is not compatible with indeterminism either. In short, incompatibilist free will could not exist *whatever* the truth should be about determinism. By sharing theses (1) and (2), what these successor views have in common with Edwards's hard determinism is that they reject both *compatibilism* (including *soft determinism*) and *libertarian* views. They hold (1) that free will is not compatible with determinism (as compatibilists and soft determinists would contend) and yet (2) incompatibilist free will does not exist either (as libertarians would contend); so free will cannot exist. Hard determinism and its successor views thus constitute a third option in free will debates to both compatibilism and libertarianism. What is your assessment of these successor views? They cannot be criticized in the same way that Edwards's view can be. Are they therefore sound views? How would one criticize them?

3.   One other modern successor view to hard determinism is even more unusual. This is the view of Israeli philosopher Saul Smilansky in a recent work, *Free Will and Illusion* (2000). Smilansky also agrees with Edwards, Honderich, and Pereboom that (1) free will (in the true responsibility-entailing sense) is not compatible with determinism and that (2) incompatibilist or libertarian free will cannot exist (because free will is not compatible with indeterminism either). But, in contrast to Honderich and Pereboom, Smilansky thinks that widespread belief that we in fact do not possess free will would have dire consequences for morality and human social life. One would have to give up the idea that persons are ultimately responsible and accountable for their actions and that they are ultimately deserving of praise or blame, punishment or reward. And Smilansky believes this would undermine morality and the ethical and social bonds that make human societies viable. Do you agree with Smilansky about this or do you think that both morality and society would survive, though changed somewhat, if it was generally believed that we lacked free will?

4. Smilansky's own view is that the *illusion* of free will ought to be maintained even though he believes we do not really have it. He does not mean that political elites ought to induce illusory beliefs in people – in the manner of *Brave New World*. Rather he believes that (illusory) beliefs about free will are already "in place" in society. Most people already think they have free will in an incompatibilist sense and don't question it; and those who are compatibilists assume they have all the freedom and responsibility they need. Smilansky thinks these illusory beliefs play a largely positive role in upholding morality and society and therefore ought to remain in place. Illusion, he thinks, is not always bad. Do you agree with him? Do you think Smilansky's view is more plausible or less plausible than the views of Edwards, Honderich or Pereboom?

Suggested Reading

Few contemporary philosophers besides Edwards defend hard determinism in its classical form, but successor views to hard determinism such as those of Honderich, Pereboom, and Smilansky present challenging alternatives to both compatibilism and libertarianism. See Honderich's *How Free Are You?* (1993), Pereboom's *Living Without Free Will* (2001) and Smilansky's *Free Will and Illusion* (2000). Another prominent philosopher who also defends the two basic theses of successor views to classical hard determinism, (1) free will is incompatible with determinism and yet (2) libertarian free will cannot exist, is Galen Strawson. See his *Freedom and Belief* (1986).

Part II:

The Compatibility/ Incompatibility Question: Alternative Possibilities and Moral Responsibility

5

The Incompatibility of Free Will and Determinism

Peter van Inwagen

Editor's Introduction

Peter van Inwagen was for many years Professor of Philosophy at Syracuse University and is now John Cardinal O'Hara Professor of Philosophy at the University of Notre Dame. The selections reprinted here are from his influential book, *An Essay on Free Will* (1983), in which he defends several versions of a widely discussed argument for the incompatibility of free will and determinism often called the "consequence argument." The argument, informally stated, is this:

> If determinism is true, then our acts are the consequences of the laws of nature and events in the remote past. But it is not up to us what went on before we were born, and neither is it up to us what the laws of nature are. Therefore the consequences of these things (including our present acts) are not up to us. (p. 56)

In the reading that follows, van Inwagen develops a formal version of this argument in order to lay out its presuppositions and defend it. To do so, he first introduces an expression "Np" which is to be interpreted as follows (where "p" may represent any sentence, such as "all men are mortal"):

"Np" means "p (is the case) and no one has, or ever had, any choice about whether p (is the case)."

Thus "N all men are mortal" means "all men are mortal and no one has, or ever had, any choice about whether all men are mortal." Note that "N" is designed to do the work of the expression "it was not up to us" in the informal statement of the consequence argument. "N all men are mortal" expresses the idea that "it is not up to us that all men are mortal."

Van Inwagen thinks there are two inference rules governing this expression "N" that are presupposed by the consequence argument and he thinks both are valid. The first rule he calls

Rule (α): if $\Box p$, then one can infer that Np

The symbol "$\Box$" is the logician's symbol for necessity, so that "$\Box p$" is to be read "It is necessary that p." Rule (α) thus says that if something is *necessary*, or necessarily true (e.g., that $2 + 2 = 4$), then no one has or ever had a choice about whether or not it was true. Van Inwagen thinks this rule is obviously valid since no one can change what is necessarily so. The second rule is more controversial, but van Inwagen thinks it is also valid. He calls it

Rule (β): if Np and N($p \supset q$), then one can infer Nq

The symbol "$\supset$" is the standard logician's symbol of implication and is read "implies" or "if ... then." So Rule (β) says "if p is the case and no one has, or ever had, a choice about whether p is the case, and if p implies q, and no one has or ever had a choice about whether p implies q, then one can infer that q is the case and no one has, or ever had, a choice about whether q is the case. For example, if a large meteor struck the earth 65 million years ago (p) and no one has or ever had a choice about whether the meteor struck (p), and (assuming the laws of nature) if a meteor this large struck the earth, then dinosaurs would become extinct (q), and no one had a choice about whether the meteor's striking given the laws implied the extinction of the dinosaurs, then no one has, or ever had, a choice about whether the dinosaurs became extinct (q).

With the expression "N" and these two rules in hand, van Inwagen's version of the consequence argument proceeds as follows. Let "L" represent a conjunction of true statements describing the laws of nature and let "P_0" represent a conjunction of true statements describing the state of the world at some earlier time before any living things existed. Finally, let P represent any true statement whatever, for example "I just raised my arm." If determinism is true, then

(1) $\Box(P_0 \,\&\, L) \supset P$

That is, necessarily ($\Box$), P (e.g., "I just raised my arm") is implied by a conjunction of true sentences describing the laws of nature (L) and a conjunction of true sentences about the state of the world at remote past time before any living things existed (P_0). This premise is meant to capture the first sentence of the consequence argument: "if determinism is true, then our acts are the (necessary) consequences of the laws of nature and events in the remote past." Now from premise (1) we can deduce by elementary rules of logic

(2) $\Box(P_0 \supset (L \supset P))$

Roughly paraphrased, if determinism is true, it is also true that necessarily ($\Box$), if the past was a certain way before any living things existed (P_0), then, if the laws of nature are as they are (L), it would follow that P ("I just raised my arm"). At this point, Rule (α) is introduced to infer from (2) that

(3) $N(P_0 \supset (L \supset P)$

You should verify that the move from (2) to (3) is an instance of Rule (α) – if $\Box p$, then one can infer Np – where "$P_0 \supset (L \supset P)$" is substituted for "$p$". For example, if it is necessarily true ($\Box$) that the events in the remote past plus the laws of nature entail that I just raised my arm, then no one has, or ever had, a choice (N) about whether or not I just raised my arm.

But now it seems true that no one has, or ever had, a choice about what went on in the remote past, which can be written

(4) NP_0

So we can invoke Rule (β) to infer from (3) and (4) that

(5) $N(L \supset P)$

No one has, or ever had, a choices about whether the laws of nature imply P (that I raised my arm). Once again you should verify that the move from (3) and (4) to (5) is an instance of Rule (β) – if Np and N($p \supset q$), then one can infer Nq.

But it also seems true that no one has, and no one ever had, a choice about what the laws of nature are, which can be written

(6)   NL

So by another application of Rule (β), this time to steps (5) and (6), we arrive at the conclusion

(7)   NP

which says that P (e.g., I just raised my arm), and no one has, or ever had a choice about whether or not P (I just raised my arm). Having formulated the consequence argument in this way, van Inwagen proceeds to explain its meaning and defend it in the following selection. The "deduction" he refers to at the beginning of this selection is the argument we have just presented from premise (1) to conclusion (7).

Peter van Inwagen: selections from *An Essay On Free Will* (1983)

This deduction shows that if determinism is true, then no one ever has any choice about anything, since any sentence that expresses a truth may replace "P" in it. Consider, for example, the question whether anyone had a choice about whether Richard Nixon would receive a pardon for any offences he might have committed while in office. Nixon did receive such a pardon. Therefore, if determinism is true,

$\square$(P$_0$ & L. $\supset$ Richard Nixon received a pardon for any offences he might have committed while in office).

Therefore, if (α) and (β) are valid rules, and if NL and NP$_0$, then we have:

No one had any choice about whether Richard Nixon received a pardon for any offences he might have committed while in office.

Most of us, I presume, think this conclusion is false. Most of us think Gerald Ford had a choice about whether Nixon would receive a pardon. (Even if someone thinks that Ford's actions were wholly controlled by some cabal, he none the less thinks *someone* had a choice about whether Nixon would receive a pardon.) But the above deduction (i.e., our formal argument) shows that if we wish to accept this conclusion we must reject one of the following five propositions:

Determinism is true;
NP_0;
NL;
Rule (α) is valid;
Rule (β) is valid.

My choice, of course, is to reject determinism. But let us examine the alternatives.

I do not see how anyone can reject "NP_0" or "NL" ... The proposition that P_0 is a proposition about the remote past. We could, if we like, stipulate that it is a proposition about the distribution and momenta of atoms and other particles in the inchoate, presidereal nebulae. Therefore, surely, no one has any choice about whether P_0. The proposition that L is a proposition that "records" the laws of nature. If it is a law of nature that angular momentum is conserved, then no one has any choice about whether angular momentum is conserved, and, more generally, since it is a law of nature that L, no one has any choice about whether L.

I do not see how anyone could reject Rule (α). If (α) is invalid, then it could be that someone has a choice about what is necessarily true. Hardly anyone besides Descartes has been willing to concede such a capability even to God. No one, so far as I know, has ever suggested that human beings could have a choice about what is necessarily true....

Only Rule (β) remains to be considered. The validity of (β) is, I think, the most difficult of the premises of the argument to defend. How might one go about defending it? [...]

I must confess that my belief in the validity of (β) has only two sources, one incommunicable and the other inconclusive. The former source is what philosophers are pleased to call "intuition": when I carefully consider (β), it seems to be valid. But I can't expect anyone to be very impressed by this fact. People's intuitions, after all, have led them to accept all sorts of crazy propositions and many sane but false propositions. (The Unrestricted Comprehension Principle in set theory and the Galilean Law of the Addition of Velocities in physics are good examples of propositions in the second category.) The latter source is the fact that I can think of no instances of (β) that have, or could possibly have, true premisses and a false conclusion. Consider, for example, these two instances of (β):

> Alice has asthma and no one has, or ever had, any choice about whether she has asthma;
>
> If Alice has asthma, she sometimes has difficulty breathing, and no one has, or ever had, any choice about whether, if she has asthma, she sometimes has difficulty breathing;

hence, Alice sometimes has difficulty breathing, and no one has, or ever had, any choice about whether Alice sometimes has difficulty breathing.

> The sun will explode in 2000 AD, and no one has, or ever had, any choice about whether the sun will explode in 2000 AD;
>
> If the sun explodes in 2000 AD, all life on earth will end in 2000 AD, and no one has, or ever had, any choice about whether, if the sun explodes in 2000 AD, all life on earth will end in 2000 AD;

hence, All life on earth will end in 2000 AD, and no one has, or ever had, any choice about whether all life on earth will end in 2000 AD.

These arguments are clearly valid. There is simply no way things could be arranged that would be sufficient for the truth of their premisses and the falsity of their conclusions. Take the second. Conceivably we could do something to prevent the explosion of the sun. Then perhaps the conclusion of this argument would be false; but its first premiss would also be false. Perhaps we could erect an enormous shield that would protect the earth from the explosion of the sun; if we could do this, the conclusion would be false. But the second premiss would also be false. Perhaps we could spread a poison that would destroy all life on earth before 2000 AD; but in that case too the second premiss would be false. I cannot help feeling that the reader who makes a serious attempt at constructing a counter-example to (β) will begin to appreciate, even if he does not come to share, the intuition that I have expressed by saying, "when I carefully consider (β), it seems to be valid".

It is interesting to note that rule (β) seems to figure in recent discussions of the philosophical and social implications of socio-biology and the question whether certain widespread features of human social behaviour are genetically determined. Consider, for example, the proposition (P) that there are certain jobs (jobs that both sexes are physically capable of performing) such that, in every society, these jobs devolve almost entirely upon women. Suppose a socio-biologist alleges that there is a certain fact or set of facts (F) about the evolutionary history of our species that explains why P is true. Anyone who says this is likely to be the target of some such criticism as this:

> What you are saying is that "women's role" is genetically determined, and thus that all attempts at changing the role of women in this or any other society are doomed by biology. This doctrine is pernicious. You are not a scientist but an ideologue, and the ideology you are peddling makes you a most useful prop for the existing system.

Anyone who is the target of such criticism is likely to defend himself in some way pretty much like this:

> Not so. While I believe that F explains why P is true, I do not say that F makes P *inevitably* true. Given F, there is a tendency for P to be true, but tendencies can be resisted. I do not say that "biology is destiny". It may well be that we have a choice about whether we shall behave in accordance with this tendency that our evolutionary heritage has presented us with.

Now I am not so much interested in where the right lies in disputes that take this form – after all, where it lies may depend on what is substituted for "F" and for "P" – as I am in its underlying logic. I believe that the logical skeleton of this dispute looks something like this:

CRITIC: It follows from your position that the premisses of the following valid argument are true:
N F obtains
N(F obtains ⊃ P is true)
hence, N P is true

SOCIO-BIOLOGIST: The first premiss is certainly true, but the second does *not* follow from my position and may very well be false.

It would probably never occur to the socio-biologist to deny that the conclusion of the argument he has been charged with endorsing actually does follow from its premises. And if he did deny this, then the critic would rightly charge him with sophistry, for if it is granted that no one has any choice about whether, given that our history is such-and-such, we do so-and-so, and if it is granted that our history *is* such-and-such and that we have no choice about this, then it just obviously does follow that no one has any choice about whether we do so-and-so. This does not, of course, entail that (β) is valid, for it may be that while this instance of (β) is valid, other instances of (β) are invalid. But I think that anyone who said that, while the argument the critic has formulated is valid, (β) is *not* valid, would be saying something that is not on the face of it very plausible. The validity of (β), in its full generality, certainly does seem to be part of the "common ground" in the socio-biological dispute I have imagined. (Despite the fact that I have imagined it, its logical structure is typical of disputes about biological determinism.) That is, (β) seems to be accepted, and properly so, by both sides in the dispute; the dispute seems to turn simply on *what* – according to socio-biology – we have a choice about, and not on any questions about the validity of inferences involving "having a choice about". People who accept, or are accused of accepting, "special determinisms" – that is, theories that say, or are sometimes interpreted as saying, that some important aspect of human behaviour is determined by this or that factor outside our control – tend to find themselves embroiled in disputes about the freedom of the will. I have used a socio-biologist as an example of such a person because I am writing now, but the "biology is destiny" debate is not the only one of its type. If I had been writing a few years ago, I should have constructed an example involving a Freudian or a Marxist and the point of my example would have been the same. Anyone who denies the validity of (β), it seems to me, must react to such disputes in one of two ways. He must either call them pseudo-disputes that arise because both parties to the dispute wrongly accept (β), or he must contend that the dispute does not really involve (β) after all. In the former case, he should recommend that the socio-biologist reply to the critic like this:

I admit that F is a fact about the history of our species and that that's something no one has a choice about. I admit *if* F is a fact about the history of a given species, then, in societies that comprise members of that species, certain jobs will devolve almost entirely upon women, and that no one has any choice about *that*. Still, we *do* have a choice about whether, in our society, these jobs will devolve almost entirely upon women.

I cannot imagine anyone saying this with a straight face. In the latter case, he owes us an account of these disputes that shows how the apparent acceptance of (β) by both parties is merely apparent.

The point of this discussion may be summed up in a question: Why is none of the participants in the debates about biological determinism a compatibilist? Perhaps the answer is that the participants in these debates take the idea of biological determinism much more seriously than philosophers are accustomed to take the idea of "universal" or "Laplacian" determinism, and that compatibilism with respect to a given type of determinism is possible only for people who do not take that type of determinism very seriously.

I said above that I could think of no instances of (β) that had, or could possibly have had, true premises and a false conclusion. I meant, of course, that I could think of no instances of (β) that could be seen to have true premises and a false conclusion independently of the question whether free will is compatible with determinism. If free will is compatible with determinism, and if determinism is true, then, presumably, at least one of the following two instances of (β) has true premises and a false conclusion:

$N (P_o \supset (L \supset \text{Nixon received a pardon}))$
$N P_o$
hence, $N (L \supset \text{Nixon received a pardon})$.

$N (L \supset \text{Nixon received a pardon})$
$N L$
hence, N Nixon received a pardon.

But it would be nice to see a counter-example to (β) that did not presuppose the compatibility of free will and determinism. After all, the examples I gave in support of (β) did not presuppose the *incompatibility* of free will and determinism. I should think that if there are *any* counter-examples to (β), then some of them, at least, could be shown to be such independently of the question whether free will and determinism are compatible. [...]

Some compatibilists, when they are confronted with arguments for the incompatibility of free will and determinism, say something like this: "Your argument simply demonstrates that when you use phrases like 'could have done otherwise' or 'has a choice about', you are giving them some meaning other than the meaning they have in our actual debates about moral responsibility". This criticism is equally applicable, *mutatis mutandis*, to all three of our arguments for incompatibilism. And my answer to it is essentially the same in each case. But this answer can be presented very compactly and efficiently in terms of the vocabulary employed in the above argument. Therefore, I shall answer only this charge: "When you use the phrase 'has a choice' you are giving it a meaning different from the meaning it has in our actual debates about moral responsibility", and I will leave to the reader the mechanical task of adapting this answer to the requirements of the other arguments. My answer consists simply in a reinterpretation of "N":

Np =_{df} p and, in just the sense of *having a choice* that is relevant in debates about moral responsibility, no one has, or ever had, any choice about whether p.

If there is anything to the objection we are considering, then at least one of the four propositions,

NP_o,
NL,
Rule (α) is valid,
Rule (β) is valid,

is false, given that "N" – which occurs in (α) and (β) – is interpreted as above. But this does not seem to be the case. If one carefully retraces the steps of the Third Argument, one will find, I think, that no step becomes doubtful under our new interpretation of "N". The conclusion of the present chapter is, therefore, that if determinism is true, then no one has any choice about anything, in just that sense of *having a choice* that is relevant in debates about moral responsibility.

Comments and Questions on Peter van Inwagen's "The Incompatibility of Free Will and Determinism"

Assess the following criticisms that have been made of van Inwagen's version of the consequence argument.
1.   The consequence argument tries to show that if determinism is true, no one could have done otherwise than perform the action that was actually performed (that is, no one really had a choice about whether or not to do it). Compatibilists have argued against the consequence argument that if you analyze "could have done otherwise" in the *hypothetical*

or *conditional* way they favor, then van Inwagen's Rule (β) will not be valid and the consequence argument will fail. For on the hypothetical or conditional analysis, an agent "could have done otherwise" means only that the agent "would have done otherwise, if the agent had wanted or desired to do otherwise." (Such a conditional analysis of "could have done otherwise" is defended in the Nielsen reading.) Or, putting it in van Inwagen's terminology, the agent "had a choice about whether or not to do P" means the agent "would have done P, if the agent had wanted or desired to do it." Would such an interpretation indeed invalidate rule (β) and the consequence argument, as compatibilist critics claim? Show *why* it would or would not invalidate rule (β) and the consequence argument. If hypothetical analyses of "could have done otherwise" do invalidate the argument, incompatibilists such as van Inwagen would have to show that hypothetical interpretations are mistaken (as Chisholm tries to show in his reading).

2. Other critics of van Inwagen's version of the consequence argument have proposed interesting counterexamples to Rule (β) in the attempt to show it is not valid. One such counterexample is suggested by Thomas McKay and David Johnson (1996). If Alfred throws a fair die in an honest game of dice, we would normally assume that no one (including the thrower) has a choice about what number will come up. But we also assume that gamblers do have a choice about whether to throw dice in the first place. But this gives us an instance of Rule (β) that could have true premises and a false conclusion (thus showing the Rule invalid):

N Alfred throws a six
N (Alfred throws a six $\supset$ Alfred plays dice)
Hence, N Alfred plays dice

But while Alfred has no choice about whether he throws a six, he does have a choice about whether he plays dice. So the first premise seems true, but the conclusion false. (The second premise is also true by Rule (α) since the sentence embedded in it is necessarily true.) So it seems Rule (β) has counterexamples and is not a valid rule. How might van Inwagen respond to this objection? Does Alfred really have no choice about whether he throws a six? Assuming this is a counterexample, might Rule (β) be reformulated in some way to accommodate cases of this sort and still make the consequence argument valid?

3. Tomis Kapitan (1996) offers another rejoinder to the consequence argument. Another way of interpreting "NP" (where "P" describes an action) is to say that the agent is *unable* or lacks the *ability* to do other than

perform the action described by P (the agent "has no choice" about it). But this leads us to focus on what we mean by saying that agents are "able" or "unable" to do things. Suppose Sam's office window is closed during a 20 minute interval and he does not open it. Does Sam, who is sitting in his office, have the *ability* to open the window during that period even though he did not in fact do so? It seems that he does, says Kapitan, for Sam is physically able to go to the window if he wants to (he is not paralyzed or too physically weak), and he has the opportunity to do so. He is in the office and nothing is blocking his way to the window. And finally, Sam understands what it would reliably take to open the window. But these are the conditions we ordinarily require, Kapitan argues, for saying that an agent is *strictly able* to do something. He understands what it would take to reliably do it (e.g., open the window) and he has both the *capacity* and the *opportunity* to do what it would take. But it follows by these conditions that even though Sam did not in fact open the window and even if his not doing so was determined, he *was* strictly able to do it because all the above conditions for strict ability are satisfied. So NP (where "P" describes Sam's opening the window") is false even if determinism is true; and Rule (β) and the consequence argument would fail. Assess this argument. Do you think it succeeds? Why or why not?

Suggested Reading

Van Inwagen's *An Essay on Free Will* (1983: chapter 3) has a fuller discussion of the consequence argument and discusses two other versions of it. Other defenses of alternative versions of the consequence argument are by Carl Ginet (1966, 1990), David Wiggins (1973), James Lamb (1977), David Widerker (1987), Thomas Talbott (1988), William Hasker (1989), Timothy O'Connor (1993a, 2000), John Martin Fischer (1994), and Ted Warfield (1996). Critics of the argument in addition to those mentioned above include Andre Gallois (1977), Jan Narveson (1977), Michael Slote (1982), David Lewis (1983), Daniel Dennett (1984), Terence Horgan (1985), Bernard Berofsky (1987), Gary Watson (1987), Thomas Flint (1987), Kadri Vivhelin (1988), Richard Double (1991), and Christopher Hill (1992). General discussions of the issues may be found in Robert Kane (1996: chapter 4) and Laura Ekstrom (2000: chapter 2).

6

I Could Not Have Done Otherwise – So What?

Daniel Dennett

Editor's Introduction

Daniel Dennett is Distinguished Professor of Arts and Sciences and Director of the Center of Cognitive Studies at Tufts University. In the following reading, Dennett mounts a more radical attack upon a widely held assumption that lies behind the consequence argument and most other arguments for the incompatibility of free will and determinism. This is the assumption that an agent is responsible for an act only if the agent could have refrained from performing the act, i.e., only if the agent could have done otherwise. Dennett offers a number of challenging arguments to show that the assumption is not as obviously true as it appears. He also argues that if the ability to do otherwise is not in fact required for moral responsibility, then (contra van Inwagen and other incompatibilists) determinism would be no threat to free will.

Wherever progress is stalled on a philosophical problem, a tactic worth trying is to find some shared (and hence largely unexamined) assumption and deny it. The problem of free will is such a problem, and, as Peter van Inwagen notes:

> ... almost all philosophers agree that a necessary condition for holding an agent responsible for an act is believing that the agent *could have* refrained from performing that act.[1]

Perhaps van Inwagen is right; perhaps most philosophers agree on this. If so, this shared assumption, which I will call CDO (for "could have done otherwise"), is a good candidate for denial, especially since there turns out to be so little to be said in support of it, once it is called in question. I will argue that, just like those people who are famous only for being famous, this assumption owes its traditional high regard to nothing more than its traditional high regard. It is almost never questioned. And the tradition itself, I will claim, is initially motivated by little more than inattentive extrapolation from familiar cases.

To engage the issue, I assert that it simply does not matter at all to moral responsibility whether the agent in question could have done otherwise in the circumstances. Now how does a friend of CDO set about showing that I am obviously wrong? Not by reminding me, unnecessarily, of the broad consensus in philosophy in support of the CDO principle, or by repeating it, firmly and knowingly. The inertia of a tradition is by itself scant recommendation, and if it is claimed that the assumption is not questioned because it is obvious or self-evident, I can at least ask for some supporting illustration of the self-evidence of the assumption in application to familiar cases. Can anyone give me an example of someone withholding a judgment of responsibility until he has determined (to his own satisfaction) whether the agent could have done otherwise?

It will perhaps appear that I must be extraordinarily inattentive to the topics of daily conversation if I can ask that question with a straight face. A prominent feature of many actual inquiries into the responsibility of particular agents is the asking of the question "Could he have done otherwise?" The question is raised in trials, both civil and criminal, and much more frequently in the retrospective discussions between individuals concerning blame or excuse for particular regretted acts of omission or commission.

Before turning to a closer examination of those cases, it is worth noting that the question plays almost no role in discussions of praise or reward for felicitous, unregretted acts – except in the formulaic gracious demurrer of the one singled out for gratitude or praise: "What else could I do?" ("Anyone else would have done the same." "Shucks; 'twarn't nothin'.") And in these instances we do not take the agent to be disavowing responsibility at all, but just declaring that being responsible under those conditions was not difficult.

Perhaps one reason we do not ask "Could he have done otherwise?" when trying to assess responsibility for good deeds and triumphs is that (thanks to our generosity of spirit) we give agents the benefit of the doubt when they have done well by us, rather than delving too scrupulously into facts of ultimate authorship. Such a charitable impulse may play a role, but there are better reasons, as we shall see. And we certainly do ask the question when an act is up for censure. But when we do, we never use the familiar question to inaugurate the sort of investigation that would actually shed light on the traditional philosophical issue the question has been presumed to raise. Instead we proceed to look around for evidence of what I call a pocket of *local fatalism*: a particular circumstance in the relevant portion of the past which ensured that the agent would not have done otherwise (during the stretch of local fatalism) *no matter what he had tried, or wanted, to do.* A standard example of local fatalism is being locked in a room.[2]

If the agent was locked in a room (or in some other way had his will rendered impotent), then independently of the truth or falsity of determinism and no matter what sort of causation reigns within the agent's brain (or Cartesian soul, for that matter), we agree that "he could not have done otherwise." The readily determinable empirical fact that an agent was a victim of local fatalism terminates the inquiry into causation. (It does not always settle the issue of responsibility, however, as Harry Frankfurt shows[3]; under special circumstances an agent may still be held responsible.) And if our investigation fails to uncover any evidence of such local fatalism, this also terminates the inquiry. We consider the matter settled: the agent was responsible after all; [...]

The first point I wish to make is that if the friends of CDO look to everyday practice for evidence for the contention that *ordinary people* "agree that a necessary condition for holding an agent responsible for an act is believing that the agent *could have* refrained from performing that act," they in fact will find no such support. When the act in question is up for praise, people manifestly ignore the question and would seem bizarre if they didn't. And when assessing an act for blame, although people do indeed ask "Could he have done otherwise?", they show no interest in pursuing that question beyond the point where they have satisfied their curiosity about the existence or absence of local fatalism – a phenomenon that is entirely neutral between determinism or indeterminism. For instance, people never withhold judgment about responsibility until after they have consulted physicists (or metaphysicians or neuroscientists) for their opinions about the ultimate status – deterministic or indeterministic – of the neural or mental events that governed the agent's behavior. And so far as I know, no defense attorney has ever gone into court to mount a defense based on an effort to establish, by expert testimony, that the accused was determined to make the decision that led to the dreadful act, and hence could not have done otherwise, and hence ("obviously") is not to be held responsible for it.

So the CDO principle is not something "everybody knows" even if most philosophers agree on it. The principle requires supporting argument. My second point is that any such supporting argument must challenge an abundance of utterly familiar evidence suggesting that often, when we seem to be interested in the question of whether the agent could have done otherwise, it is because we wish to draw the opposite conclusion about responsibility from that which the philosophical tradition endorses.

"Here I stand," Luther said. "I can do no other." Luther claimed that he could do no other, that his conscience made it *impossible* for him to recant. He might, of course, have been wrong, or have been deliberately overstating the truth, but even if he was – perhaps especially if he was – his declaration is testimony to the fact that we simply do not exempt someone from blame or praise for an act because we think he could do no other. Whatever Luther was doing, he was not trying to duck responsibility.

There are cases where the claim "I can do no other" is an avowal of frailty: suppose what I ought to do is get on the plane and fly to safety, but I stand rooted on the ground and confess I can do no other – because of my irrational and debilitating fear of flying. In such a case I can do no other, I claim, because my rational control faculty is impaired. This is indeed an excusing condition. But in other cases, like Luther's, when I say I cannot do otherwise I mean that I cannot because I see so clearly what the situation is and because my rational control faculty is *not* impaired. It is too obvious what to do; reason dictates it; I would have to be mad to do otherwise, and, since I happen not to be mad, I cannot do otherwise.

I hope it is true – and think it very likely is true – that it would be impossible to induce me to torture an innocent person by offering me a thousand dollars. "Ah" – comes the objection – "but what if some evil space pirates were holding the whole world ransom, and promised not to destroy the world if only you would torture an innocent person? Would that be something you would find impossible to do?" Probably not, but so what? That is a vastly different case. If what one is interested in is whether *under the specified circumstances* I could have done otherwise, then the other case mentioned is utterly irrelevant. I claimed it would not be possible to induce me to torture someone *for a thousand dollars*. Those who hold the CDO principle dear are always insisting that we should look at whether one could have done otherwise in *exactly* the same circumstances. I claim something stronger; I claim that I could not do otherwise even in any roughly similar case. I would *never* agree to torture an innocent person for a thousand dollars. It would make no difference, I claim, what tone of voice the briber used, or whether I was tired and hungry, or whether the proposed victim was well illuminated or partially concealed in shadow. I am, I hope, immune to all such offers.

Now why would anyone's intuitions suggest that, if I am right, then if and when I ever have occasion to refuse such an offer, my refusal would not count as a responsible act? Perhaps this is what some people think: they think that if I were right when I claimed I could not do otherwise in such cases, I would be some sort of zombie, "programmed" always to refuse thousand-dollar bribes. A genuinely free agent, they think, must be more volatile somehow. If I am to be able to listen to reason, if I am to be flexible in the right way, they think, I mustn't be too dogmatic. Even in the most preposterous cases, then, I must be able to see that "there are two sides to every question." I must be able to pause, and weigh up the pros and cons of this suggested bit of lucrative torture. But the only way I could be constituted so that I can always "see both sides" – no matter how preposterous one side is – is by being constituted so that *in any particular case* "I could have done otherwise."

That would be fallacious reasoning. Seeing both sides of the question does not require that one not be overwhelmingly persuaded, in the end, by one side. The flexibility we want a responsible agent to have is the flexibility to recognize the one-in-a-zillion case in which, thanks to that thousand dollars, not otherwise obtainable, the world can be saved (or whatever). But the general capacity to respond flexibly in such cases does not at all require that one could have done otherwise in the particular case, or in any particular case, but only that under some variations in the circumstances – the variations that matter – one would do otherwise. Philosophers have often noted, uneasily, that the difficult moral problem cases, the decisions that "might go either way", are not the only, or even the most frequent, sorts of decisions for which we hold people responsible. They have seldom taken the hint to heart, however, and asked whether the CDO principle was simply wrong.

If our responsibility really did hinge, as this major philosophical tradition insists, on the question of whether we ever could do otherwise than we in fact do *in exactly those circumstances*, we would be faced with a most peculiar problem of ignorance: it would be unlikely in the extreme, given what now seems to be the case in physics, that anyone would ever know whether anyone has ever been responsible. For today's orthodoxy is that indeterminism reigns at the subatomic level of quantum mechanics; so, in the absence of any general and accepted argument for universal determinism, it is possible for all we know that our decisions and actions truly are the magnified, macroscopic effects of quantum-level indeterminacies occurring in our brains. But it is also possible for all we know that, even though indeterminism reigns in our brains at the subatomic quantum-mechanical level, our macroscopic decisions and acts are all themselves determined; the quantum effects could just as well be self-canceling, not amplified (as if by organic Geiger counters in the neurons). And it is extremely unlikely, given the complexity of the brain at even the molecular level (a complexity for which the word "astronomical" is a vast understatement), that we could ever develop good evidence that any particular act was such a large-scale effect of a critical subatomic indeterminacy. So if someone's responsibility for an act did hinge on whether, at the moment of decision, that decision was (already) determined by a prior state of the world, then barring a triumphant return of universal determinism in microphysics (which would rule out all responsibility on this view), the odds are very heavy that we will never have *any* reason to believe of any particular act that it was or was not responsible. The critical difference would be utterly inscrutable from every macroscopic vantage point and practically inscrutable from the most sophisticated microphysical vantage point imaginable. [. . .]

If it is unlikely that it matters whether a person could have done otherwise – when we look microscopically closely at the causation involved – what is the other question that we are (and should be) interested in when we ask "But could he have done otherwise?"? Consider a similar question that might arise about a robot, destined (by hypothesis) to live its entire life as a deterministic machine on a deterministic planet. Even though this robot is, by hypothesis, completely deterministic, it can be controlled by "heuristic" programs that invoke "random" selection – of strategies, policies, weights, or whatever – at various points. All it needs is a pseudo-random number generator, either a preselected list or table of pseudo-random numbers to consult deterministically when the occasion demands or an algorithm that generates a pseudo-random sequence of digits. Either way it can have a sort of bingo-parlor machine for providing it with a patternless and arbitrary series of digits on which to pivot some of its activities.

Whatever this robot does, it could not have done otherwise, if we mean that in the strict and metaphysical sense of those words that philosophers have concentrated on. Suppose then that one fine Martian day it makes a regrettable mistake: it concocts and executes some scheme that destroys something valuable – another robot, perhaps. I am not supposing, for the moment, that *it* can regret anything, but just that its designers, back on Earth, regret what it has done and find themselves wondering a wonder that might naturally be expressed: *Could it have done otherwise?* Let us suppose that they first satisfy themselves that no obvious local fatalism (locked room, dead battery) has afflicted their robot. But still they press their question: Could it have done otherwise? They know it is a deterministic system, of course; so they know better than to ask the metaphysical question. Their question concerns the design of the robot; for in the wake of this regrettable event they may wish to redesign it slightly, to make this *sort* of event less likely in the future.[5] What they want to know, of course, is what information the robot was relying on, what reasoning or planning it did, and whether it did "enough" of the right sort of reasoning or planning.

Of course in one sense of "enough" they know the robot did not do enough of the right sort of reasoning; if it had, it would have done the right thing. But it may be that the robot's design in this case could not really be improved. For it may be that it was making optimal use of optimally designed heuristic procedures – but this time, unluckily, the heuristic chances it took didn't pay off. Put the robot in a *similar* situation in the future, and, thanks to no more than the fact that its pseudo-random number generator is in a different state, it will do something different; in fact it will usually do the right thing. It is tempting to add: it *could* have done the right thing on this occasion – meaning by this that it was well enough designed, at the time, to have done the right thing (its "character" is not impugned); its failure depended on nothing but the fact that something *undesigned* (and unanticipatable) happened to intervene in the process in a way that made an unfortunate difference. [. . .]

What concerns the engineers when they encounter misperformance in their robot is whether the misperformance is a telling one: does it reveal something about a pattern of systematic weakness, likely to recur, or an inappropriate and inauspicious linking between sorts of circumstances and sorts of reactions? Is this *sort* of thing apt to happen again, or was it due to the coincidental convergence of fundamentally independent factors, highly unlikely to recur? So long as their robot is *not* misperforming but rather making the "right" decisions, the point in asking whether it could have done otherwise is to satisfy themselves that the felicitous behavior was not a fluke or mere coincidence but rather the outcome of good design. They hope that their robot, like Luther, will be imperturbable in its mission.

To get evidence about this they ignore the micro-details, which will never be the same again in any case, and just average over them, analyzing the robot into a finite array of *macro*scopically defined states, organized in such a way that there are links between the various degrees of freedom of the system. The question they can then ask is this: Are the links the right links for the task?

This rationale for ignoring micro-determinism (wherever it may "in principle" exist) and squinting just enough to blur such fine distinctions into probabilistically related states and regions that can be *treated as* homogeneous is clear, secure, and unproblematic in science, particularly in engineering and biology. That does not mean, of course, that this is also just the right way to think of people, when we are wondering whether they have acted responsibly. But there is a lot to be said for it.

Why do we ask "Could he have done otherwise?"? We ask it because something has happened that we wish to interpret. An act has been performed, and we wish to understand how the act came about, why it came about, and what meaning we should attach to it. That is, we want to know what conclusions to draw from it about the future. Does it tell us anything about the agent's character, for instance? Does it suggest a criticism of the agent that might, if presented properly, lead the agent to improve his ways in some regard? Can we learn from this incident that this is or is not an agent who can be trusted to behave *similarly* on *similar* occasions in the future? If one held his character constant, but changed the circumstances in minor – even major – ways, would he almost always do the same lamentable sort of thing? Was what we observed a fluke, or was it a manifestation of a robust trend – a trend that persists, or is constant, over an interestingly wide variety of conditions?[6]

When the agent in question is oneself, this rationale is even more plainly visible. Suppose I find I have done something dreadful. *Who cares* whether, in exactly the circumstances and state of mind I found myself, I could have done something else? I didn't do something else, and it's too late to undo what I did. But when I go to interpret what I did, what do I learn about myself? Ought I to practice the sort of maneuver I botched, in hopes of making it more reliable, less vulnerable to perturbation, or would that be wasted effort? Would it be a good thing, so far as I can tell, for me to try to adjust my habits of thought in such sorts of cases in the future?[...]

It does not matter for the robot, someone may retort, because a robot could not *deserve* punishment or blame for its moments of malfeasance. For us it matters because we are candidates for blame and punishment, not mere redesign. You can't *blame* someone for something he did, if he could not have done otherwise. This, however, is just a reassertion of the CDO principle, not a new consideration, and I am denying that principle from the outset. Why indeed shouldn't you blame someone for doing something he could not have refrained from doing? After all, if he did it, what difference does it make that he was determined to do it?

"The difference is that if he was determined to do it, then he *had no chance not to do it*." But this is simply a *non sequitur*, unless one espouses an extremely superstitious view of what a chance is. Compare the following two lotteries for fairness. In Lottery A, after all the tickets are sold, their stubs are placed in a suitable mixer, and, after suitable mixing (involving some genuinely – quantum-mechanically – random mixing if you like), the winning ticket is blindly drawn. In Lottery B, this mixing and drawing takes place *before* the tickets are sold, but otherwise the lotteries are conducted the same. Many people think the second lottery is unfair. It is unfair, they think, because the winning ticket is determined before people even buy their tickets; one of those tickets is *already* the winner; the other tickets are so much worthless paper, and selling them to unsuspecting people is a sort of fraud. But in fact, of course, the two lotteries are equally fair: *everyone has a chance of winning*. The timing of the selection of the winner is an utterly inessential feature. The reason the drawing in a lottery is typically postponed until after the sale of the tickets is to provide the public with first-hand eyewitness evidence that there have been no shenanigans. No sneaky agent with inside knowledge has manipulated the distribution of the tickets, because the knowledge of the winning ticket did not (and could not) exist in any agent until after the tickets were sold.

It is interesting that not all lotteries follow this practice. Publishers' Clearinghouse and Reader's Digest mail out millions of envelopes each year that say in bold letters on them "YOU MAY ALREADY HAVE WON" – a million dollars or some other prize. Surely these expensive campaigns are based on market research that shows that in general people do think lotteries with pre-selected winners are fair so long as they are honestly conducted. But perhaps people go along with these lotteries uncomplainingly because they get their tickets for free. Would many people *buy* a ticket in a lottery in which the winning stub, sealed in a special envelope, was known to be deposited in a bank vault from the outset? I suspect that most ordinary people would be untroubled by such an arrangement, and would consider themselves to have a real opportunity to win. I suspect, that is, that most ordinary people are less superstitious than those philosophers (going back to Democritus and Lucretius) who have convinced themselves that, without a continual supply of genuinely random *cruces* to break up the fabric of causation, there cannot be any real opportunities or chances.

If our world is determined, then we have pseudo-random number generators in us, not Geiger counter randomizers. That is to say, if our world is determined, all our lottery tickets were drawn at once, eons ago, put in an envelope for us, and doled out as we needed them through life. "But that isn't fair!" some say, "For some people will have been dealt more winners than others." Indeed, on any particular deal, some people have more high cards than others, but one should remember that the luck averages out. "But if all the drawings take place before we are born, some people are *destined* to get more luck than others!" But that will be true even if the drawings are held not before we are born, but periodically, on demand, throughout our lives.

Once again, it makes no difference – this time to fairness and, hence, to the question of desert – whether an agent's decision has been determined for eons (via a fateful lottery ticket lodged in his brain's decision-box, waiting to be used), or was indeterministically fixed by something like a quantum effect at, or just before, the moment of ultimate decision.

It is open to friends of the CDO principle to attempt to provide other grounds for allegiance to the principle, but since at this time I see nothing supporting that allegiance but the habit of allegiance itself, I am constrained to conclude that the principle should be dismissed as nothing better than a long-lived philosophical illusion. I may be wrong to conclude this, of course, but under the circumstances I cannot do otherwise.

Notes

1 "The Incompatibility of Free Will and Determinism," *Philosophical Studies*, xxvii, 3 (March 1975): 185–99, p. 188, reprinted in Gary Watson, ed., *Free Will* (New York: Oxford, 1982): 46–58, p. 50.
2 The misuse of this standard example – e.g., in the extrapolation to the theme that, if determinism is true, the whole world's a prison – is described in my *Elbow Room: The Varieties of Free Will Worth Wanting* (Cambridge, Mass.: Bradford/MIT Press, 1984), from which portions of the present argument are drawn.
3 "Alternate Possibilities and Moral Responsibility," The Journal of Philosophy, lxv, 23 (Dec. 4, 1969): 829–33.
4 This is shown in "Designing the Perfect Deliberator," in *Elbow Room, op. cit.*
5 "We are scarcely ever interested in the performance of a communication-engineering machine for a single input. To function adequately it must give a satisfactory performance for a whole class of inputs, and this means a statistically satisfactory performance for the class of inputs which it is statistically expected to receive." Norbert Wiener, *Cybernetics* (Cambridge, Mass: Technology Press: New York: Wiley, 1948), p. 55.

6 We are interested in trends and flukes in both directions (praiseworthy and regretted); if we had evidence that Luther was just kidding himself, that his apparently staunch stand was a sort of comic-opera coincidence, our sense of his moral strength would be severely diminished. "He's not so stalwart," we might say. "He could well have done otherwise."

Comments and Questions on Daniel Dennett's "I Could Not Have Done Otherwise – So What?"

1.   Dennett says: "it is worth noting that the question ['could he have done otherwise?'] plays almost no role in discussions of praise or reward" for good acts – "except in the formulaic gracious demurrer of one singled out for gratitude or praise: 'What else could I do?' ('Anyone else would have done the same.' 'Shucks; twarn't nothin'). And in these instances we do not take the agent to be disavowing responsibility at all, but just declaring that being responsible under these conditions was not difficult." Dennett concludes from this that we do not assume that "could have done otherwise" is required for responsible or praiseworthy acts. Is he right? And if so, does this mean that determinism is no threat to free will, as he assumes?

2.   Dennett discusses the case of Martin Luther, who said "Here I stand. I can do no other" when breaking with the Church in Rome. Are we not inclined to think that Luther acted "from his own free will" in this act which was the most responsible act of his life, even if he was right that at that moment he could have done no other? Dennett thinks so, and thus he again argues that free will and responsibility do not require "could have done otherwise." Do you agree with him about this Luther case; and if not, where do you think he goes wrong in accounting for it?

3.   Dennett argues that when we do ask in ordinary circumstances whether someone could have done otherwise, we do not mean whether they could have done otherwise *in exactly the same circumstances*. Why does he think it is important to show this, if his ultimate goal is to show that free will and moral responsibility are compatible with determinism? Dennett introduces an example of a robot "destined ... to live its entire life as a deterministic machine on a deterministic planet" in order to show that when we ask whether someone could have done otherwise we do not mean whether they could have done otherwise in exactly the same circumstances. How is the example of the robot suppose to show this? Does it succeed?

Suggested Reading

Dennett's *Elbow Room: The Varieties of Free Will Worth Wanting* (1984) is a lively and readable statement of the compatibilist position on free will that he defends in this reading.

7

Frankfurt-style Examples, Responsibility and Semi-compatibilism

John Martin Fischer

Editor's Introduction

John Martin Fischer is Professor of Philosophy and Director of the University Honors Program at the University of California, Riverside. In the following reading, Fischer discusses some intriguing examples introduced into modern debates about moral responsibility and free will by Harry Frankfurt (1969) which have come to be known as Frankfurt-style examples. Fischer argues that these examples provide further support for the claim that moral responsibility does not require alternative possibilities (or the power to do otherwise) and hence they provide support for the claim that moral responsibility is compatible with determinism. On this key point, Fischer sides with Dennett against van Inwagen. But Fischer's view is unusual, since he also believes that the consequence argument shows that *freedom* is not compatible with determinism, because freedom *does* require alternative possibilities or the power to do otherwise. On this point Fischer sides with van Inwagen against Dennett. These arguments lead Fischer to the unusual view which he calls "*semicompatibilism*": freedom is not compatible with determinism because it requires alternative possibilities, but moral responsibility is compatible with determinism because it does not require alternative possibilities. Frankfurt-style examples are the key to Fischer's position because they supposedly show that moral responsibility does not require alternative possibilities. The following reading is an instructive discussion of Frankfurt-style examples and the arguments for and against them.

It is a quite basic and pervasive assumption that in order to be morally responsible for one's behavior, one must have had (at some relevant point along the path to the behavior) alternative possibilities of a certain sort. This basic idea is encapsulated in the "Principle of Alternative Possibilities," the various versions of which require that moral responsibility be associated with the presence of alternative possibilities.[1] Now there are powerful reasons to think that causal determinism would rule out alternative possibilities.[2] So it has appeared to many philosophers that causal determinism is incompatible with moral responsibility.

There are however various ways of challenging the Principle of Alternative Possibilities. One way employs a thought-experiment with a distinctive structure; such thought-experiments are frequently called "Frankfurt-type examples," because of Harry Frankfurt's seminal presentation of them (1969). The examples contain a failsafe mechanism that does not actually play any role in the relevant agent's deliberations, choices, and behavior, but whose presence ensures that the agent deliberates, chooses, and behaves just as he actually does.

Frankfurt-type Examples

The first "Frankfurt-type case" was given by John Locke in *An Essay Concerning Human Understanding*. Locke's example is a case in which "a man be carried whilst fast asleep into a room where is a person he longs to see and speak with, and be there locked fast in, beyond his power to get out; he awakes and is glad to find himself in so desirable company, which he stays willingly in . . ."[3] In Locke's example, the man stays in the room voluntarily and it seems that he does so "freely" (although Locke himself would use the term "voluntarily," rather than "freely") and can be morally responsible for doing so, although unbeknownst to him he could not have left the room. Of course, the man *does* have various alternative possibilities (apart from special assumptions): he can choose to leave the room and try to leave the room, and so forth.

Frankfurt can be seen to be entering the debate at this point. Frankfurt seeks to construct examples in which even *these* sorts of alternative possibilities have been eliminated. To do this, Frankfurt employs the apparatus of a "counterfactual intervener"[4] who can monitor the brain and intervene in it, should the agent be about to choose to do otherwise. In order to flesh out these examples – although Frankfurt did not explicitly do this – it is useful to posit a "prior sign" that can be read by the counterfactual intervener and guide him in his activity. (This was David

Blumenfeld's innovation: Blumenfeld 1971.) If the sign indicates that the agent is about to choose to do what the counterfactual intervener wants him to choose, the intervener does not intervene. If, contrary to fact, the agent were about to choose differently, the prior sign would inform the counterfactual intervener (and he would intervene).

Here is a particular version of a "Frankfurt-type case." Suppose Jones is in a voting booth deliberating about whether to vote for Gore or Bush. After reflection, he chooses to vote for Gore, and does vote for Gore by marking his ballot in the normal way. Unbeknownst to him, Black, a liberal neurosurgeon working with the Democratic party, has implanted a device in Jones' brain which monitors Jones' brain activities. If he is about to choose to vote Democratic, the device simply continues monitoring and does not intervene in the process in any way. If, however, Jones is about to choose to vote (say) Republican, the device triggers an intervention which involves electronic stimulation of the brain sufficient to produce a choice to vote for the Democrat (and a subsequent Democratic vote).

How can the device tell whether Jones is about to choose to vote Republican or Democratic? This is where the "prior sign" comes in. If Jones is about to choose at $T2$ to vote for Gore at $T3$, he shows some involuntary sign – say a neurological pattern in his brain – at $T1$. Detecting this, Black's device does not intervene. But if Jones is about to choose at $T2$ to vote for Bush at $T3$, he shows an involuntary sign – a different neurological pattern in his brain – at $T1$. This brain pattern would trigger Black's device to intervene and cause Jones to choose at $T2$ to vote for Gore, and to vote for Gore at $T3$.

Given that the device plays no role in Jones' deliberations and act of voting, it seems to me that Jones acts freely and is morally responsible for voting for Gore. And given the presence of Black's device, it is plausible to think that Jones does not have alternative possibilities with regard to his choice and action. Thus, the Frankfurt-type examples seem to be counterexamples to the Principle of Alternative Possibilities. [...]

The Flicker of Freedom Strategy

...The original case of Jones is supposed to be one in which Jones is morally responsible for his choice and his act of voting for Gore, although he lacks alternative possibilities. At this point it may be objected that, despite the initial appearance, Jones *does* have at least *some* alternative possibility. Although Jones cannot choose or vote differently, he can still exhibit a different neurological pattern in his brain N^* (from the one he actually exhibits, N). I have called such an alternative possibility a "flicker of freedom" (Fischer 1994). The flicker theorist contends that our moral responsibility always can be traced back to some suitably placed flicker of freedom; our responsibility is grounded in and derives from such alternative possibilities.

It seems that one can always find a flicker of freedom in the Frankfurt-type cases insofar as they are developed as "prior-sign" cases. That is, the agent will always at least have the power to exhibit an alternative sign. But I contend that the mere involuntary display of some sign – such as a neurological pattern in the brain, a blush, or a furrowed brow – is too thin a reed on which to rest moral responsibility. The power involuntarily to exhibit a different sign seems to me to be insufficiently robust to ground our attributions of moral responsibility.

Note that in the alternative sequence (in which Jones shows neurological pattern N^*, which is indicative of an impending decision to vote for Bush), the sign is entirely involuntary and the subsequent decision and vote are produced electronically. Thus, in the alternative sequence Jones cannot be said to be choosing and acting freely, and similarly, cannot be thought to be morally responsible for his choice and action... This sort of alternative possibility cannot ground ascriptions of moral responsibility. It is insufficiently robust: it lacks "voluntary oomph." [...]

I believe that this problem of lack of robustness – lack of voluntary oomph – plagues various versions of the Flicker of Freedom strategy or response to the Frankfurt-type examples. For example, suppose one follows Margery Bedford Naylor (1984) in arguing that what one is "really" morally responsible for is (say) acting "on one's own" (and not as a result of coercion, manipulation, and so forth). Now if this is so one could say that the agent does indeed have an alternative possibility – the option of not acting on one's own in this sense. But I would contend that this sort of alternative possibility is a mere flicker of freedom and insufficiently robust to ground attributions of moral responsibility.

This is because in the alternative sequence of a Frankfurt-type case the agent would not be voluntarily choosing not to perform the action on his own. That is, it is true that (in the alternative sequence of a Frankfurt-type case) the agent would not be choosing and acting on his own, but these features of the sequence would not be voluntarily adopted by him – they would be entirely fortuitous, from the point of view of his deliberations. It would then seem to me that the sort of alternative possibility identified by Naylor lacks voluntary oomph.

A Dilemma for the Proponent of Frankfurt-type Examples

An important challenge to the position I have sketched above (against the flicker theorist) has been presented by such philosophers as David Widerker (1995a and b), Robert Kane (1985: 51; 1996: 142–5),[5] Carl Ginet (1996), and Keith Wyma (1997). I will boil down the various versions of the argument into the following. It begins with a dilemma: either the proponent of the Frankfurt-type examples is presupposing the truth of causal determinism or indeterminism.

Let us start with the presupposition that causal determinism obtains. Now it appears as if the relevant agent – Jones, in the example above – cannot choose or do otherwise (cannot choose at $T2$ to vote for Bush or vote for Bush at $T3$). This is because the "counterfactual intervener" – the liberal neurosurgeon Black – can know, given the prior sign exhibited by Jones at $T1$, that Jones will indeed choose to vote for Gore at $T2$. If Jones were to choose at $T2$ to vote for Bush, the prior sign would have had to have been different; thus, Jones cannot at $T2$ choose to vote for Bush at $T3$. But the problem is that the contention that Jones is morally responsible for choosing to vote for Gore and actually voting for Gore is put in doubt, given the assumption of causal determinism. That is, if causal determinism is explicitly presupposed, it does not seem that someone could say that Jones is obviously morally responsible for his actual choice and action, in a context in which the relationship between causal determinism and moral responsibility are at issue. To do so would appear to beg the question against the incompatibilist.

Now suppose that indeterminism (of a certain relevant sort) obtains. Under this supposition it would not be dialectically inappropriate to claim that Jones is morally responsible for his actual choice at $T2$ to vote for Gore and his vote for Gore at $T3$. But now the contention that Jones cannot choose at $T2$ to vote for Bush at $T3$ is called into question. This is because there is no deterministic relationship between the prior sign exhibited by Jones at $T1$ and Jones' subsequent choice at $T2$. So, if we consider the time just prior to $T2$, everything about the past can be just as it is consistently with Jones' choosing at $T2$ to vote for Bush at $T3$. Someone might think that if it takes some time for Jones to make the choice, Black can intervene to prevent the completion of the choice; but then Jones will still have the possibility of "beginning to make the choice," which is surely more robust than a mere flicker of freedom (say an involuntary twitch, blush, or neurological pattern). After all, beginning to make a choice is a voluntary undertaking (even if it is truncated through no fault of one's own) – it presumably has sufficient voluntary oomph to ground ascriptions of moral responsibility.

The proponents of the Frankfurt-type examples contend that they are non-question-begging cases in which an agent is morally responsible for his choice and action and yet the agent has no sufficiently robust alternative possibilities. But the counter-argument of Widerker, Kane, Ginet, and Wyma appears to show that the examples in question are either not uncontroversial cases in which the agent is morally responsible for his choice and subsequent behavior or not cases in which the agent lacks the alternative possibilities. This is clearly an important argument, and it has been quite influential. Indeed, in a recent paper Ted A. Warfield (1996: 221) claims that the rejection of the Frankfurt-type examples (as cases in which an agent is morally responsible yet lacks alternative possibilities) is "increasingly common."

A Reply on Behalf of the Proponent of the Frankfurt-type Examples

Despite this rising chorus I still remain convinced that the Frankfurt-type cases help to establish that moral responsibility does not require alternative possibilities.

The assumption of causal determinism

Begin with the first horn of the dilemma: the assumption that causal determinism obtains. I agree that one cannot now simply and precipitously conclude, from consideration of the examples, that the agent is morally responsible for his choice and behavior. But in any case this is not how I would have proceeded; I never have envisaged a simple "one-step" argument to the conclusion that (say) Jones is morally responsible for his choice and action. Rather, I employ the Frankfurt-type examples as the first (but obviously important) step of a slightly more complex argument to the conclusion that Jones is morally responsible for his choice and action (despite lacking alternative possibilities).

The argument goes as follows. First, one carefully considers the Frankfurt-type cases. Upon reflection, I believe that one should conclude that in these cases the lack of alternative possibilities does not in itself ground a claim that the agent is not morally responsible for his choice and action. In other words, I think that the examples make highly plausible the preliminary conclusion that *if* Jones is not morally responsible for his choice and action, this is *not* simply because he lacks alternative possibilities. After all, everything that has any causal (or any other kind of) influence on Jones would be exactly the same, if we "subtracted" Black entirely from the scene. And Jones' moral responsibility would seem to be supervenient on what has an influence or impact on him in some way.

So the relevant (preliminary) conclusion is: if Jones is not morally responsible for his choice and action, this is not simply because he lacks alternative possibilities. And it does *not* appear to beg the question to come to this conclusion, even if causal determinism obtains. The first step is to argue – based on the Frankfurt-type examples – that intuitively it is plausible that alternative possibilities are irrelevant to ascriptions of moral responsibility. One is supposed to see the irrelevance of alternative possibilities simply by reflecting on the examples. I do not know how to *prove* the irrelevance thesis, but I find it extremely plausible intuitively. When Louis Armstrong was asked what the definition of jazz is, he allegedly said, "If you have to ask, you ain't never gonna know." I am inclined to say the same thing here: if you have to ask *how* the Frankfurt-type cases show the irrelevance of alternative possibilities to moral responsibility, you ain't never gonna know.

The *second* step in the argument consists in asking whether causal determinism *in itself and apart from ruling out alternative possibilities* threatens moral responsibility. I have considered various possible reasons why someone might think that causal determinism does threaten moral responsibility in itself and apart from ruling out alternative possibilities, and I have come to the conclusion that it is not plausible to accept any of these reasons.[6] It seems to me that this two-stage argument is highly plausible and does *not* beg the question against the incompatibilist, even on the assumption of causal determinism. Thus I believe that the use of the "prior-sign" cases can be defended against the charge of begging the question.

The assumption of indeterminism

Let us now move to the second horn of the dilemma: the assumption of indeterminism. Here I admit that the prior-sign cases will not be cases in which the agent does not have alternative possibilities. But I want to sketch three strategies for modifying the Frankfurt-type case to address this difficulty.[7]

Hunt's approach. A Frankfurt-type case which works as the ones sketched previously in this paper is a "prior-sign" case. But recall that the original "Frankfurt-type" case was presented by John Locke in *An Essay Concerning Human Understanding*. It is important to see that there can be *another* sort of Frankfurt-type case, which takes its cue more closely from Locke's example; I shall refer to such a case, developed by David Hunt (Forthcoming [2000]), as a "blockage case." Note that in Locke's example the door to the room is actually locked *no matter whether the man is inclined to choose to stay in the room or not*. Imagine, then, that although the actual neural processes in one's brain (one is here supposing that the mind supervenes on the brain) take place indeterministically, *all other neural pathways are blocked*.[8] This is a way of bringing the locked door – the blockage – into the brain. Just as with Locke's locked door, the pathways are actually blocked; in contrast to the structure of the prior-sign cases, the pathways being blocked are not dependent on prior features of Jones. This, then, is a different way of solving precisely the problem Frankfurt sought to solve – one that more simply and naturally takes its cue from Locke. And, importantly, it does *not* appear to introduce alternative possibilities.

Mele and Robb's approach.   Here is a second way of modifying the Frankfurt-type cases so that they (allegedly) "work" in a causally indeterministic context. Hunt's strategy involves "blockage" which is not sensitive to prior signs. The second strategy, developed by Alfred Mele and David Robb, involves two simultaneously operating sequences, one of which is indeterministic, the other of which is causally deterministic; the indeterministic sequence actually leads to the result in question, but the deterministic sequence (the operation of which is not sensitive to prior signs) would have issued in the same sort of result, if the indeterministic sequence had not. Mele and Robb (1998) develop their ingenious example as follows (changing our cast of characters slightly):

> At *T1*, Black initiates a certain deterministic process *P* in Bob's brain with the intention of thereby causing Bob to decide at *T2* (an hour later, say) to steal Ann's car. The process, which is screened off from Bob's consciousness, will deterministically culminate in Bob's deciding at *T2* to steal Ann's car unless he decides on his own at *T2* to steal it or is incapable at *T2* of making a decision (because, *e.g.*, he is dead by *T2*). (Black is unaware that it is open to Bob to decide on his own at *T2* to steal the car; he is confident that *P* will cause Bob to decide as he wants Bob to decide.) The process is in no way sensitive to any "sign" of what Bob will decide. As it happens, at *T2* Bob decides on his own to steal the car, on the basis of his own indeterministic deliberation about whether to steal it, and his decision has no deterministic cause. But if he had not just then decided on his own to steal it, *P* would have deterministically issued, at *T2*, in his deciding

to steal it. Rest assured that *P* in no way influences the indeterminstic decision-making process that actually issues in Bob's decision. (pp. 101–2)

The actual sequence in the Mele/Robb example is indeterministic, and yet the agent could not have done otherwise due to the unfolding of a deterministic causal sequence that preemptively overdetermines the actual decision. And the relevant agent seems to be morally responsible for his decision and behavior.

Stump's approach. The third strategy for modifying the Frankfurt-type cases to accommodate indeterministic contexts is developed by Eleonore Stump (1990; 1996; 1999a, 1999b which is a response to Goetz 1999). Stump assumes that there is some sort of one–many correlation between a mental act or state and the firings of neurons in the brain:

> When I suddenly recognize my daughter's face across a crowded room, that one mental act of recognition, which feels sudden, even instantaneous, to me, is correlated with many neural firings as information from the retina is sent through the optic nerve, relayed through the lateral geniculate nucleus of the thalamus, processed in various parts of the occipital cortex, which take account of figure, motion, orientation in space, and color, and then processed further in cortical asociation areas. Only when the whole sequence of neural firings is completed, do I have the mental act of recognizing my daughter. Whatever neural firings are correlated with an act of will or intellect, I take it that in this case, as in all others, the correlation between the mental act and the firing of the relevant neurons is a one–many relation. (1999b: 417)

On Stump's approach, it is crucial that if the firing of the whole neural sequence correlated with a mental act is not completed, the result is not some truncated or incomplete mental act (say, the beginning of a choice or decision). It is no mental act at all. She says:

> If the neural sequence correlated with my recognizing my daughter's face across a crowded room is interrupted at the level of the thalamus, say, then I will have no mental act having to do with seeing her. I won't for example think to myself, "For a moment there, I thought I saw my daughter, but now I'm not sure." I won't have a sensation of almost but not quite seeing her. I won't have a premonition that I was about to see her, and then I mysteriously just don't see her. I will simply have no mental act regarding recognition of her at all. (1999b: 417–18)

Let us suppose now that a mental event is identical to a series of neural firings.[9] A particular mental event, say, a choice, can be assumed to be the result of an indeterministic process. Further, there can be a counterfactual intervener associated with the agent who could notice (in an alternative scenario) that a different neural sequence was beginning, and could then interrupt it before it can be completed. If Black – the counterfactually intervening liberal neurosurgeon – did interrupt a neural sequence which was beginning to unfold (and which is such that, if it were completed, it would constitute – or correlate with – a decision to vote for Bush), Jones would *not* (according to Stump) have engaged in the mental act of *beginning to make a decision*. Jones would have *no* mental act, just as Stump would not have begun to recognize her daughter, if the sequence of neural firings beginning in her retina had been terminated in the thalamus (1999b: 418).

Thus, in Stump's version of the Frankfurt-type cases, the agent's choice is not causally determined, and it is also true that the agent cannot have chosen (or behaved) differently from how he actually chooses (and behaves). And yet it seems entirely plausible that the agent be morally responsible for his choice and behavior in these cases.

Despite the force and influence of the argument (presented by Widerker, Kane, Ginet, and Wyma) against the contention that in the Frankfurt-type cases the agent is morally responsible although he has no alternative possibilities, there is an attractive strategy of response. Even if causal determinism is true, it does not appear to be question-begging to use the cases as part of a two-stage argument (rather than an argument that simply assumes that the relevant agents are morally responsible in the cases). And if causal determinism is false (in certain ways), it still seems (at least at first blush) to be possible to construct versions of the Frankfurt-type cases in which it is plausible to say that the agent is morally responsible and yet lacks alternative possibilities.

Analysis of the Indeterministic Cases

It is contentious however whether the indeterministic cases presented by such philosophers as Hunt, Mele and Robb, and Stump really work. Let's start by focusing on Hunt's approach. Recall that Hunt envisages a case in which the neural events resulting in the relevant choice are indeterministic, and yet all *other* neural pathways in the brain are "blocked" (as in Locke's "locked-door" example). The question could now be put as follows: Does the agent have access to a scenario in which his neural path makes contact with or "bumps up against" the blockage? If so, it would seem that the alternative possibility in question does after all exist, because if the neural path "bumps up against" the blockage, then presumably the agent is no longer the author of the subsequent act (and is not morally responsible for it).

But how exactly can the agent (or his neural events) bump up against the blockage? It would seem that in order to have access to the blockage, there would have to be an intermediate set of neural events, different from the actual neural events, that is, as it were, a "bridge" between the actual neural process and the blockage. (In Locke's example, the agent would have to walk over to the door and try to open it.) But even these intermediate events are presumed to be blocked in Hunt's example. So it may seem that Hunt has indeed provided an example of the required sort, *i.e.*, one in which the agent is morally responsible and yet does not have *any* alternative possibilities.

But the example is difficult to imagine (and thus properly to evaluate). If casual indeterminism obtains in the actual neural pathway, how exactly can it be the case that the agent does not have access to events consisting in bumping up against any of the barriers (intermediate or terminal)? And if the agent really does not have access to any such "bumping" events, how can it be the case that causal determinism does not actually obtain?

Consider the following somewhat rough analogy. Suppose one is driving on a freeway, with some space (as is safe!) between one's car and other vehicles. But imagine also that all of the off-ramps to the freeway are entirely bottled up with traffic, right from the beginnings of the off-ramps. The spaces between the cars represents that one's actual driving on the freeway corresponds to causal indeterminism, and the off-ramps' being blocked corresponds to the lack of alternative possibilities.

But now someone will ask why, if there is indeed space between the vehicles, the driver cannot at least begin to guide his car toward an off-ramp. And if there are such possibilities of changing direction, then these would seem to be alternative possibilities of the relevant sort, *i.e.*, with sufficient voluntary oomph. So the example needs to be changed so that one is driving along on the freeway absolutely "up against" the bumpers of the cars in front and back, but not being pushed or pulled in any way by those cars. Of course, if one were being pushed or pulled along, then this would correspond to actual-sequence causal determination. The idea is that it at least seems possible to be driving in such a manner that one is not being pushed or pulled by the contiguous cars and yet (because of the positions of the cars) one does not have the power to change the direction of the car at all. But here again there seems to be the alternative possibility that involves pressure's being exerted on the contiguous cars. That is, the "bumping events" seem to be ineradicable features of the analogy, and thus it is hard to see how completely to eradicate the "bumping events" from the brain. (For another sort of reply to the blockage strategy, see Robert Kane forthcoming [2000a].)

David Hunt has also suggested that the context of God's foreknowledge of future events is relevantly similar to Frankfurt-type examples.[10] Let us suppose that God exists within the same time framework as humans, is essentially omniscient, and can know future contingent truths. Let us further assume that causal indeterminism obtains. (Of course, each of these assumptions is contentious, as is their combination.) I believe that it follows from the conjunction of these assumptions (suitably interpreted) that human agents cannot choose or do otherwise; and yet (given certain assumptions about God) God's knowledge plays absolutely no role in human choices and actions. Just as with the "counterfactual intervener" in a Frankfurt-type case, one could "subtract" God from the situation and everything that has a causal impact on the agent's choices and behavior would be exactly the same. If all the above is correct, then the context of God's foreknowledge would seem to be one in which an agent could be held morally responsible for his choice and behavior, and yet have no alternative possibilities. Here the problem of the apparent ineradicability of the "bumping" events is eliminated, but, of course, the package of assumptions necessary to do the trick is controversial.

To take stock. It seems to me that both the approaches of Hunt and Mele and Robb are promising, but that they posit something that is contentious: that the actual sequence can be indeterministic and nevertheless there are absolutely no alternative possibilities (even including bumping events). This problem comes out in Mele and Robb at the point at which they contend that the deterministic process P "in no way influences" the indeterministic process X which actually issues in the decision, and yet that the agent has absolutely no alternative possibility. How exactly is it possible for P to "neutralize" all non-actual neural pathways without issuing in causal determination in the actual pathway? I do not think it is obvious that the critiques are decisive, but on the other hand it is unclear whether we have here plausible Frankfurt-type examples that work in indeterministic contexts. God's foreknowledge (envisaged in a certain way) *may* do the trick. Also, if Stump is correct, then "bumping" events may well be insufficiently robust to ground moral responsibility attributions, because the neural bumping events would not be sufficient for a mental event with voluntary oomph.[11] [...]

Conclusion

These controversies notwithstanding, it is my view that the Frankfurt-type cases provide very strong reasons to think that moral responsibility does not require alternative possibilities. Of course, they fall short of providing *decisive* reason to abandon the Principle of Alternative Possibilities. But they should make a reasonable person turn away from endlessly seeking to identify some sort of alternative possibility, and set about the task of saying what it is about the actual sequence of events leading to an action (or omission or consequence) that grounds ascriptions of moral responsibility. [...]

My position here is that the argument for the incompatibility of causal determinism and alternative possibilities is *considerably stronger* than the argument that causal determinism rules out moral responsibility...I believe that reasonable people, not already committed to a particular position on the free will debate, would find it highly plausible that causal determinism rules out alternative possibilities. But moral responsibility is another matter. If moral responsibility does not require alternative possibilities, as Frankfurt-style examples seem to show, it would not follow that moral responsibility is incompatible with determinism even if determinism is incompatible with alternative possibilities. Further, given that that there are strong motivations toward compatibilism about causal determinism and moral responsibility – especially the desire to protect our status as morally responsible agents from esoteric scientific discoveries about the form of the equations that describe the universe – I am inclined to adopt "semicompatibilism" – the doctrine that causal determinism is compatible with moral responsibility, even if causal determinism were to rule out alternative possibilities.

Of course, there are various ways of specifying and developing an "actual-sequence" approach to moral responsibility...The approach I favor contends that when one "decodes" the information embedded in the actual sequence in which there is moral responsibility, one will find a certain sort of "control." Whereas typically it is thought that control must involve alternative possibilities, I believe there are two species of control. "Regulative control" does indeed involve alternative possibilities, but "guidance control" does not; guidance control is the sort of control displayed by agents in the actual sequences of Frankfurt-type examples, and, in general, by agents who are morally responsible for their behavior.

My project has been to lay out an analysis of guidance control and to show that this sort of control is compatible with moral responsibility. (See Fischer 1994 and Fischer and Ravizza 1998.) In my view, guidance control of one's behavior has two components: the behavior must issue from one's own mechanism, and this mechanism must be appropriately responsive to reasons. I have sought to give accounts of both components – mechanism ownership and reasons-responsiveness, and I have defended the idea that guidance control, so analyzed, is compatible with causal determinism.[12]

Notes

1   Some philosophers prefer "alternate possibilities," whereas others prefer "alternative possibilities." Harry Frankfurt offers a (somewhat curmudgeonly) defense of his use of the term "alternate possibilities," in Frankfurt 1999: 372.
2   See, for example, Ginet in Lehrer, ed., 1996: 87–104; and 1990; Wiggins in Honderich, ed., 1973: 31–62; Van Inwagen 1983; and Fischer 1994.
3   Book II, Chapter XI, Sec. 10.
4   This term was introduced in Fischer 1982.
5   As far as I know, Kane was the first to articulate this strategy in reply to the Frankfurt examples: Kane 1985: 51.
6   Fischer 1994, pp. 147–154. For further discussion of this issue, see Kane 1996: 40–43; and Mele 1996: 123–141.
7   For yet another approach, see: Fischer 1995; Widerker and Katzoff, 1996; Hunt 1996; and Speak 1999.
8   I borrow this example from Hunt (Forthcoming [2000]). He develops this – and related – examples further in "Freedom, Foreknowledge, and Frankfurt," unpublished manuscript.
9   This supposition is just for simplicity's sake; Stump's view is compatible with other stories as to the precise relationship between mental states and brain events.
10   Hunt, working paper.
11   It should be noted that the original proponents of the "indeterminist" strategy of reply to the Frankfurt examples, such as Kane and Widerker, have attempted to respond to the challenges of Fischer, Hunt, Mele and Robb, and Stump. Kane attempts to respond to Hunt and Fischer on blockage cases in Kane forthcoming [2000]. He attempts to respond to Mele and Robb in "Responsibility, Incompatibilism and Frankfurt-Style Examples," unpublished manuscript to be published in a collection edited by McKenna and Widerker, and to Stump in "The Dual Regress of Free Will and the Role of Alternative Possibilities," forthcoming in *Philosophical Perspectives* (vol. 14). Widerker attempts to respond to all three strategies in "Frankfurt's Attack on the Principle of Alternative Possibilities," forthcoming in *Philosophical Perspectives* (vol. 14).

12   This paper builds on – and relies considerably on – previously published work. In particular, I am grateful for permission from the University of Chicago Press to reprint parts of Fischer 1999a, and from Kluwer Academic Publishers to reprint parts of 1999b.

Comments and Questions on John Martin Fischer's "Frankfurt-style Examples, Responsibility and Semi-compatibilism"

1.   Frankfurt-style examples are meant to refute the Principle of Alternative Possibilities (often designated PAP): an act is morally responsible only if the agent could have done otherwise than perform it. One of the critics of Frankfurt-style examples, David Widerker, has pointed out that it is a crucial assumption of such examples that the mechanism (say, in the brain) which would prevent the agent from doing otherwise *plays no actual role in the situation* when the agent acts on his or her own. Why is this assumption crucial to the success of Frankfurt-style examples in refuting PAP?

2.   What does Fischer mean by a "flicker of freedom" strategy for refuting Frankfurt-style examples? He argues that flickers of freedom are not sufficiently "robust" to ground ascriptions of moral responsibility. Why does he think this, and do you agree?

3.   According to the objection made against Frankfurt-style examples in the third section of Fischer's paper (the objection by Widerker, Kane, Ginet and Wyma), a Frankfurt-style case does not work if the free and responsible choice in question is *causally undetermined* (as incompatibilists and libertarians about free choice assume it must be). Why not? How is indeterminism suppose to undermine or thwart Frankfurt-style control? Fischer discusses three attempts – by David Hunt, by Alfred Mele and David Robb, and by Eleonore Stump – to save Frankfurt-style arguments from this "indeterministic" objection by offering more refined versions of Frankfurt-style examples. In your view, do the Frankfurt-style arguments proposed by Hunt, Mele/Robb and Stump save Frankfurt-style examples from this indeterministic objection? If so, why? If not, why not?

Suggested Reading

There is further discussion of Frankfurt-style examples in Fischer's *The Metaphysics of Free Will: A Study of Control* (1994). Fischer develops his semicompatibilist view of responsibility further in *Responsibility and Control: A Theory of Moral*

Responsibility (1998) (coauthored with Mark Ravizza). Critics of Frankfurt-style examples include Widerker (1995 a and b), Kane (1985, 1996), Ginet (1996), Wyma (1997), Copp (1997), Goetz (1999), Ekstrom (2000). Defenders include Stump (1990, 1999), Mele and Robb (1998), Haji (1998), Hunt (1999), among others. A useful collection of readings on Frankfurt-style examples by these and other authors is *Freedom, Responsibility and Agency: Essays on the Importance of Alternative Possibilities* edited by David Widerker and Michael McKenna (forthcoming 2002). Another collection, *Perspectives on Moral Responsibility* (1993) edited by Fischer and Mark Ravizza, contains one section of essays on Frankfurt-style examples.

8

The Explanatory Irrelevance of Alternative Possibilities

Derk Pereboom

Editor's Introduction

Derk Pereboom is Professor and Chair of the Department of Philosophy at the University of Vermont. In the following reading, he offers a different perspective from Fischer's on Frankfurt-style examples and their relevance to the free will/determinism controversy. Pereboom argues that the novel Frankfurt-style examples put forward by Eleonore Stump, David Hunt, and others do not successfully answer critics of Frankfurt-style examples. But he thinks such critics can be answered none the less; and he offers an intriguing Frankfurt-style example of his own to show this. A number of things should be noted about Pereboom's overall position that are not explicitly discussed in his paper, but help to understand where he is coming from. Pereboom agrees with Fischer that Frankfurt-style examples show that moral responsibility does not require alternative possibilities. But Pereboom does not follow Fischer in concluding that moral responsibility is compatible with *determinism,* for he thinks there is another way to argue that free will and moral responsibility are incompatible with determinism without invoking alternative possibilities. (This alternative route to incompatibilism is actually discussed in a later reading by Kane.) Pereboom thus rejects Fischer's semicompatibilism, since he believes that *both* free will and moral responsibility are incompatible with determinism, even though neither requires alternative possibilities. Finally, while Pereboom is thus an incompatibilist about free will, he does not think an incompatibilist free will exists because he thinks human behavior is for all intents and purposes determined. He therefore calls his view "hard incompatibilism." See the comments on this hard incompatibilist view at the end of the Paul Edwards reading.

The claim that moral responsibility for an action requires that the agent could have done otherwise is surely attractive. Moreover, it seems reasonable to contend that a requirement of this sort is not merely a necessary condition of little consequence, but that it plays a significant role in *explaining why* an agent is morally responsible. For if an agent is to be blameworthy for an action, it seems crucial that she could have done something to avoid being blameworthy – that she could have done something to get herself off the hook. If she is to be praiseworthy for an action, it seems important that she could have done something less admirable. Libertarians have often grounded their incompatibilism precisely in such intuitions. As a result, they have often defended principles of alternative possibilities like the following:

> An action is free in the sense required for moral responsibility only if the agent could have done otherwise than she actually did.

I shall argue that despite resourceful attempts to defend conditions of this kind, this sort of requirement is irrelevant to explaining why an agent is morally responsible for an action.[1]

A Libertarian Objection to Frankfurt-style Arguments

Familiarly, Frankfurt-style arguments are designed to show that alternative possibilities are not required for moral responsibility.[2] An important kind of objection to these kinds of arguments was initially raised by Robert Kane and then independently developed by David Widerker.[3] The example Widerker uses is one in which Jones wants to kill Smith, but Black is afraid that Jones might become fainthearted, and so he is prepared to intervene if Jones fails to show a sign that he will kill Smith. The prior sign that he will kill Smith is Jones's blushing at t1. But Jones does indeed blush at t1, and he kills Smith without Black having to intervene. This case is designed to generate the intuition that Jones is morally responsible even though he could not have refrained from deciding to kill Smith. This scenario was originally devised by John Fischer as one in which the prior sign could fail to occur – as one in which Jones could fail to blush – but in Fischer's conception this alternative possibility is too "flimsy and exiguous" to ground Jones's moral responsibility. To use his term, this alternative possibility is insufficiently *robust*.[4]

The salient features of the example are these:

(1) If Jones is blushing at t1, then, provided no one intervenes, he will decide at t2 to kill Smith.
(2) If Jones is not blushing at t1, then, provided no one intervenes, he will not decide at t2 to kill Smith.
(3) If Black sees that Jones shows signs that he will not decide at t2 to kill Smith, that is, he sees that Jones is *not* blushing at t1, then Black will force Jones to decide at t2 to kill Smith; but if he sees that Jones is blushing at t1, then he will do nothing.

Finally, suppose that Black does not have to show his hand, because

(4) Jones is blushing at t1, and decides at t2 to kill Smith for reasons of his own.[5]

Although this scenario is meant to elicit the conviction that Jones is morally responsible despite the fact that he could not have done otherwise, Widerker claims that this conclusion is not forced on the libertarian. He asks, first of all: What would ground the truth of (1), that is, what would make it true that if Jones is blushing at t1, then, provided no one intervenes, he will decide at t2 to kill Smith? If the example is to convince the libertarian that alternative possibilities are not required for moral responsibility, then the truth of (1) cannot be grounded in the fact that Jones's blushing at t1 causally determines his decision to kill Smith, or that it indicates a state that causally determines that decision. For then the libertarian would deny that Jones is morally responsible. On the other hand, if the truth of (1) is not grounded in causal determinism, then the following options are available to the libertarian to support the contention that Jones has alternative possibilities after all. He could reject (1), claiming that the most that he would allow is

(1a) If Jones is blushing at t1, then Jones will *probably* decide at t2 to kill Smith. But (1a) is clearly compatible with Jones's having an alternative possibility – to refrain from deciding at t2 to kill Smith. Or else the libertarian may reconstrue (1) as a "conditional of freedom":
(1b) If Jones is blushing at t1, then Jones will *freely* decide at t2 to kill Smith (in a sense that allows that the agent could have decided otherwise).

On this assumption, the libertarian obviously can again claim that in the actual situation when Jones is blushing at t1 he can refrain from deciding at t2 to kill Smith.[6]

The Kane/Widerker objection is very significant, and it serves as a test for the effectiveness of any Frankfurt-style argument. One point of clarification: if the libertarian that Kane and Widerker suppose Frankfurt must convince is simply presupposing a principle of alternative possibilities, then one could not expect that a Frankfurt-style argument would dislodge his view. But Kane and Widerker clearly do not intend that the libertarian simply presuppose this principle, but rather only the claim that moral responsibility is incompatible with an action's having a deterministic causal history. I will proceed with this understanding of the Kane/Widerker objection.

Problems for Recent Attempts to Answer Kane and Widerker.

Several critics have tried to construct Frankfurt-style arguments that escape this objection. The cases used in these arguments divide into two categories:

(a)   those in which the relationship between the prior sign and the action is causally deterministic, and the indeterminism that makes for the agent's libertarian freedom is present in the causal history of the action before the prior sign.

(b)   those in which the prior sign is eliminated altogether.

Eleonore Stump and Ishtiyaque Haji have devised examples in category (a),[7] while David Hunt, and Alfred Mele together with David Robb, have conceived scenarios in category (b).[8]

In my view, the cases that have been devised in each of these categories face significant problems.[9] First, (a)-type situations are difficult to construct so that they are effective against Widerker's objection. Consider Stump's case as a representative. In her example, Grey, the neurosurgeon, wants to ensure that Jones will vote for Reagan. Grey finds that every time Jones decides to vote for Republicans, the decision regularly correlates with *the completion* of a sequence of neural firings in Jones' brain that always includes, near the beginning, the firing of neurons a, b, and c. Jones' deciding to vote for Democratic candidates is correlated with the completion of a neural sequence that always includes, near the beginning, the firing of neurons x, y, and z. Whenever Grey's neuroscope detects the firing of x, y, and z, it disrupts that sequence, with the result that this sequence is not brought to completion. Instead, the device activates a coercive mechanism that makes Jones vote Republican. Crucially, Stump specifies that the firing of x, y, and z does not constitute a decision, and in her view the occurrence of this sequence would not count as a robust alternative possibility – one that could ground an agent's moral responsibility. If, on the other hand, the neuroscope detects the firing of a, b, and c, it allows the sequence to proceed to completion and the decision to vote Republican to occur.[10] Stump specifies that the decision is indeed a causal outcome of the neural sequence.[11] What makes the agent libertarian is that the neural sequence is not the outcome of a causal chain that originates in a cause outside him. Rather, it is the outcome of a causal chain that originates, at least to a significant extent, *in an act of the agent which is not the outcome of a causal chain that originates in a cause outside the agent.* Here Stump suggests the Aquinas-inspired view that the neural sequence is the outcome of a causal chain that originates in the agent's intellect and will.[12]

But as Stewart Goetz points out, to assess this case, one needs to know more about the psychological features of the act performed by the agent to cause the neural process. If this originating act is causally determined, then Stump's agent would appear not to be free in the libertarian sense. If it is not causally determined, then he might well have robust alternative possibilities for action. If the originating act is an intention to make a decision, for example, and if the indeterminism of that act allows for the agent to have avoided intending to make the decision, then the case might well include a robust alternative possibility after all.[13] Note that in Stump's setup, the agent's performance of that act – which constitutes the agent's crucial libertarian causal role – precedes the possible intervention.[14]

More generally, the challenge for Stump is to characterize the agent's causal role so that (1) her action is not causally determined (by factors beyond her control) and (2) her action does not involve robust alternative possibilities. A case of the sort that Stump devises is subject to the following dilemma: if the indeterminism (whether or not it is a characteristic of the sort of agent's act she has in mind) that occurs prior to the neural sequence is significant enough to make the action a libertarian freely-willed action, then it has not been ruled out that the indeterministic juncture features a robust alternative possibility. If Stump were to reject the claim that there is a robust alternative possibility at this point, then it would remain open to a libertarian (like Kane or Widerker) to deny that the agent has genuine libertarian free will. I doubt that there could be a plausible Frankfurt-style case in which the action is not causally determined by factors beyond the agent's control (in a way that would satisfy the libertarian) and she lacks robust alternative possibilities if the intervention would occur after the crucial indeterministic juncture.

Frankfurt-style Scenarios Without Prior Signs.

Cases in category (b) exemplify a different kind of strategy for opposing alternative-possibility conditions. In these cases there are no prior signs to guide intervention, not even nonrobust flickers of freedom. An important version of this strategy has become known as "blockage," and has been developed by Hunt.[15] Here is a way of presenting this sort of approach that I think is especially powerful. Consider two situations.

> *Situation A*: Ms. Scarlet deliberately chooses to kill Colonel Mustard at t1, and there are no factors beyond her control that deterministically produce her choice. When she chooses to kill the Colonel, she could have chosen not to kill him. There are no causal factors that would prevent her from not making the choice to kill Colonel Mustard.

In these circumstances, Ms. Scarlet could be morally responsible for her choice. But then, against an alternative-possibilities principle one might employ a counterfactual version of this situation:

> *Situation B*: Ms. Scarlet's choice to kill Colonel Mustard has precisely the same actual causal history as in A. But before she even started to think about killing Colonel Mustard, a neurophysiologist had blocked all the neural pathways not used in Situation A, so that no neural pathway other than the one employed in that situation could be used. Let us suppose that it is causally determined that she remain a living agent, and if she remains a living agent, some neural pathway has to be used. Thus every alternative for Ms. Scarlet is blocked except the one that realizes her choice to kill the Colonel. But the blockage does not affect the actual causal history of Ms. Scarlet's choice, because the blocked pathways would have remained dormant.

One might, at least initially, have the intuition that Ms. Scarlet could be morally responsible for her choice in B as well. Yet for an incompatibilist this intuition might well be undermined upon more careful reflection on whether in B Ms. Scarlet retains libertarian freedom. One important question about such blockage cases is one Fischer asks: *Could* neural events bump up against, so to speak, the blockage?[16] If so, there still may be alternative possibilities for the agent. But if not, it might seem, as Kane suggests, that the neural events are causally determined partly by virtue of the blockage.[17]

In response, one might point out that in the standard Frankfurt-style cases the relevant action is inevitable, but the intuition that the agent is morally responsible for it depends on the fact that it does not have an actual causal history by means of which it is made inevitable. What makes the action inevitable is rather some fact about the situation that is not a feature of its actual causal history, and hence, the action's being inevitable need not make it the case that it is causally determined. But then how is the blockage case different from the standard Frankfurt-style cases? After all, the blockage does not seem to affect the actual causal history of the action.

Nevertheless, perhaps Kane's response can be defended. Two-situation cases of the above sort might be misleading just because it is natural to assume that the actual causal history of an event is essentially the same in each, given that the only difference between them is a restriction that would seem to have no actual effect on the event. But consider a simple two-situation case modeled on a reflection of Hunt's.[18] Imagine a universe correctly described by Epicurean physics: at the most fundamental level all that exists is atoms and the frictionless void, and there is a determinate downwards direction in which all atoms naturally fall – except if they undergo uncaused swerves.

> *Situation C*: A spherical atom is falling downward through space, with a certain velocity and acceleration. Its actual causal history is indeterministic because at any time the atom can be subject to an uncaused swerve. Suppose that the atom can swerve in any direction other than upwards. In actual fact, from t1 to t2 it does not swerve.

A counterfactual situation diverges from C only by virtue of a device that eliminates alternative possibilities and all differences thereby entailed:

> *Situation D*: The case is identical to C, except that the atom is falling downward through a straight and vertically oriented tube whose interior surface is made of frictionless material, and whose interior is precisely wide enough to accommodate the atom. The atom would not have swerved during this time interval, and the trajectory, velocity, and acceleration of the atom from t1 to t2 are precisely what they are in C.

One might initially have the intuition that the causal history of the atom from t1 to t2 in these two situations is in essence the same. However, this intuition could be challenged by the fact that the restrictions present in D but not in C may change this causal history from one that is essentially indeterministic to one that is essentially deterministic. For since the tube prevents any alternative motion, it would seem that it precludes any indeterminism in the atom's causal history from t1 to t2. And if the tube precludes indeterminism in this causal history, it would appear to make the causal history deterministic. Whether this line of argument is plausible is difficult to ascertain, but it is not obviously implausible.

This problem could make it hard to assess moral responsibility in blockage cases. Sympathy for Frankfurt-style arguments is generated by the sense that moral responsibility is very much a function of the features of the actual causal history of an action, to which restrictions that exist but would seem to play no actual causal role are irrelevant. However, in a scenario in which such restrictions, despite initial appearances, could be relevant to the nature of the actual causal history of an action after all, one's intuitions about whether the agent is morally responsible might become unstable. My own view is not that actual causal histories in blockage cases are clearly deterministic, but only that these considerations show that they may be. This type of problem should make one less confident when evaluating these difficult kinds of Frankfurt-style cases.[19]

A New Frankfurt-style Scenario

I propose a case of a different sort, one that doesn't fit either category (a) or (b):

Tax evasion, Part 1: Joe is considering whether to claim a tax deduction for the substantial local registration fee that he paid when he bought a house. He knows that claiming the deduction is illegal, that he probably won't be caught, and that if he is, he can convincingly plead ignorance. Suppose he has a very powerful but not always overriding desire to advance his self-interest no matter what the cost to others, and no matter whether advancing his self-interest involves illegal activity. Furthermore, he is a libertarian free agent. Crucially, his psychology is such that the only way that in this situation he could fail to choose to evade taxes is for moral reasons. (As I use the phrase here, *failing to choose to evade taxes* will encompass both not choosing to evade taxes and choosing not to evade taxes.) His psychology is not, for example, such that he could fail to choose to evade taxes for no reason or simply on a whim. In fact, it is causally necessary for his failing to choose to evade taxes in this situation that a moral reason occur to him *with a certain force*. A moral reason can occur to him with that force either involuntarily or as a result of his voluntary activity (e.g., by his willing to consider it, or by his seeking out a vivid presentation of such a reason). However, a moral reason occurring to him with such force is not causally sufficient for his failing to choose to evade taxes. If a moral reason were to occur to him with that force, Joe could, with his libertarian free will, either choose to act on it or refrain from doing so (without the intervener's device in place). But to ensure that he choose to evade taxes, a neuroscientist now implants a device which, were it to sense a moral reason occurring with the specified force, would electronically stimulate his brain so that he would choose to evade taxes. In actual fact, no moral reason occurs to him with such force, and he chooses to evade taxes while the device remains idle.[20]

In this situation, Joe could be morally responsible for choosing to evade taxes despite the fact that he could not have chosen otherwise. This scenario is not a (b)-type case, since it does indeed feature alternative possibilities, which involve a moral reason occurring to him with a certain force. In one type of possibility Joe makes this happen voluntarily. But such a possibility is insufficiently robust to ground his moral responsibility for deciding to evade taxes. For the deeper intuition underlying alternative-possibilities requirements is that if, for example, an agent is to be blameworthy for an action, it is crucial that she could have done something to avoid this blameworthiness. If alternative possibilities were to play a role in explaining an agent's moral responsibility for an action (that is, if they were to be robust), it would be because as a result of securing an alternative possibility instead, he would thereby have avoided the responsibility he has for the action he performed. However, if Joe had made a reason for an alternative action occur to him with a certain force, he would not thereby have avoided responsibility for deciding to evade taxes. For his making the reason for an alternative action occur to him is compatible with his never deciding to perform the alternative action, or even ever being inclined to perform that action, and choosing to evade taxes instead.[21]

It is important to the example that the trigger for intervention be that a moral reason occur to Joe with a certain force, and not simply that a moral reason occur to him. For one might plausibly argue that it is a necessary condition of blameworthiness that the agent understands that his action is morally wrong, which in Joe's case requires would seem to require some awareness of moral reasons.[22] At the same time, Joe's blameworthiness would not require that moral reasons occur to him with any particularly strong force.

The core of the Kane/Widerker objection is that if the inevitability of the action given the prior sign is grounded in causal determinism, then the libertarian cannot be expected to agree that the agent is morally responsible for the action, but if we eliminate the causal determination then the agent has alternative possibilities after all. But in tax evasion, the inevitability of the action given the prior sign is not grounded in causal determinism (and this is what differentiates it from an (a)-type case), while at the same time no robust alternative possibilities are available to the agent. In this example, the connection between the prior sign and the action is expressed in the following proposition (the analogue of Widerker's (1)):

(5)   If a moral reason does not occur to Joe with a certain force, then, provided no one intervenes, he will decide to evade taxes.

Clearly, the truth of (5) is not grounded in causal determinism. For the absence of what would trigger the intervention at some particular time, that is, the nonoccurrence of a moral reason with the requisite force at some particular time, or a state indicated by this absence, will not, together with all the other actual facts about the situation, causally determine the decision. To see this, first remove the intervener from the scenario – we can do so safely, for by hypothesis, the intervener exerts no actual causal influence on Joe's deciding to evade taxes, so removing the intervener won't have any implications for whether Joe is causally determined to make this decision. There is no relevant time at which refraining from deciding to evade taxes in the future is impossible for Joe, since he can always make the moral reason with the right force occur to him, whereupon he can freely refrain from deciding to evade taxes – or else freely decide to evade taxes. Suppose he does in fact come to decide to evade taxes and he never makes the moral reason occur to him with the requisite force. Nevertheless, one cannot point to a deterministic process that results in his deciding to evade taxes, for it is never determined that he will refrain from making the moral reason occur to him with the right force, and if he did make such a reason occur to him with this force, he could then refrain from deciding to evade taxes – or indeed still decide to evade taxes instead.

At the same time, the decision *will* occur, and not just probably occur, in the absence of what would trigger the intervention, even though it is not causally determined by this absence, because what would trigger the intervention is causally necessary for the decision's failing to be made. Nonetheless, because the agent is not causally determined to make the decision he does, there is a libertarian sense in which he decides *freely*, but *without* its being the case that he could have decided otherwise.

Seeing how this example responds to Kane's version of the objection highlights the value of having the cue for intervention be causally necessary but not sufficient for the action, while ensuring that up to the time of the decision itself, the agent is not causally determined to make it. Kane argues, first of all, that supposing a Frankfurt-style case is to convince the libertarian, then if the agent in the example decides on his own, this decision must be causally undetermined. Now if the intervention does occur, the agent is not morally responsible. But if the neuroscientist "does not intervene to predetermine the outcome and the indeterminacy remains in place until the choice is made – so that the outcome is [a 'self-forming willing'] – then the agent... is ultimately responsible for it. However, then it is also the case that the agent *could have done otherwise.*"[23] However, let the cue for intervention be the relevant sort of causally necessary condition, such as, in our example, the occurrence to the agent of a moral reason with a certain force. Then if the neuroscientist does not intervene, even though the indeterminacy remains in place until the choice is made, *it is not the case*, contrary to Kane's supposition, that the agent could have decided or could have done otherwise. For in order to decide otherwise, a moral reason would have had to occur to the agent with the requisite force, and then the device would have been activated. Consequently, the Kane/Widerker objection can be answered. Even presupposing libertarianism, it appears that the availability of alternative possibilities does not have significant role in explaining moral responsibility.[24]

Notes

1 I maintain instead that the most plausible and fundamentally explanatory incompatibilist principles concern the causal history of an action, and not alternative possibilities. This claim leaves open the prospect of alternative-possibilities conditions necessary for moral responsibility but nevertheless irrelevant to explaining why an agent is morally responsible. I develop my argument for this view in *Living Without Free Will*, Chapters 1–4; the argument is summarized on pp. 127–8. See a list of others that have endorsed a position of this kind on p. 2, note 1.
2 Harry G. Frankfurt, "Alternate Possibilities and Moral Responsibility" (1969), John Martin Fischer, "Responsibility and Control," in *Moral Responsibility*, Fischer, ed. (1986). For a general account of such cases, see the preceding article in this volume by Fischer.

122 *Derk Pereboom*

3 Robert Kane, *Free Will and Values* (1985), p. 51 n. 25, and *The Significance of Free Will* (1996), pp. 142–4, 191–2; David Widerker, "Libertarianism and Frankfurt's Attack on the Principle of Alternative Possibilities" (1995a), cf. Ishtiyaque Haji, *Moral Appraisability* (1998), pp. 34–5. Carl Ginet develops a related objection in his "In Defense of the Principle of Alternative Possibilities: Why I Don't Find Frankfurt's Arguments Convincing" (1996); see also Keith D. Wyma, "Moral Responsibility and Leeway for Action" (1997). Fischer provides a clear and helpful account of these views in "Recent Work on Moral Responsibility" (1999a), pp. 111–12.
4 Fischer, *The Metaphysics of Free Will* (1994), pp. 131–59.
5 Widerker, "Libertarianism and Frankfurt's Attack on the Principle of Alternative Possibilities," pp. 249–50.
6 Ibid., p. 250.
7 Eleonore Stump, "Libertarian Freedom and the Principle of Alternative Possibilities" (1996), pp. 73–88; Haji, *Moral Appraisability* (1998), p. 36.
8 Alfred Mele and David Robb, "Rescuing Frankfurt-Style Cases" (1998); David Hunt, "Moral Responsibility and Avoidable Action" (2000).
9 Recently Widerker has criticized these arguments in "Frankfurt's Attack on the Principle of Alternative Possibilities: A Further Look," *Philosophical Perspectives* 14 (2000), pp. 181–202.
10 Stump, "Libertarian Freedom and the Principle of Alternative Possibilities" (1996), pp. 77–8.
11 Ibid., p. 79.
12 Ibid., pp. 80–5.
13 Stewart Goetz, "Stumping for Widerker" (1999).
14 Stump replies to Goetz's objection in "Dust, Determinism and Frankfurt: A Reply to Goetz" (1999b), but in my view she does not lay to rest the worry I just described.
15 Hunt, "Moral Responsibility and Avoidable Action" (2000). See also Fischer (2000) *The Significance of Free Will* by Robert Kane, in *Philosophy and Phenomenological Research* 60, pp. 141–8.
16 Fischer, "Recent Work on Moral Responsibility" (1999a), p. 119.
17 Kane suggests this response in his reply to Fischer in "Responses to Bernard Berofsky, John Martin Fischer and Galen Strawson" (2000), p. 162:

> In [a case in which every other alternative is blocked except the agent's making A at t], of course, there *are* no alternative possibilities left to the agent; every one is blocked except the agent's choosing A at t. But now we seem to have determinism pure and simple. By implanting the mechanism in this fashion, a controller would have predetermined exactly what the agent would do (and when); and, as a consequence, the controller, not the agent, would be ultimately responsible for the outcome. Blockage by a controller that rules out all relevant alternative possibilities is simply

predestination; and on my view at least, predestination runs afoul of ultimate responsibility.

18 From Hunt's personal correspondence with Fischer, cited in Fischer's "Recent Work on Moral Responsibility" (1999a), pp. 119–20.

19 An ingenious scenario in this category (b) is the one devised by Alfred Mele and David Robb (see the description of this example in Fischer's "Frankfurt-Type Examples, Responsibility and Semi-compatibilism," this volume). Their development of this case appears to involve blockage, and if it indeed does, it would then be subject to the problem just raised. See my "Alternative Possibilities and Causal Histories" (2000), and *Living Without Free Will* (2001), pp. 14–18.

20 Independently, Hunt, in "Moral Responsibility and Avoidable Action" (2000), pp. 214–16, also considers making the prior sign a necessary condition of the alternative decision, but there he expresses skepticism about this approach.

21 The final notion of robustness that I advocate incorporates an epistemic dimension. For an agent's moral responsibility is implausibly explained by the availability of an alternative possibility if she fails to understand that willing the alternative possibility would preclude her from the responsibility she has for her actual choice. Hence, for an alternative possibility to be relevant to explaining why an agent is morally responsible for an action it must satisfy the following characterization: she could have willed something different from what she actually willed such that she understood that by willing it she would thereby be precluded from moral responsibility for the action. See my *Living Without Free Will* (2001), p. 26.

22 Thanks to Michael McKenna for suggesting that I make this point explicit.

23 Kane, *The Significance of Free Will* (1996), p. 142.

24 This article derives from my "Alternative Possibilities and Causal Histories" (2000). Some of the themes are also discussed in my *Living Without Free Will* (2001). I wish to thank David Christensen, John Fischer, Michael McKenna, Robert Kane, Hilary Kornblith, and Alfred Mele for helpful comments and conversations.

Comments and Questions on Derk Pereboom's "The Explanatory Irrelevance of Alternative Possibilities"

1. Pereboom does not think the novel Frankfurt-style examples of Stump and Hunt adequately answer the "indeterministic" criticisms of Frankfurt-style examples by Widerker and Kane. Why does he think the Stump and Hunt examples fail? Do you think he is right?

2.   Pereboom offers a novel Frankfurt-style example of his own to refute the indeterministic objection. What is unique about his example which in his view makes it succeed where others fail? Do you think Pereboom's example does succeed where others fail in showing that moral responsibility (and any free will that entails moral responsibility) does not require alternative possibilities?

3.   Pereboom seems convinced that Frankfurt-style examples show that moral responsibility does not require alternative possibilities. But he does not conclude (as Fischer does) that moral responsibility is compatible with determinism. Do you think it is plausible to be convinced (as Pereboom is) that Frankfurt-style examples show that moral responsibility does not require alternative possibilities and yet hold on to one's intuitions that moral responsibility is incompatible with determinism? If so, how?

Suggested Readings

See Pereboom's *Living Without Free Will* (2001) for further defense of his "hard incompatibilist" position. Also see the suggested readings following the essay by Paul Edwards in this volume ("Hard and Soft Determinism") for views similar to, but different from, Pereboom's. For other readings on Frankfurt-style examples, see the suggested readings at the end of the previous selection by Fischer.

Part III:

Hierarchical Motivation, Deep Self Theories and Reactive Attitudes: New Compatibilist Theories

9

Freedom of the Will and the Concept of a Person

Harry Frankfurt

Editor's Introduction

Harry Frankfurt is Professor of Philosophy at Princeton University and a past president of the American Philosophical Association. In the following paper, he argues that the problem of free will is intimately related to the question of what it means to be a person or self. Persons, such as human persons, are distinguished from other creatures by the structures of their *wills*. Unlike other animals, human persons not only have first-order desires for food or warmth and the like. They are also capable of "hierarchical motivation" – that is, of having second- and higher-order desires about which of their first-order desires they want to be effective in action. By being able to have higher-order desires or motives of such kinds, persons are thus capable of "reflective-self evaluation" about the motives they have and ought to have. Frankfurt develops a novel account of free will in terms of these ideas. By discussing various cases, he shows that "wantons," unwilling drug addicts, and others would lack free will in the sense he describes. Frankfurt also argues that if we view free will in the "hierarchical" way he suggests, we can explain much of what we believe about free will without supposing it must be incompatible with determinism.

What philosophers have lately come to accept as analysis of the concept of a person is not actually analysis of *that* concept at all. Strawson, whose usage represents the current standard, identifies the concept of a person as "the concept of a type of entity such that *both* predicates ascribing states of consciousness *and* predicates ascribing corporeal characteristics ...are equally applicable to a single individual of that single type."[1] But

there are many entities besides persons that have both mental and physical properties. As it happens – though it seems extraordinary that this
should be so – there is no common English word for the type of entity
Strawson has in mind, a type that includes not only human beings but
animals of various lesser species as well. Still, this hardly justifies the
misappropriation of a valuable philosophical term.

Whether the members of some animal species are persons is surely not
to be settled merely by determining whether it is correct to apply to them,
in addition to predicates ascribing corporeal characteristics, predicates
that ascribe states of consciousness. It does violence to our language to
endorse the application of the term "person" to those numerous creatures which do have both psychological and material properties but
which are manifestly not persons in any normal sense of the word. This
misuse of language is doubtless innocent of any theoretical error. But
although the offense is "merely verbal," it does significant harm. For it
gratuitously diminishes our philosophical vocabulary, and it increases
the likelihood that we will overlook the important area of inquiry with
which the term "person" is most naturally associated. It might have been
expected that no problem would be of more central and persistent concern to philosophers than that of understanding what we ourselves
essentially are. Yet this problem is so generally neglected that it has
been possible to make off with its very name almost without being
noticed and, evidently, without evoking any widespread feeling of
loss.[...]

Our concept of ourselves as persons is not to be understood, therefore,
as a concept of attributes that are necessarily species-specific. It is conceptually possible that members of novel or even of familiar nonhuman
species should be persons; and it is also conceptually possible that some
members of the human species are not persons. We do in fact assume, on
the other hand, that no member of another species is a person. Accordingly, there is a presumption that what is essential to persons is a set of
characteristics that we generally suppose – whether rightly or wrongly –
to be uniquely human.

It is my view that one essential difference between persons and other
creatures is to be found in the structure of a person's will. Human beings
are not alone in having desires and motives, or in making choices. They
share these things with the members of certain other species, some of
whom even appear to engage in deliberation and to make decisions based
upon prior thought. It seems to be peculiarly characteristic of humans,
however, that they are able to form what I shall call "second-order
desires" or "desires of the second order."

Besides wanting and choosing and being moved *to do* this or that, men may also want to have (or not to have) certain desires and motives. They are capable of wanting to be different, in their preferences and purposes, from what they are. Many animals appear to have the capacity for what I shall call "first-order desires" or "desires of the first order," which are simply desires to do or not to do one thing or another. No animal other than man, however, appears to have the capacity for reflective self-evaluation that is manifested in the formation of second-order desires.[2]

I

[...]As I shall understand them, statements of the form "*A* wants to *X*" cover a rather broad range of possibilities.[3] ... When *A* is unaware of any feelings concerning *X*-ing, when he is unaware that he wants to *X*, when he deceives himself about what he wants and believes falsely that he does not want to *X*, when he also has other desires that conflict with his desire to *X*, or when he is ambivalent. The desires in question may be conscious or unconscious, they need not be univocal, and *A* may be mistaken about them. There is a further source of uncertainty with regard to statements that identify someone's desires, however, and here it is important for my purposes to be less permissive.

Consider first those statements of the form "*A* wants to *X*" which identify first-order desires – that is, statements in which the term "to *X*" refers to an action. A statement of this kind does not, by itself, indicate the relative strength of *A*'s desire to *X*. It does not make it clear whether this desire is at all likely to play a decisive role in what *A* actually does or tries to do. For it may correctly be said that *A* wants to *X* even when his desire to *X* is only one among his desires and when it is far from being paramount among them. Then it may be true that *A* wants to *X* when he strongly prefers to do something else instead; and it may be true that he wants to *X* despite the fact that, when he acts, it is not the desire to *X* that motivates him to do what he does. On the other hand, someone who states that *A* wants to *X* may mean to convey that it is this desire that is motivating or moving *A* to do what he is actually doing and that *A* will in fact be moved by this desire (unless he changes his mind) when he acts.

It is only when it is used in the second of these ways that, given the special usage of "will" that I propose to adopt, the statement identifies *A*'s will. To identify an agent's will is either to identify the desire (or desires) by which he is motivated in some action he performs or to identify the desire (or desires) by which he will or would be motivated when or if he acts. An agent's will, then, is identical with one or more of his first-order desires. But the notion of the will, as I am employing it, is not coextensive with the notion of first-order desires. It is not the notion of something that merely inclines an agent in some degree to act in a certain way. Rather, it is the notion of an *effective* desire – one that moves the will or would move a person all the way to action. Thus the notion of the will is not coextensive with the notion of what an agent intends to do. For even though someone may have a settled intention to do X, he may nonetheless do something else instead of doing X because, despite his intention, his desire to do X proves to be weaker or less effective than some conflicting desire.

Now consider those statements of the form "A wants to X" which identify second-order desires – that is, statements in which the term "to X" refers to a desire of the first order. There are also two kinds of situation in which it may be true that A wants to want to X. In the first place, it might be true of A that he wants to have a desire to X despite the fact that he has a univocal desire, altogether free of conflict and ambivalence, to refrain from X-ing. Someone might want to have a certain desire, in other words, but univocally want that desire to be unsatisfied.

Suppose that a physician engaged in psychotherapy with narcotics addicts believes that his ability to help his patients would be enhanced if he understood better what it is like for them to desire the drug to which they are addicted. Suppose that he is led in this way to want to have a desire for the drug. If it is a genuine desire that he wants, then what he wants is not merely to feel the sensations that addicts characteristically feel when they are gripped by their desires for the drug. What the physician wants, insofar as he wants to have a desire, is to be inclined or moved to some extent to take the drug.

It is entirely possible, however, that, although he wants to be moved by a desire to take the drug, he does not want this desire to be effective. He may not want it to move him all the way to action. He need not be interested in finding out what it is like to take the drug. And insofar as he now wants only to *want* to take it, and not to *take* it, there is nothing in what he now wants that would be satisfied by the drug itself. He may now have, in fact, an altogether univocal desire *not* to take the drug; and he may prudently arrange to make it impossible for him to satisfy the desire he would have if his desire to want the drug should in time be satisfied.

It would thus be incorrect to infer, from the fact that the physician now wants to desire to take the drug, that he already does desire to take it. His second-order desire to be moved to take the drug does not entail that he has a first-order desire to take it. If the drug were now to be administered to him, this might satisfy no desire that is implicit in his desire to want to take it. While he wants to want to take the drug, he may have *no* desire to take it; it may be that *all* he wants is to taste the desire for it. That is, his desire to have a certain desire that he does not have may not be a desire that his will should be at all different than it is.

Someone who wants only in this truncated way to want to X stands at the margin of preciosity, and the fact that he wants to want to X is not pertinent to the identification of his will. There is, however, a second kind of situation that may be described by "*A* wants to want to X"; and when the statement is used to describe a situation of this second kind, then it does pertain to what *A* wants his will to be. In such cases the statement means that A wants the desire to X to be the desire that moves him effectively to act. It is not merely that he wants the desire to X to be among the desires by which, to one degree or another, he is moved or inclined to act. He wants this desire to be effective – that is, to provide the motive in what he actually does. Now when the statement that *A* wants to want to X is used in this way, it does entail that *A* already has a desire to X. It could not be true both that *A* wants the desire to X to move him into action and that he does not want to X. It is only if he does want to X that he can coherently want the desire to X not merely to be one of his desires but, more decisively, to be his will.[4]

Suppose a man wants to be motivated in what he does by the desire to concentrate on his work. It is necessarily true, if this supposition is correct, that he already wants to concentrate on his work. This desire is now among his desires. But the question of whether or not his second-order desire is fulfilled does not turn merely on whether the desire he wants is one of his desires. It turns on whether this desire is, as he wants it to be, his effective desire or will. If, when the chips are down, it is his desire to concentrate on his work that moves him to do what he does, then what he wants at that time is indeed (in the relevant sense) what he wants to want. If it is some other desire that actually moves him when he acts, on the other hand, then what he wants at that time is not (in the relevant sense) what he wants to want. This will be so despite the fact that the desire to concentrate on his work continues to be among his desires.

II

Someone has a desire of the second order either when he wants simply to have a certain desire or when he wants a certain desire to be his will. In situations of the latter kind, I shall call his second-order desires "second-order volitions" or "volitions of the second order." Now it is having second-order volitions, and not having second-order desires generally, that I regard as essential to being a person. It is logically possible, however unlikely, that there should be an agent with second-order desires but with no volitions of the second order. Such a creature, in my view, would not be a person. I shall use the term "wanton" to refer to agents who have first-order desires but who are not persons because, whether or not they have desires of the second order, they have no second-order volitions.[5]

The essential characteristic of a wanton is that he does not care about his will. His desires move him to do certain things, without its being true of him either that he wants to be moved by those desires or that he prefers to be moved by other desires. The class of wantons includes all non-human animals that have desires and all very young children. Perhaps it also includes some adult human beings as well. In any case, adult humans may be more or less wanton; they may act wantonly, in response to first-order desires concerning which they have no volitions of the second order, more or less frequently.

The fact that a wanton has no second-order volitions does not mean that each of his first-order desires is translated heedlessly and at once into action. He may have no opportunity to act in accordance with some of his desires. Moreover, the translation of his desires into action may be delayed or precluded either by conflicting desires of the first order or by the intervention of deliberation. For a wanton may possess and employ rational faculties of a high order. Nothing in the concept of a wanton implies that he cannot reason or that he cannot deliberate concerning how to do what he wants to do. What distinguishes the rational wanton from other rational agents is that he is not concerned with the desirability of his desires themselves. He ignores the question of what his will is to be. Not only does he pursue whatever course of action he is most strongly inclined to pursue, but he does not care which of his inclinations is the strongest.

Thus a rational creature, who reflects upon the suitability to his desires of one course of action or another, may nonetheless be a wanton. In maintaining that the essence of being a person lies not in reason but in will, I am far from suggesting that a creature without reason may be a person. For it is only in virtue of his rational capacities that a person is capable of becoming critically aware of his own will and of forming volitions of the second order. The structure of a person's will presupposes, accordingly, that he is a rational being.

The distinction between a person and a wanton may be illustrated by the difference between two narcotics addicts. Let us suppose that the physiological condition accounting for the addiction is the same in both men, and that both succumb inevitably to their periodic desires for the drug to which they are addicted. One of the addicts hates his addiction and always struggles desperately, although to no avail, against its thrust. He tries everything that he thinks might enable him to overcome his desires for the drug. But these desires are too powerful for him to withstand, and invariably, in the end, they conquer him. He is an unwilling addict, helplessly violated by his own desires.

The unwilling addict has conflicting first-order desires: he wants to take the drug, and he also wants to refrain from taking it. In addition to these first-order desires, however, he has a volition of the second order. He is not a neutral with regard to the conflict between his desire to take the drug and his desire to refrain from taking it. It is the latter desire, and not the former, that he wants to constitute his will; it is the latter desire, rather than the former, that he wants to be effective and to provide the purpose that he will seek to realize in what he actually does.

The other addict is a wanton. His actions reflect the economy of his first-order desires, without his being concerned whether the desires that move him to act are desires by which he wants to be moved to act. If he encounters problems in obtaining the drug or in administering it to himself, his responses to his urges to take it may involve deliberation. But it never occurs to him to consider whether he wants the relations among his desires to result in his having the will he has. The wanton addict may be an animal, and thus incapable of being concerned about his will. In any event he is, in respect of his wanton lack of concern, no different from an animal.

The second of these addicts may suffer a first-order conflict similar to the first-order conflict suffered by the first. Whether he is human or not, the wanton may (perhaps due to conditioning) both want to take the drug and want to refrain from taking it. Unlike the unwilling addict, however, he does not prefer that one of his conflicting desires should be paramount over the other; he does not prefer that one first-order desire rather than the other should constitute his will. It would be misleading to say that he is neutral as to the conflict between his desires, since this would suggest that he regards them as equally acceptable. Since he has no identity apart from his first-order desires, it is true neither that he prefers one to the other nor that he prefers not to take sides.

It makes a difference to the unwilling addict, who is a person, which of his conflicting first-order desires wins out. Both desires are his, to be sure;

and whether he finally takes the drug or finally succeeds in refraining from taking it, he acts to satisfy what is in a literal sense his own desire. In either case he does something he himself wants to do, and he does it not because of some external influence whose aim happens to coincide with his own but because of his desire to do it. The unwilling addict identifies himself, however, through the formation of a second-order volition, with one rather than with the other of his conflicting first-order desires. He makes one of them more truly his own and, in so doing, he withdraws himself from the other. It is in virtue of this identification and withdrawal, accomplished through the formation of a second-order volition, that the unwilling addict may meaningfully make the analytically puzzling statements that the force moving him to take the drug is a force other than his own, and that it is not of his own free will but rather against his will that this force moves him to take it.

The wanton addict cannot or does not care which of his conflicting first-order desires wins out. His lack of concern is not due to his inability to find a convincing basis for preference. It is due either to his lack of the capacity for reflection or to his mindless indifference to the enterprise of evaluating his own desires and motives.[6] There is only one issue in the struggle to which his first-order conflict may lead: whether the one or the other of his conflicting desires is the stronger. Since he is moved by both desires, he will not be altogether satisfied by what he does no matter which of them is effective. But it makes no difference to *him* whether his craving or his aversion gets the upper hand. He has no stake in the conflict between them and so, unlike the unwilling addict, he can neither win nor lose the struggle in which he is engaged. When a *person* acts, the desire by which he is moved is either the will he wants or a will he wants to be without. When a *wanton* acts, it is neither.

III

There is a very close relationship between the capacity for forming second-order volitions and another capacity that is essential to persons – one that has often been considered a distinguishing mark of the human condition. It is only because a person has volitions of the second order that he is capable both of enjoying and of lacking freedom of the will. The concept of a person is not only, then, the concept of a type of entity that has both first-order desires and volitions of the second order. It can also be construed as the concept of a type of entity for whom the freedom of its will may be a problem. This concept excludes all wantons, both infrahuman and human, since they fail to satisfy an essential condition for the enjoyment of freedom of the will. And it excludes those supra-human beings, if any, whose wills are necessarily free.

Just what kind of freedom is the freedom of the will? This question calls for an identification of the special area of human experience to which the concept of freedom of the will, as distinct from the concepts of other sorts of freedom, is particularly germane. In dealing with it, my aim will be primarily to locate the problem with which a person is most immediately concerned when he is concerned with the freedom of his will.

According to one familiar philosophical tradition, being free is funda-mentally a matter of doing what one wants to do. Now the notion of an agent who does what he wants to do is by no means an altogether clear one: both the doing and the wanting, and the appropriate relation be-tween them as well, require elucidation. But although its focus needs to be sharpened and its formulation refined, I believe that this notion does capture at least part of what is implicit in the idea of an agent who *acts* freely. It misses entirely, however, the peculiar content of the quite different idea of an agent whose *will* is free.

We do not suppose that animals enjoy freedom of the will, although we recognize that an animal may be free to run in whatever direction it wants. Thus, having the freedom to do what one wants to do is not a sufficient condition of having a free will. It is not a necessary condition either. For to deprive someone of his freedom of action is not necessarily to undermine the freedom of his will. When an agent is aware that there are certain things he is not free to do, this doubtless affects his desires and limits the range of choices he can make. But suppose that someone, without being aware of it, has in fact lost or been deprived of his freedom of action. Even though he is no longer free to do what he wants to do, his will may remain as free as it was before. Despite the fact that he is not free to translate his desires into actions or to act according to the determin-ations of his will, he may still form those desires and make those deter-minations as freely as if his freedom of action had not been impaired.

When we ask whether a person's will is free we are not asking whether he is in a position to translate his first-order desires into actions. That is the question of whether he is free to do as he pleases. The question of the freedom of his will does not concern the relation between what he does and what he wants to do. Rather, it concerns his desires themselves. But what question about them is it?

It seems to me both natural and useful to construe the question of whether a person's will is free in close analogy to the question of whether an agent enjoys freedom of action. Now freedom of action is (roughly, at least) the freedom to do what one wants to do. Analogously, then, the statement that a person enjoys freedom of the will means (also roughly) that he is free to want what he wants to want. More precisely, it means that he is free to will what he wants to will, or to have the will he wants. Just as the question about the freedom of an agent's action has to do with whether it is the action he wants to perform, so the question about the freedom of his will has to do with whether it is the will he wants to have.

It is in securing the conformity of his will to his second-order volitions, then, that a person exercises freedom of the will. And it is in the discrepancy between his will and his second-order volitions, or in his awareness that their coincidence is not his own doing but only a happy chance, that a person who does not have this freedom feels its lack. The unwilling addict's will is not free. This is shown by the fact that it is not the will he wants. It is also true, though in a different way, that the will of the wanton addict is not free. The wanton addict neither has the will he wants nor has a will that differs from the will he wants. Since he has no volitions of the second order, the freedom of his will cannot be a problem for him. He lacks it, so to speak, by default.

People are generally far more complicated than my sketchy account of the structure of a person's will may suggest. There is as much opportunity for ambivalence, conflict, and self-deception with regard to desires of the second order, for example, as there is with regard to first-order desires. If there is an unresolved conflict among someone's second-order desires, then he is in danger of having no second-order volition; for unless this conflict is resolved, he has no preference concerning which of his first-order desires is to be his will. This condition, if it is so severe that it prevents him from identifying himself in a sufficiently decisive way with *any* of his conflicting first-order desires, destroys him as a person. For it either tends to paralyze his will and to keep him from acting at all, or it tends to remove him from his will so that his will operates without his participation. In both cases he becomes, like the unwilling addict though in a different way, a helpless bystander to the forces that move him.

Another complexity is that a person may have, especially if his second-order desires are in conflict, desires and volitions of a higher order than the second. There is no theoretical limit to the length of the series of desires of higher and higher orders; nothing except common sense and, perhaps, a saving fatigue prevents an individual from obsessively refusing to identify himself with any of his desires until he forms a desire of the next higher order. The tendency to generate such a series of acts of forming desires, which would be a case of humanization run wild, also leads toward the destruction of a person.

It is possible, however, to terminate such a series of acts without cutting it off arbitrarily. When a person identifies himself *decisively* with one of his first-order desires, this commitment "resounds" throughout the potentially endless array of higher orders. Consider a person who, without reservation or conflict, wants to be motivated by the desire to concentrate on his work. The fact that his second-order volition to be moved by this desire is a decisive one means that there is no room for questions concerning the pertinence of desires or volitions of higher orders. Suppose the person is asked whether he wants to want to want to concentrate on his work. He can properly insist that this question concerning a third-order desire does not arise. It would be a mistake to claim that, because he has not considered whether he wants the second-order volition he has formed, he is indifferent to the question of whether it is with this volition or with some other that he wants his will to accord. The decisiveness of the commitment he has made means that he has decided that no further question about his second-order volition, at any higher order, remains to be asked. It is relatively unimportant whether we explain this by saying that this commitment implicitly generates an endless series of confirming desires of higher orders, or by saying that the commitment is tantamount to a dissolution of the pointedness of all questions concerning higher orders of desire.

Examples such as the one concerning the unwilling addict may suggest that volitions of the second order, or of higher orders, must be formed deliberately and that a person characteristically struggles to ensure that they are satisfied. But the conformity of a person's will to his higher-order volitions may be far more thoughtless and spontaneous than this. Some people are naturally moved by kindness when they want to be kind, and by nastiness when they want to be nasty, without any explicit forethought and without any need for energetic self-control. Others are moved by nastiness when they want to be kind and by kindness when they intend to be nasty, equally without forethought and without active resistance to these violations of their higher-order desires. The enjoyment of freedom comes easily to some. Others must struggle to achieve it.

IV

My theory concerning the freedom of the will accounts easily for our disinclination to allow that this freedom is enjoyed by the members of any species inferior to our own. It also satisfies another condition that must be met by any such theory, by making it apparent why the freedom of the will should be regarded as desirable. The enjoyment of a free will means the satisfaction of certain desires of the second or of higher orders – whereas its absence means their frustration. The satisfactions at stake are those which accrue to a person of whom it may be said that his will is his own. The corresponding frustrations are those suffered by a person of whom it may be said that he is estranged from himself, or that he finds himself a helpless or a passive bystander to the forces that move him.

A person who is free to do what he wants to do may yet not be in a position to have the will he wants. Suppose, however, that he enjoys both freedom of action and freedom of the will. Then he is not only free to do what he wants to do; he is also free to want what he wants to want. It seems to me that he has, in that case, all the freedom it is possible to desire or to conceive. There are other good things in life, and he may not possess some of them. But there is nothing in the way of freedom that he lacks.

It is far from clear that certain other theories of the freedom of the will meet these elementary but essential conditions: that it be understandable why we desire this freedom and why we refuse to ascribe it to animals. Consider, for example, Roderick Chisholm's quaint version of the doctrine that human freedom entails an absence of causal determination.[7] Whenever a person performs a free action, according to Chisholm, it's a miracle. The motion of a person's hand, when the person moves it, is the outcome of a series of physical causes; but some event in this series, "and presumably one of those that took place within the brain, was caused by the agent and not by any other events" (18). A free agent has, therefore, "a prerogative which some would attribute only to God: each of us, when we act, is a prime mover unmoved" (23).

This account fails to provide any basis for doubting that animals of subhuman species enjoy the freedom it defines. Chisholm says nothing that makes it seem less likely that a rabbit performs a miracle when it moves its leg than that a man does so when he moves his hand. But why, in any case, should anyone *care* whether he can interrupt the natural order of causes in the way Chisholm describes? Chisholm offers no reason for believing that there is a discernible difference between the experience of a man who miraculously initiates a series of causes when he moves his hand and a man who moves his hand without any such breach of the normal causal sequence. There appears to be no concrete basis for prefering to be involved in the one state of affairs rather than in the other.[8]

It is generally supposed that, in addition to satisfying the two conditions I have mentioned, a satisfactory theory of the freedom of the will necessarily provides an analysis of one of the conditions of moral responsibility. The most common recent approach to the problem of understanding the freedom of the will has been, indeed, to inquire what is entailed by the assumption that someone is morally responsible for what he has done. In my view, however, the relation between moral responsibility and the freedom of the will has been very widely misunderstood. It is not true that a person is morally responsible for what he has done only if his will was free when he did it. He may be morally responsible for having done it even though his will was not free at all.

A person's will is free only if he is free to have the will he wants. This means that, with regard to any of his first-order desires, he is free either to make that desire his will or to make some other first-order desire his will instead. Whatever his will, then, the will of the person whose will is free could have been otherwise; he could have done otherwise than to constitute his will as he did. It is a vexed question just how "he could have done otherwise" is to be understood in contexts such as this one. But although this question is important to the theory of freedom, it has no bearing on the theory of moral responsibility. For the assumption that a person is morally responsible for what he has done does not entail that the person was in a position to have whatever will he wanted.

This assumption *does* entail that the person did what he did freely, or that he did it of his own free will. It is a mistake, however, to believe that someone acts freely only when he is free to do whatever he wants or that he acts of his own free will only if his will is free. Suppose that a person has done what he wanted to do, that he did it because he wanted to do it, and that the will by which he was moved when he did it was his will because it was the will he wanted. Then he did it freely and of his own free will. Even supposing that he could have done otherwise, he would not have done otherwise; and even supposing that he could have had a different will, he would not have wanted his will to differ from what it was. Moreover, since the will that moved him when he acted was his will because he wanted it to be, he cannot claim that his will was forced upon him or that he was a passive bystander to its constitution. Under these conditions, it is quite irrelevant to the evaluation of his moral responsibility to inquire whether the alternatives that he opted against were actually available to him.[9]

In illustration, consider a third kind of addict. Suppose that his addiction has the same physiological basis and the same irresistible thrust as the addictions of the unwilling and wanton addicts, but that he is altogether delighted with his condition. He is a willing addict, who would not have things any other way. If the grip of his addiction should somehow weaken, he would do whatever he could to reinstate it; if his desire for the drug should begin to fade, he would take steps to renew its intensity.

The willing addict's will is not free, for his desire to take the drug will be effective regardless of whether or not he wants this desire to constitute his will. But when he takes the drug, he takes it freely and of his own free will. I am inclined to understand his situation as involving the overdetermination of his first-order desire to take the drug. This desire is his effective desire because he is physiologically addicted. But it is his effective desire also because he wants it to be. His will is outside his control, but, by his second-order desire that his desire for the drug should be effective, he has made this will his own. Given that it is therefore not only because of his addiction that his desire for the drug is effective, he may be morally responsible for taking the drug.

My conception of the freedom of the will appears to be neutral with regard to the problem of determinism. It seems conceivable that it should be causally determined that a person is free to want what he wants to want. If this is conceivable, then it might be causally determined that a person enjoys a free will. There is no more than an innocuous appearance of paradox in the proposition that it is determined, ineluctably and by forces beyond their control, that certain people have free wills and that others do not. There is no incoherence in the proposition that some agency other than a person's own is responsible (even *morally* responsible) for the fact that he enjoys or fails to enjoy freedom of the will. It is possible that a person should be morally responsible for what he does of his own free will and that some other person should also be morally responsible for his having done it.[10]

On the other hand, it seems conceivable that it should come about by chance that a person is free to have the will he wants. If this is conceivable, then it might be a matter of chance that certain people enjoy freedom of the will and that certain others do not. Perhaps it is also conceivable, as a number of philosophers believe, for states of affairs to come about in a way other than by chance or as the outcome of a sequence of natural causes. If it is indeed conceivable for the relevant states of affairs to come about in some third way, then it is also possible that a person should in that third way come to enjoy the freedom of the will.

Notes

1   P. F. Strawson, *Individuals* (London: Methuen, 1959), pp. 101–102. Ayer's usage of "person" is similar: "it is characteristic of persons in this sense that besides having various physical properties...they are also credited with various forms of consciousness" [A. J. Ayer, *The Concept of a Person* (New York: St. Martin's, 1963), p. 82]. What concerns Strawson and Ayer is the problem of understanding the relation between mind and body, rather than the quite different problem of understanding what it is to be a creature that not only has a mind and a body but is also a person.

2   For the sake of simplicity, I shall deal only with what someone wants or desires, neglecting related phenomena such as choices and decisions. I propose to use the verbs "to want" and "to desire" interchangeably, although they are by no means perfect synonyms. My motive in forsaking the established nuances of these words arises from the fact that the verb "to want", which suits my purposes better so far as its meaning is concerned, does not lend itself so readily to the formation of nouns as does the verb "to desire". It is perhaps acceptable, albeit graceless, to speak in the plural of someone's "wants." But to speak in the singular of someone's "want" would be an abomination.

3   What I say in this paragraph applies not only to cases in which "to X" refers to a possible action or inaction. It also applies to cases in which "to X" refers to a first-order desire and in which the statement that "*A* wants to X" is therefore a shortened version of a statement – "*A* wants to want to X" – that identifies a desire of the second order.

4   It is not so clear that the entailment relation described here holds in certain kinds of cases, which I think may fairly be regarded as nonstandard, where the essential difference between the standard and the nonstandard cases lies in the kind of description by which the first-order desire in question is identified. Thus, suppose that *A* admires *B* so fulsomely that, even though he does not know what *B* wants to do, he wants to be effectively moved by whatever desire effectively moves *B*; without knowing what *B*'s will is, in other words, *A* wants his own will to be the same. It certainly does not follow that *A* already has, among his desires, a desire like the one that constitutes *B*'s will. I shall not pursue here the questions of whether there are genuine counterexamples to the claim made in the text or of how, if there are, that claim should be altered.

5   Creatures with second-order desires but no second-order volitions differ significantly from brute animals, and, for some purposes, it would be desirable to regard them as persons. My usage, which withholds the designation "person" from them, is thus somewhat arbitrary. I adopt it largely because it facilitates the formulation of some of the points I wish to make. Hereafter, whenever I consider statements of the form "*A* wants to want to X," I shall have in mind statements identifying second-order volitions and not statements identifying second-order desires that are not second-order volitions.

6   In speaking of the evaluation of his own desires and motives as being characteristic of a person, I do not mean to suggest that a person's second-order volitions necessarily manifest a *moral* stance on his part toward his first-order desires. It may not be from the point of view of morality that the person evaluates his first-order desires. Moreover, a person may be capricious and irresponsible in forming his second-order volitions and give no serious consideration to what is at stake. Second-order volitions express evaluations only in the sense that they are preferences. There is no essential restriction on the kind of basis, if any, upon which they are formed.

7   "Freedom and Action," in K. Lehrer, ed., *Freedom and Determinism* (New York: Random House, 1966), pp. 11–44.

8   I am not suggesting that the alleged difference between these two states of affairs is unverifiable. On the contrary, physiologists might well be able to show that Chisholm's conditions for a free action are not satisfied, by establishing that there is no relevant brain event for which a sufficient physical cause cannot be found.

9   For another discussion of the considerations that cast doubt on the principle that a person is morally responsible for what he has done only if he could have done otherwise, see my "Alternate Possibilities and Moral Responsibility," *The Journal of Philosophy*, LXVI, 23 (Dec. 4, 1969): 829–839.

10   There is a difference between being *fully* responsible and being *solely* responsible. Suppose that the willing addict has been made an addict by the deliberate and calculated work of another. Then it may be that both the addict and this other person are fully responsible for the addict's taking the drug, while neither of them is solely responsible for it. That there is a distinction between full moral responsibility and sole moral responsibility is apparent in the following example. A certain light can be turned on or off by flicking either of two switches, and each of these switches is simultaneously flicked to the "on" position by a different person, neither of whom is aware of the other. Neither person is solely responsible for the light's going on, nor do they share the responsibility in the sense that each is partially responsible; rather, each of them is fully responsible.

Comments and Questions on Harry Frankfurt's "Freedom of the Will and the Concept of a Person"

1.   Frankfurt argues that both the *wanton* and the *unwilling drug addict* lack free will in his sense. But the wanton and unwilling drug addict lack free will for different reasons. Explain what he means by a wanton and an unwilling drug addict and why each is supposed to lack free will. Do you think he is correct in thinking that both the wanton and the unwilling

addict lack free will? If so, do you think he correctly explains *why* they lack it?

2.   The *willing* addict is a different sort of character than the unwilling addict. Since the willing addict indulges in his habit happily and without qualms, it would seem that he "has the will he wants to have" and so has free will in Frankfurt's sense. But is the willing addict really free in the sense required by free will? How does Frankfurt answer this question in the reading? Do you think his handling of this case of the willing addict is correct or incorrect, and why?

3.   A common objection to Frankfurt's hierarchical account of free will was first made by Gary Watson. The objection is stated this way by another critic, Richard Double (1991): could one not also be a wanton in Frankfurt's sense with respect to one's second- and higher-order desires as well as one's first-order desires? "Suppose," says Double, "I decisively identify with my first-order desire . . . to sacrifice my life if my religious leader asks me to. If I do so in a completely nonreflective way, it is difficult to see how I have more freedom than a wanton, despite the fact that, according to Frankfurt's . . . account these decisions are clearly mine" (p. 35). Would not free will require that one has to be reflective about second-order desires by bringing some of them into conformity with one's third-order desires, and so on to higher orders? Why stop at the second or any higher level? But since our reflectivity cannot go on to infinity, how are we ever really free rather than just more sophisticated wantons after all? How, if at all, does Frankfurt try to answer this sort of objection? Can he answer it successfully in your opinion?

4.   Another objection to Frankfurt takes the following line. Suppose someone has manipulated us into having the higher-order desires we do have. (Go back to Skinner's *Walden Two* here and imagine that this was done by the behavioral engineers.) Might we not then have free will in Frankfurt's sense (might we not identify wholeheartedly with our wills or have the wills we want to have) despite being so manipulated? And does this not suggest that we would not have free will after all? How do you think Frankfurt might answer this objection? Can he answer it success-fully?

Suggested Reading

Frankfurt's views on free will, personhood, and many other topics are further developed in his *The Importance of What We Care About* (1988). For critical discussions of Frankfurt's hierarchical view, see Gary Watson (1975), David Zimmerman (1981), David Shatz (1985), John Martin Fischer (1986), Richard Double (1991), and Robert Kane (1996). Also see the essays in *The Contours of Agency: Essays in Honor of Harry Frankfurt* (2001), edited by Sarah Buss and Lee Overton, for critical discussions of Frankfurt's views.

10

Sanity and the Metaphysics of Responsibility

Susan Wolf

Editor's Introduction

Susan Wolf is Professor of Philosophy at Johns Hopkins University. In the following selection, she critically examines Frankfurt's "hierarchical theory" of motivation and free will along with several other new views of free will suggested by Gary Watson and Charles Taylor. Wolf refers to the views of Frankfurt, Watson and Taylor as "Deep Self" views because they hold that one has free will when one acts from one's *deep* or *real* or *authentic* self, whether that real or authentic self is defined in terms of one's higher-order motives (Frankfurt), or one's values (Watson) or the strong valuations (Taylor) one is most committed to. Wolf thinks there is some truth to Deep Self theories, but she also argues that they fall short of giving us a fully adequate account of freedom and responsibility. She illustrates this by discussing the imagined case of JoJo, "the favorite son of Jo the First, an evil and sadistic dictator of a small underdeveloped country." Through this example she tries to show that something more than acting from one's Deep Self must be required for free will; and this leads her to consider the role of sanity and insanity – and the role of appreciating right from wrong and understanding the True and the Good – in free and responsible action.

Philosophers who study the problems of free will and responsibility have an easier time than most in meeting challenges about the relevance of their work to ordinary, practical concerns. Indeed, philosophers who study these problems are rarely faced with such challenges at all, since questions concerning the conditions of responsibility come up so obviously and so frequently in everyday life. Under scrutiny, however, one might question whether the connections between philosophical and nonphilosophical concerns in this area are real.

In everyday contexts, when lawyers, judges, parents, and others are concerned with issues of responsibility, they know, or think they know, what in general the conditions of responsibility are. Their questions are questions of application: Does this or that particular person meet this or that particular condition? Is he mature enough, or informed enough, or sane enough to be responsible? Was he acting under posthypnotic suggestion or under the influence of a mind-impairing drug? It is assumed, in these contexts, that normal, fully developed adult human beings are responsible beings. The questions have to do with whether a given individual falls within the normal range.

By contrast, philosophers tend to be uncertain about the general conditions of responsibility, and they care less about dividing the responsible from the nonresponsible agents than about determining whether, and if so why, any of us are ever responsible for anything at all.

In the classroom, we might argue that the philosophical concerns grow out of the nonphilosophical ones, that they take off where the nonphilosophical questions stop. In this way, we might convince our students that even if they are not plagued by the philosophical worries, they ought to be. If they worry about whether a person is mature enough, informed enough, and sane enough to be responsible, then they should worry about whether he is metaphysically free enough, too.

The argument I shall make in this essay, however, goes in the opposite direction. My aim is not to convince people who are interested in the apparently nonphilosophical conditions of responsibility that they should go on to worry about the philosophical conditions as well, but rather to urge those who already worry about the philosophical problems not to leave the more mundane, prephilosophical problems behind. In particular, I shall suggest that the mundane recognition that *sanity* is a condition of responsibility has more to do with the murky and apparently metaphysical problems that surround the issue of responsibility than at first meets the eye. Once the significance of the condition of sanity is fully appreciated, at least some of the apparently insuperable metaphysical aspects of the problem of responsibility will dissolve.

My strategy will be to examine a recent trend in philosophical discussions of responsibility, a trend that tries, but I think ultimately fails, to give an acceptable analysis of the conditions of responsibility and that fails due to what at first appear to be deep and irresolvable metaphysical problems. It is here that I shall suggest that the condition of sanity comes to the rescue. What at first appears to be an impossible requirement for responsibility – namely, the requirement that the responsible agent must have created himself – turns out to be the vastly more mundane and noncontroversial requirement that the responsible agent must, in a fairly standard sense, be sane.

Frankfurt, Watson, and Taylor

The trend I have in mind is exemplified by the writings of Harry Frankfurt, Gary Watson, and Charles Taylor. I shall briefly discuss each of their separate proposals, and then offer a composite view that, while lacking the subtlety of any of the separate accounts, will highlight some important insights and some important blindspots that they share.

In his seminal article, "Freedom of the Will and the Concept of a Person,"[1] Harry Frankfurt notes a distinction between freedom of action and freedom of the will. A person has freedom of action, he points out, if she has the freedom to do whatever she wills to do – the freedom to walk or sit, to vote liberal or conservative, to publish a book or open a store, in accordance with her strongest desires. Even a person who has freedom of action may fail to be responsible for her actions, however, if the wants or desires she has the freedom to convert into action are themselves not subject to her control. Thus, the person who acts under posthypnotic suggestion, the victim of brainwashing, the kleptomaniac might all possess freedom of action. In the standard contexts in which these examples are raised, it is assumed that none of the individuals are locked up or bound. Rather, these individuals are understood to act on what, at one level at least, must be called *their own desires*. Their exemption from responsibility stems from the fact that their own desires (or, at least the ones governing their actions) are not up to them. These cases may be described in Frankfurt's terms as cases of people who possess freedom of action but who fail to be responsible agents because they lack freedom of the will.

Philosophical problems about the conditions of responsibility naturally focus on an analysis of this latter kind of freedom: What *is* freedom of the will, and under what conditions can we reasonably be thought to possess it? Frankfurt's proposal is to understand freedom of the will by analogy to freedom of action. As freedom of action is the freedom to do whatever one wills to do, freedom of the will is the freedom to will whatever one wants to will. To make this point clearer, Frankfurt introduces a distinction between first-order and second-order desires. First-order desires are desires to do or to have various things, second-order desires are desires about what desires to have or what desires to make effective in action. In order for an agent to have both freedom of action and freedom of the will, she must be capable of governing her actions by her first-order desires *and* capable of governing her first-order desires by her second-order desires.

Gary Watson's view of free agency[2] – free and responsible agency, that is – is similar to Frankfurt's in holding that an agent is responsible for an action only if the desires expressed by that action are of a particular kind. While Frankfurt identifies the right kind of desires as desires that are supported by second-order desires, Watson draws a distinction between "mere" desires, so to speak, and desires that are *values*. According to Watson, the difference between free action and unfree action cannot be analyzed by reference to the logical form of the desires from which these various actions arise, but rather must relate to a difference in the quality of their source. Whereas some of my desires are just appetites or conditioned responses which I find myself "stuck with," others are expressions of judgments on my part that the objects I desire are good. Insofar as my actions can be governed by the latter type of desire – governed, that is, by my values or valuational system – they are actions that I perform freely and for which I am responsible.

Both Frankfurt's and Watson's accounts offer ways of cashing out the intuition that in order to be responsible for one's actions, one must be responsible for the self that performs these actions. Charles Taylor, in an article entitled "Responsibility for Self"[3] discusses the same intuition. While Taylor does not describe his view in terms of different levels or types of desire, his view is related, for he claims that our freedom and responsibility depends on our ability to reflect on, criticize, and revise ourselves. Like Frankfurt and Watson, Taylor seems to believe that if the characters from which our actions flowed were simply and permanently *given* to us, implanted by heredity, environment, or God, then we would be mere vehicles through which the causal forces of the world traveled – no more responsible than dumb animals or young children or machines. But like the others, he points out that, for most of us, our characters and desires are not so brutely implanted – or, at any rate, if they are, they are subject to revision by our own reflecting, valuing, or second-order desiring selves. We human beings – and as far as we know, only we human beings – have the ability to step back from ourselves and decide whether we are the selves we want to be. Because of this, these philosophers think, we are responsible for ourselves and for the actions that we produce.

Although there are subtle and interesting differences among the accounts of Frankfurt, Watson, and Taylor, my concern is with features of their views that are common to them all. All share the idea that responsible agency involves something more than intentional agency. All agree that if we are responsible agents, it is not just because our actions are within the control of our wills, but because, in addition, our wills are not just psychological states *in* us, but expressions of characters that come *from* us, or that at any rate are acknowledged and affirmed *by* us. For Frankfurt, this means that our wills must be ruled by our second-order desires; for Watson, that our wills must be governable by our system of values; for Taylor, that our wills must issue from selves that are subject to self-assessment and redefinition in terms of a vocabulary of worth. In one way or another, all these philosophers seem to be saying that the key to responsibility lies in the fact that responsible agents are those for whom it is not just the case that their actions are within the control of their wills, but also the case that their wills are within the control of their *selves* in some deeper sense. Because, at one level, the differences among Frankfurt, Watson, and Taylor may be understood as differences in the analysis or interpretation of what it is for an action to be under the control of this deeper self, we may speak of their separate positions as variations of one basic view about responsibility, the Deep Self View.

The Deep Self View

Much more must be said about the notion of a deep self before a fully satisfactory account of this view can be given. Providing a careful, detailed analysis of that notion poses an interesting, important, and difficult task in its own right. The degree of understanding achieved by abstraction from the views of Frankfurt, Watson, and Taylor, however, should be sufficient to allow us to recognize some important virtues as well as some important drawbacks of the Deep Self View.

One virtue is that this view explains a good portion of our pretheoretical intuitions about responsibility. It explains why kleptomaniacs, victims of brainwashing, and people acting under posthypnotic suggestion may not be responsible for their actions, although most of us typically are. In the cases of people in these special categories, the connection between the agents' deep selves and their wills is dramatically severed – their wills are governed, not by their deep selves, but by forces external to and independent from them. A different intuition is that we adult human beings can be responsible for our actions in a way that dumb animals, infants, and machines cannot be. Here the explanation is not in terms of a split between these beings' deep selves and their wills – rather the point is that these beings *lack* deep selves altogether. Kleptomaniacs and victims of hypnosis exemplify individuals whose selves are *alienated* from their actions; lower animals and machines, on the other hand, don't have the sorts of selves from which actions *can* be alienated, and so they don't have the sort of selves from which, in the happier cases, actions can responsibly flow.

At a more theoretical level, the Deep Self View has another virtue: It responds to at least one way in which the fear of determinism presents itself.

A naive reaction to the idea that everything we do is completely determined by a causal chain that extends backwards beyond the times of our births involves thinking that in that case we would have no control over our behavior whatsoever. If everything is determined, it is thought, then what happens, happens, whether we want it to or not. A common, and proper, response to this concern points out that determinism does not deny the causal efficacy an agent's desires might have on her behavior. On the contrary, determinism in its more plausible forms tends to affirm this connection, merely adding that as one's behavior is determined by one's desires, so one's desires are determined by something else.[4]

Those who were initially worried that determinism implied fatalism, however, are apt to find their fears merely transformed rather than erased. If our desires are governed by something else, they might say, they are not *really* ours after all – or, at any rate, they are ours in only a superficial sense.

The Deep Self View offers an answer to this transformed fear of determinism, for it allows us to distinguish cases in which desires are determined by forces foreign to oneself from desires which are determined *by* one's self – by one's "real," or second-order-desiring, or valuing, or deep self, that is. Admittedly, there are cases, like that of the kleptomaniac or the victim of hypnosis, in which the agent acts on desires that "belong to" her in only a superficial sense. But the proponent of the Deep Self View will point out that even if determinism is true, ordinary adult human action can be distinguished from this. Determinism implies that the desires that govern our actions are in turn governed by something else, but that something else will, in the fortunate cases, be our own deeper selves.

This account of responsibility thus offers a response to our fear of determinism. But it is a response with which many will remain unsatisfied. For, even if my actions are governed by my desires and my desires are governed by my own deeper self, there remains the question, who, or what, is responsible for this deeper self? The above response seems only to have pushed the problem further back.

Admittedly, some versions of the Deep Self View – namely, Frankfurt's and Taylor's – seem to anticipate this question by providing a place for the ideal that an agent's deep self may be governed by a still deeper self. Thus, for Frankfurt, second-order desires may themselves be governed by third-order desires, third-order desires by fourth-order desires, and so on. And Taylor points out that, as we can reflect and evaluate our prereflective selves, so we can reflect and evaluate the selves who are doing the first reflecting and evaluating, and so on. But this capacity to recursively create endless levels of depth ultimately misses the criticism's point.

First of all, even if there is no *logical* limit to the number of levels of reflection or depth a person may have, there is certainly a psychological limit – it is virtually impossible to imaginatively conceive a fourth-, much less an eighth-order desire. More importantly, no matter how many levels of self we posit, there will still, in any individual case, be a last level – a deepest self about whom the question, "What governs it?" will arise as problematic as ever. If determinism is true, it implies that even if my actions are governed by my desires, and my desires are governed by my deepest self, my deepest self will still be governed by something that must, logically, be external to myself altogether. Though I can step back from the values my parents and teachers have given me and ask whether these are the values I really want, the "I" that steps back will itself be a product of the parents and teachers I am questioning.

The problem seems even worse when one sees that one fares no better if determinism is false. For if my deepest self is not determined by something external to myself, it will still not be determined by *me*. Whether I am a product of carefully controlled forces or a result of random mutations, whether there is a complete explanation of my origin or no explanation at all, *I* am not, in any case, responsible for my existence. I am not in control of my deepest self.

Thus, though the claim that an agent is responsible for only those actions that are within the control of her deep self correctly identifies a necessary condition for responsibility – a condition that separates the hypnotized and the brainwashed, the immature and the lower animals from ourselves, for example – it fails to provide a sufficient condition of responsibility that puts all fears of determinism to rest. For one of the fears invoked by the thought of determinism seems to be connected to its implication that we are but intermediate links in a causal chain, rather than ultimate, self-initiating sources of movement and change. From the point of view of one who has this fear, the Deep Self View seems merely to add loops to the chain, complicating the picture but not really improving it. From the point of view of one who has this fear, responsibility seems to require being a prime mover unmoved, whose deepest self is itself neither random *nor* externally determined but is rather determined *by* itself – who is, in other words, self-created.

At this point, however, proponents of the Deep Self View may wonder whether this fear is legitimate. For although people evidently can be brought to the point where they feel that responsible agency requires them to be ultimate sources of power, to the point where it seems that nothing short of self-creation will do, a return to the internal standpoint of the agent whose responsibility is in question makes it hard to see what good this metaphysical status is supposed to provide or what evil its absence is supposed to impose.

From the external standpoint, which discussions of determinism and indeterminism encourage us to take up, it may appear that a special metaphysical status is required to distinguish us significantly from other members of the natural world. But proponents of the Deep Self View will suggest that this is an illusion that a return to the internal standpoint should dispel. The possession of a deep self that is effective in governing one's actions is a sufficient distinction, they will say. For while other members of the natural world are not in control of the selves that they are, we, possessors of effective deep selves, are in control. We can reflect on what sorts of beings we are, and on what sorts of marks we make on the world. We can change what we don't like about ourselves and keep what we do. Admittedly, we do not create ourselves from nothing. But as long as we can revise ourselves, they will suggest, it is hard to find reason to complain. Harry Frankfurt writes that a person who is free to do what he wants to do and also free to want what he wants to want has "all the freedom it is possible to desire or to conceive."[5] This suggests a rhetorical question: If you are free to control your actions by your desires, and free to control your desires by your deeper desires, and free to control those desires by still deeper desires, what further kind of freedom can you want?

The Condition of Sanity

Unfortunately, there is a further kind of freedom we can want, which it is reasonable to think necessary for responsible agency. The Deep Self View fails to be convincing when it is offered as a complete account of the conditions of responsibility. To see why, it will be helpful to consider another example of an agent whose responsibility is in question.

JoJo is the favorite son of Jo the First, an evil and sadistic dictator of a small undeveloped country. Because of his father's special feelings for the boy, JoJo is given a special education and is allowed to accompany his father often and observe his daily routine. In light of this treatment, it is not surprising that little JoJo takes his father as a role-model and develops values very much like his dad's. As an adult, he does many of the same sorts of things his father did, including sending people to prison or to death or to torture chambers on the basis of the slightest of his whims. He is not *coerced* to do these things, he acts according to his own desires. Moreover, these are desires that he wholly wants to have. When he steps back and asks, "Do I really want to be this sort of person?" his answer is resoundingly Yes, for this way of life expresses a crazy sort of power that forms part of his deepest ideal.

In light of JoJo's heritage and upbringing – both of which he was powerless to control – it is dubious at best that he should be regarded as responsible for what he does. For it is unclear whether anyone with a childhood such as his could have developed into anything but the twisted and perverse sort of person that he has become. But note that JoJo is someone whose actions are controlled by his desires and whose desires are the desires he wants to have. That is, his actions are governed by desires that are governed by and expressive of his deepest self.

The Frankfurt–Watson–Taylor strategy that allowed us to differentiate our normal selves from the victims of hypnosis and brainwashing will not allow us to differentiate ourselves from the son of Jo the First. In the case of these earlier victims, we were able to say that although the actions of these individuals were, at one level, in control of the individuals themselves, these individuals themselves, *qua* agents, were not the selves they more deeply wanted to be. In this respect, these people were unlike our happily more integrated selves. But we cannot say of JoJo that his self, *qua* agent, is not the self he wants it to be. It *is* the self he wants it to be. From the inside, he feels as integrated, free, and responsible as we do.

Our judgment that JoJo is not a responsible agent is one that we can only make from the outside – from reflecting on the fact, it seems, that his deepest self is not up to him. Looked at from the outside, however, our situation seems no different from his. For in the last analysis, it is not up to any of us to have the deepest selves we do. Once more, the problem seems metaphysical – and not just metaphysical, but insuperable. For, as I mentioned before, the problem is independent of the truth of determinism. Whether we are determined or undetermined, we cannot have created our deepest selves. Literal self-creation is not just empirically, but logically impossible.

If JoJo is not responsible because his deepest self is not up to him, then we are not responsible either. Indeed, in that case responsibility would be impossible for anyone ever to achieve. But I believe that the appearance that literal self-creation is required for freedom and responsibility is itself mistaken.

The Deep Self View was right in pointing out that freedom and responsibility requires us to have certain distinctive types of control over our behavior and ourselves. Specifically, our actions need to be under the control of ourselves, and our (superficial) selves need to be under the control of our deep selves. Having seen that these types of control are not enough to guarantee us the status of responsible agents, we are tempted to go on to suppose that we must have yet another kind of control to assure us that even our deepest selves are somehow up to us. But not all the things necessary for freedom and responsibility must be types of power and control. We may need simply to *be* a certain way, even though it is not within our power to determine whether we are that way or not.

Indeed, it becomes obvious that at least one condition of responsibility is of this form as soon as one remembers what, in everyday contexts, we have known all along – namely, that in order to be responsible, an agent must be *sane*. It is not ordinarily in our power to determine whether we are or are not sane. Most of us, it would seem, are lucky, but some of us are not. Moreover, being sane does not necessarily mean that one has any type of power or control that an insane person lacks. All to our distress, some insane people, like JoJo and some actual political leaders who resemble him, may have complete control of their actions, and even complete control of their acting selves. The desire to be sane is thus not a desire for another form of control. It is rather a desire that one's self be connected to the world in a certain way – we could even say it is a desire that one's self be *controlled by* the world in certain ways and not in others.

This becomes clear if we attend to the criteria for sanity that have historically been dominant in legal questions about responsibility. According to the M'Naughten Rule, a person is sane if (1) he knows what he's doing and (2) he knows that what he's doing is, as the case may be, right or wrong. Insofar as one's desire to be sane involves a desire to know what one's doing – or more generally, a desire to live in the Real World – it is a desire to be controlled – to have, in this case, one's *beliefs* controlled – by perceptions and sound reasoning that produce an accurate conception of the world rather than by blind or distorted forms of response. The same goes for the second constituent of sanity – only, in this case, one's hope is that one's *values* be controlled by processes that afford an accurate conception of the world.[6] Putting these two conditions together, we may understand sanity, then, as the minimally sufficient ability to cognitively and normatively recognize and appreciate the world for what it is.

There are problems with this definition of sanity, at least some of which will become obvious in what follows, that make it ultimately unacceptable either as a gloss on or an improvement of the meaning of the term in many of the contexts in which it is used. The definition offered does seem to bring out the interest sanity has for us in connection with issues of responsibility, however, and some pedagogical as well as stylistic purposes will be served if we use sanity hereafter in this admittedly specialized sense.

The Sane Deep Self View

So far I have argued that the conditions of responsible agency offered by the Deep Self View are necessary but not sufficient. Moreover, the gap left open by the Deep Self View seems to be one that can only be filled by a metaphysical, and as it happens, metaphysically impossible addition. I now wish to argue, however, that the condition of sanity, as characterized above, is sufficient to fill the gap. In other words, the Deep Self View, supplemented by the condition of sanity, provides a satisfying conception of responsibility. The conception of responsibility I am proposing, then, agrees with the Deep Self View in requiring that a responsible agent be able to govern her actions by her desires and to govern her desires by her deep self. In addition, my conception insists that the agent's deep self be sane and claims that this is *all* that is needed for responsible agency. By contrast to the plain Deep Self View, let us call this new proposal the Sane Deep Self View.

It is worth noting, to begin with, that this new proposal deals with the case of JoJo and related cases of deprived childhood victims, in ways that better match our pretheoretical intuitions. Unlike the plain Deep Self View, the Sane Deep Self View offers a way of explaining why JoJo is not responsible for his actions without throwing our own responsibility into doubt. For although, like us, JoJo's actions flow from desires that flow from his deep self, unlike us, JoJo's deep self is itself insane. Sanity, remember, involves the ability to know the difference between right and wrong, and a person who, even on reflection, can't see that having someone tortured because he failed to salute you is wrong plainly lacks the requisite ability.

Less obviously, but quite analogously, this new proposal explains why we give less than full responsibility to persons who, though acting badly, act in ways that are strongly encouraged by their societies – the slave-owners of the 1850s, the German Nazis of the 1930s, and many male chauvinists of our fathers' generation, for example. These are people, we imagine, who falsely believe that the ways they are acting are morally acceptable, and so, we may assume, their behavior is expressive of or at least in accordance with these agents' deep selves. But their false beliefs in the moral permissibility of their actions and the false values from which these beliefs derived may have been inevitable given the social circumstances in which they developed. If we think that the agents could not help but be mistaken about their values, we do not blame them for the actions which those values inspired.[7]

It would unduly distort ordinary linguistic practice to call the slave-owner, the Nazi, or the male chauvinist even partially or locally insane. Nonetheless the reason for withholding blame from them is at bottom the same as the reason for withholding it from JoJo. Like JoJo, they are, at the deepest level, unable to cognitively and normatively recognize and appreciate the world for what it is. In our sense of the term, their deepest selves are not fully sane.

The Sane Deep Self View thus offers an account of why victims of deprived childhood as well as victims of misguided societies may not be responsible for their actions without implying that we are not responsible for ours. The actions of these others are governed by mistaken conceptions of value that the agents in question cannot help but have. Since, as far as we know, our values are not, like theirs, unavoidably mistaken, the fact that these others are not responsible for their actions need not force us to conclude that we are not responsible for ours.

But it may not yet be clear why sanity, in this special sense, should make such a difference; why, in particular, the question of whether someone's values are unavoidably *mistaken* should have any bearing on their status as responsible agents. The fact that the Sane Deep Self View implies judgments that match our intuitions about the difference in status between characters like JoJo and ourselves provides little support for it if it cannot also defend these intuitions. So we must consider an objection that comes from the point of view we earlier considered that rejects the intuition that a relevant difference can be found.

Earlier, it seemed that the reason JoJo was not responsible for his actions was that although his actions were governed by his deep self, his deep self was not up to him. But this had nothing to do with his deep self's being mistaken or not mistaken, evil or good, insane or sane. If JoJo's values are unavoidably mistaken, our values, even if not mistaken, appear to be just as unavoidable. When it comes to freedom and responsibility, isn't it the unavoidability rather than the mistakenness that matters?

Before answering this question, it is useful to point out a way in which it is ambiguous: the concepts of avoidability and mistakenness are not unequivocally distinct. One may, to be sure, construe the notion of avoidability in a purely metaphysical way. Whether an event or state of affairs is unavoidable under this construal depends, as it were, on the tightness of the causal connections, so to speak, that bear on the event's or state of affairs' coming about. In this sense, our deep selves do seem as unavoidable for us as JoJo's and the others' are for them. For presumably we are just as influenced by our parents, our cultures, and our schooling as they are influenced by theirs. In another sense, however, our characters are not similarly unavoidable.

In particular, in the cases of JoJo and the others, there are certain features of their characters that they cannot avoid *even though these features are seriously mistaken, misguided, or bad*. This is so because, in our special sense of the term, these characters are less than fully sane. Since these characters lack the ability to know right from wrong, they are unable to revise their characters on the basis of right and wrong, and so their deep selves lack the resources and the reasons that might have served as a basis for self-correction. Since the deep selves *we* unavoidably have, however, are sane deep selves – deep selves, that is, that unavoidably *contain* the ability to know right from wrong, we unavoidably do have the resources and reasons on which to base self-correction. What this means is that though in one sense we are no more in control of our deepest selves than JoJo and others, it does not follow in our case, as it does in theirs, that we would be the way we are, even if it is a bad or wrong way to be. But, if this does not follow, it seems to me, our absence of control at the deepest level should not upset us.

Consider what the absence of control at the deepest level amounts to for us: Whereas JoJo is unable to control the fact that, at the deepest level, he is not fully sane, we are not responsible for the fact that, at the deepest level, we are. It is not up to us to *have* minimally sufficient abilities to cognitively and normatively recognize and appreciate the world for what it is. Also, presumably, it is not up to us to have lots of other properties, at least to begin with – a fondness for purple, perhaps, or an antipathy for beets. As the proponents of the plain Deep Self View have been at pains to point out, however, we do, if we are lucky, have the ability to revise ourselves in terms of the values that are held by or constitutive of our deep selves. If we are lucky enough both to have this ability and to have our deep selves be sane, it follows that although there is much in our characters that we did not choose to have, there is nothing irrational or objectionable in our characters that we are compelled to keep.

Being sane, we are able to understand and evaluate our characters in a reasonable way, to notice what there is reason to hold on to, what there is reason to eliminate, and what, from a rational and reasonable standpoint, we may retain or get rid of as we please. Being able as well to govern our superficial selves by our deep selves, then, we are able to change the things that we find there is reason to change. This being so, it seems that although we may not be *metaphysically* responsible for ourselves – for, after all, we did not create ourselves from nothing – we are *morally* responsible for ourselves, for we are able to understand and appreciate right and wrong, and to change our characters and our actions accordingly.

Self-Creation, Self-Revision, and Self-Correction

At the beginning of this chapter, I claimed that recalling that sanity was a condition of responsibility would dissolve at least some of the appearance that responsibility was metaphysically impossible. To see how this is so, and to get a fuller sense of the Sane Deep Self View, it may be helpful to put that view into perspective by comparing it to the other views we have discussed along the way.

As Frankfurt, Watson, and Taylor showed us, in order to be free and responsible, we need not only to be able to control our actions in accordance with our desires, we need to be able to control our desires in accordance with our deepest selves. We need, in other words, to be able to *revise* ourselves – to get rid of some desires and traits, and perhaps replace them with others on the basis of our deeper desires or values or reflections. Consideration of the fact that the selves who are doing the revising might themselves be either brute products of external forces or arbitrary outputs of random generation made us wonder whether the capacity for self-revision was enough to assure us of responsibility, however, and the example of JoJo added force to the suspicion that it was not. If the ability to revise ourselves is not enough, however, the ability to create ourselves does not seem necessary either. Indeed, when you think of it, it is unclear why anyone should want self-creation. Why should anyone be disappointed at having to accept the idea that one has to get one's start somewhere? It is an idea that most of us have lived with quite contentedly all along. What we do have reason to want, then, is something more than the ability to revise ourselves but less than the ability to create ourselves. Implicit in the Sane Deep Self View is the idea that what is needed is the ability to *correct* (or approve) ourselves.

Recognizing that in order to be responsible for our actions, we have to be responsible for ourselves, the Sane Deep View analyzes what is necessary in order to be responsible for our selves as (1) the ability to evaluate ourselves sensibly and accurately and (2) the ability to transform ourselves insofar as our evaluation tells us to do so. We may understand the exercise of these abilities as a process whereby we *take* responsibility for the selves that we are but did not ultimately create. The condition of sanity is intrinsically connected to the first ability; the condition that we be able to control our superficial selves by our deep selves is intrinsically connected to the second.

The difference between the plain Deep Self View and the Sane Deep Self View, then, is the difference between the requirement of the capacity for self-revision and the requirement of the capacity for self-correction. Anyone with the first capacity can *try* to take responsibility for herself. Only someone with a sane deep self, however, a deep self that can see and appreciate the world for what it is, can evaluate herself sensibly and accurately. And so, although insane selves can try to take responsibility for themselves, only sane selves will properly be accorded responsibility.

Two Objections Considered

At least two problems with the Sane Deep Self View are so glaring as to have certainly struck many of my readers, and, in closing, I shall briefly address them. First, some will be wondering how, in light of my specialized use of the term "sanity," I can be so sure that "we" are any saner than the nonresponsible individuals I have discussed. What justifies my confidence that, unlike the slaveowners, Nazis, and male chauvinists, not to mention JoJo himself, we are able to understand and appreciate the world for what it is? The answer to this is that nothing justifies this except widespread intersubjective agreement and the considerable success we have in getting around in the world and satisfying our needs. These are not sufficient grounds for the smug assumption that we are in a position to see the truth about *all* aspects of ethical and social life. Indeed, it seems more reasonable to expect that time will reveal blindspots in our cognitive and normative outlook, just as it has revealed errors in the outlooks of those who have lived before. But our judgments of responsibility can only be made from here, on the basis of the understandings and values that we can develop by exercising the abilities we do possess as well and as fully as possible.

If some have been worried that my view implicitly expresses an over-confidence in the assumption that we are sane and therefore right about the world, others will be worried that my view too closely connects sanity with being right about the world and fear that my view implies that anyone who acts wrongly or has false beliefs about the world is therefore insane and so not responsible for his actions. This seems to me to be a more serious worry, which I am sure I cannot answer to everyone's satisfaction.

First, it must be admitted that the Sane Deep Self View embraces a conception of sanity that is explicitly normative. But this seems to me a strength of that view rather than a defect. Sanity *is* a normative concept, in its ordinary as well as in its specialized sense, and severely deviant behavior, such as that of a serial murderer or a sadistic dictator, does constitute evidence of a psychological defect in the agent. The suggestion that the most horrendous, stomach-turning crimes could only be committed by an insane person – an inverse of Catch-22, as it were – must be regarded as a serious possibility, despite the practical problems that would accompany general acceptance of that conclusion.

But, it will be objected, there is no justification, on the Sane Deep Self View, for regarding only horrendous and stomach-turning crimes as evidence of insanity in its specialized sense. If sanity is the ability to cognitively and normatively understand and appreciate the world for what it is, then *any* wrong action or false belief will count as evidence of the absence of that ability. This point may also be granted, but we must be careful about what conclusion to draw. To be sure, when someone acts in a way that is not in accordance with acceptable standards of rationality and reasonableness, it is always appropriate to look for an explanation of why she acted that way. The hypothesis that she was unable to understand and appreciate that her action fell outside acceptable bounds will always be a possible explanation. Bad performance on a math test always suggests the possibility that the test taker is stupid. Typically, however, other explanations will be possible, too – for example, that the agent was too lazy to consider whether her action was acceptable, or too greedy to care, or in the case of the math test taker, that she was too occupied with other interests to attend class or study. Other facts about the agent's history will help us decide among these hypotheses.

This brings out the need to emphasize that sanity, in the specialized sense, is defined as the *ability* to cognitively and normatively understand and appreciate the world for what it is. According to our commonsense understandings, having this ability is one thing and exercising it is another – at least some wrong-acting, responsible agents presumably fall within the gap. The notion of "ability" is notoriously problematic, however, and there is a long history of controversy about whether the truth of determinism would show our ordinary ways of thinking to be simply confused on this matter. At this point, then, metaphysical concerns may voice themselves again – but at least they will have been pushed into a narrower, and perhaps a more manageable corner.

The Sane Deep Self View does not, then, solve all the philosophical problems connected to the topics of free will and responsibility, and if anything, it highlights some of the practical and empirical problems rather than solves them. It may, however, resolve some of the philosophical, and particularly, some of the metaphysical problems, and reveal how intimate are the connections between the remaining philosophical problems and the practical ones.

Notes

1 Harry G. Frankfurt, "Freedom of the Will and the Concept of a Person," *Journal of Philosophy* 68 (1971), 5–20.
2 Gary Watson, "Free Agency," *Journal of Philosophy* 72 (1975), 205–20.
3 Charles Taylor, "Responsibility for Self," in G. Watson, ed. *Free Will* (Oxford: Oxford University Press, 1982), 111–26.
4 See, e.g., David Hume, *A Treatise of Human Nature* (Oxford: Oxford University Press, 1967), 399–406, and R. E. Hobart, "Free Will as Involving Determination and Inconceivable Without It," *Mind* (1934).
5 Frankfurt, "Freedom of the Will," p. 72.
6 Strictly speaking, perception and sound reasoning may not be enough to ensure the ability to achieve an accurate conception of what one is doing and especially to achieve a reasonable normative assessment of one's situation. Sensitivity and exposure to certain realms of experience may also be necessary for these goals. For the purposes of this essay, I shall understand "sanity" to include whatever it takes to enable one to develop an adequate conception of one's world. In other contexts, however, this would be an implausibly broad construal of the term.
7 Admittedly, it is open to question whether these individuals were in fact unable to help having mistaken values, and indeed, whether recognizing the errors of their society would even have required exceptional independence or

strength of mind. This is presumably an empirical question, the answer to which is extraordinarily hard to determine. My point here is simply that *if* we believe that they are unable to recognize that their values are mistaken, we do not hold them responsible for the actions that flow from these values, and *if* we believe that their ability to recognize their normative errors is impaired, we hold them less than fully responsible for the relevant actions.

Comments and Questions on Susan Wolf "Sanity and the Metaphysics of Responsibility"

1.   What does Wolf mean by a Deep Self View of responsibility? The views of Frankfurt, Watson, and Taylor are all Deep Self Views on her account. Why is each of them a Deep Self View? Yet the three views differ in certain ways. How do they differ?
2.   Wolf argues that all Deep Self Views, including these three, fail "due to what at first appear to be deep and irresolvable metaphysical problems." What are these deep and irresolvable metaphysical problems to which all Deep Self Views are subject, according to Wolf? And what do these problems have to do with the issue of free will and determinism? Do you think her critique of Deep Self Views is correct? How might defenders of a hierarchical view of freedom and responsibility such as Frankfurt's try to answer her critique and could they successfully answer it?
3.   Wolf introduces the example of JoJo in order to show what is missing in Deep Self Views of responsibility. What is missing, she thinks, is not some esoteric metaphysical condition of free will (such as indeterminism), but rather the more "mundane" condition of sanity. How is the example of JoJo suppose to show this? Does it effectively show that sanity is the missing piece in Deep Self Views of responsibility in your opinion? Indeed, is JoJo insane? What do you think she means by sanity and do you agree with her account of it?
4.   Assess Wolf's "Sane Deep Self View" of responsibility. Is it really an improvement over the Deep Self Views of Frankfurt, Watson, and Taylor that she criticizes? Near the end of the reading, she considers the objection that her Sane Deep Self View "embraces a conception of sanity that is explicitly normative." What she seems to mean by this is that we judge people like JoJo insane in part because they do things that are horrendous and unspeakable *according to our value or moral system*, or views about right or wrong; and this might seem to make judgments about whether someone is insane a matter of personal or subject value judgment rather

than of objective fact. How does Wolf answer this objection? Do you think she answers it adequately or successfully?

Suggested Reading

Wolf's "Sane Deep Self View" is more fully developed in her book *Freedom Within Reason* (1990), where she calls it a "Reason View" of freedom and responsibility. Watson's view is most clearly articulated in "Free Agency" (1975), in which he also criticizes Frankfurt's view. Taylor's view is presented in "Responsibility for Self" (1982). Wolf's view is criticized in a number of works, including John Fischer and Mark Ravizza, *Responsibility and Control* (1998, pp. 55–61) and Alfred Mele, *Autonomous Agents* (1995, pp. 162–5). Other views of free will that have an evaluative or normative component, but are different from Wolf's, are put forward by Paul Benson, "Freedom and Value" (1987) and Phillip Pettit and Michael Smith, "Freedom in Belief and Desire" (1996). Views that have some affinities with those of Frankfurt, Watson, or Wolf, but strike out in new directions of their own are those of Michael Bratman, "Identification, Decision and Treating as a Reason" (1996), Kevin Magill, *Experience and Freedom: Self-determination Without Illusions* (1997) and Hilary Bok, *Freedom and Responsibility* (1998)

11

Responsibility and the Limits of Evil: Variations on a Strawsonian Theme

Gary Watson

Editor's Introduction

Gary Watson is Professor of Philosophy at the University of California at Riverside. In the following reading, he considers issues of responsibility, sanity, morality, and punishment in relation to free will by focusing on the fascinating real life case of Robert Harris, the psychopathic multiple murderer who was on death row in California at the time Watson was writing. The story of Harris's family and troubled life leading up to his brutal crimes leads Watson to some deep reflections on the roots of evil and the limits of free will and responsibility. Watson also uses the Harris case to critically examine another influential modern compatibilist view to free will, the "reactive attitude" theory of P. F. Strawson (which Watson calls an "expressive theory" of responsibility). Watson is attracted to Strawson's influential view, but in this reading he poses questions for Strawson's theory about how we are to determine when persons like Harris are inside or outside the "moral community" so that they are fit subjects for the reactive attitudes such as resentment, admiration, gratitude, indignation, guilt, blame and the like.

Our practices do not merely exploit our natures, they express them.
Peter Strawson, "Freedom and Resentment"

Introduction

Regarding people as responsible agents is evidently not just a matter of belief. So regarding them means something in practice. It is shown in an embrace or a thank you, in an act of reprisal or obscene gesture, in a feeling of resentment or sense of obligation, in an apology or demand for an apology. To regard people as responsible agents is to be ready to treat them in certain ways.

In "Freedom and Resentment,"[1] Peter Strawson is concerned to describe these forms of treatment and their presuppositions. As his title suggests, Strawson's focus is on such attitudes and responses as gratitude and resentment, indignation, approbation, guilt, shame, (some kinds of) pride, hurt feeling, (asking and giving) forgiveness, and (some kinds of) love. All traditional theories of moral responsibility acknowledge connections between these attitudes and holding one another responsible. What is original to Strawson is the way in which they are linked. Whereas traditional views have taken these attitudes to be secondary to seeing others as responsible, to be practical corollaries or emotional side effects of some independently comprehensible belief in responsibility, Strawson's radical claim is that these "reactive attitudes" (as he calls them) are *constitutive* of moral responsibility; to regard oneself or another as responsible just is the proneness to react to them in these kinds of ways under certain conditions. There is no more basic belief which provides the justification or rationale for these reactions. The practice does not rest on a theory at all, but rather on certain needs and aversions that are basic to our conception of being human. The idea that there is or needs to be such an independent basis is where traditional views, in Strawson's opinion, have gone badly astray.

For a long time, I have found Strawson's approach salutary and appealing. Here my aim is not to defend it as superior to its alternatives, but to do something more preliminary. A comparative assessment is not possible without a better grasp of what Strawson's theory (or a Strawsonian theory)[2] *is*. As Strawson presents it, the theory is incomplete in important respects. I will investigate whether and how the incompleteness can be remedied in Strawsonian ways. In the end, I find that certain features of our practice of holding responsible are rather resistant to such remedies, and that the practice is less philosophically innocent than Strawson supposes. I hope that the issues uncovered by this investigation will be of sufficient importance to interest even those who are not as initially sympathetic to Strawson's approach as I am.[3]

Strawson's theory

Strawson presents the rivals to his view as responses to a prima facie problem posed by determinism. One rival – consequentialism – holds that blaming and praising judgments and acts are to be understood, and justified, as forms of social regulation. Apart from the question of its extensional adequacy, consequentialism seems to many to leave out something vital to our practice. By emphasizing their instrumental efficacy, it distorts the fact that our responses are typically personal reactions to the individuals in question that we sometimes think of as eminently appropriate reactions quite aside from concern for effects. Rightly "recoiling" from the consequentialist picture, some philosophers have supposed that responsibility requires a libertarian foundation, that to bring the "vital thing" back in, we must embrace a certain metaphysics of human agency. This is the other rival.

What these otherwise very different views share is the assumption that our reactive attitudes commit us to the truth of some independently apprehensible proposition which gives the content of the belief in responsibility; and so either the search is on for the formulation of this proposition, or we must rest content with an intuition of its content. For the social-regulation theorist, this is a proposition about the standard effects of having and expressing reactive attitudes. For the libertarian, it is a proposition concerning metaphysical freedom. Since the truth of the former is consistent with the thesis of determinism, the consequentialist is a compatibilist; since the truth of the latter is shown or seen not to be, the libertarian is an incompatibilist.

In Strawson's view, there is no such independent notion of responsibility that explains the propriety of the reactive attitudes. The explanatory priority is the other way around: It is not that we hold people responsible because they *are* responsible; rather, the idea (*our* idea) that we are responsible is to be understood by the practice, which itself is not a matter of holding some propositions to be true, but of expressing our concerns and demands about our treatment of one another. These stances and responses are expressions of certain rudimentary needs and aversions: "It matters to us whether the actions of other people . . . reflect attitudes toward us of good will, affection, or esteem on the one hand or contempt, indifference, or malevolence on the other." Accordingly, the reactive attitudes are "natural human reactions to the good or ill will or indifference of others toward us [or toward those we care about] as displayed in *their* attitudes and actions" (p. 53). Taken together, they express "the demand for the manifestation of a reasonable degree of good will or regard, on the part of others, not simply towards oneself, but towards all those on whose behalf moral indignation may be felt..." (p. 57).

Hence, Strawson accuses rival conceptions of "overintellectualizing" our practices. In their emphasis on social regulation, consequentialists lose sight of sentiments these practices directly express, without which the notion of moral responsibility cannot be understood. Libertarians see the gaping hole in the consequentialist account, but rather than acknowledging that "it is just these attitudes themselves which fill the gap" (p. 64), they seek to ground these attitudes in a metaphysical intuition – "a pitiful intellectualist trinket for a philosopher to wear as a charm against the recognition of his own humanity" (p. 64). Holding responsible is as natural and primitive in human life as friendship and animosity, sympathy and antipathy. It rests on needs and concerns that are not so much to be justified as acknowledged.

Excusing and exempting

To say that holding responsible is to be explained by the range of reactive attitudes, rather than by a commitment to some independently comprehensible proposition about responsibility, is not to deny that these reactions depend on a context of belief and perceptions in particular contexts. They are not mere effusions of feeling, unaffected by facts. In one way, Strawson is anxious to insist that these attitudes have no "rationale," that they neither require nor permit a "rational justification" of some general sort. Nevertheless, Strawson has a good deal to say about the particular perceptions that elicit and inhibit them. Reactive attitudes do have internal criteria, since they are reactions to the moral qualities exemplified by an individual's attitudes and conduct.[4]

Thus, reactive attitudes depend upon an interpretation of conduct. If you are resentful when jostled in a crowd, you will see the other's behavior as rude, contemptuous, disrespectful, self-preoccupied, or heedless: in short, as manifesting attitudes contrary to the basic demand for reasonable regard. Your resentment might be inhibited if you are too tired, or busy, or fearful, or simply inured to life in the big city. These are causal inhibitors. In contrast, you might think the other was pushed, didn't realize, didn't mean to... These thoughts would provide reasons for the inhibition of resentment. What makes them reasons is, roughly, that they cancel or qualify the appearance of noncompliance with the basic demand.[5]

In this way, Strawson offers a plausible account of many of the "pleas" that in practice inhibit or modify negative reactive attitudes. One type of plea is exemplified by the aforementioned reasons for inhibited senti-ments. This type of plea corresponds to standardly acknowledged *excus-ing* conditions. It works by denying the appearance that the other failed to fulfill the basic demand; when a valid excuse obtains, the internal criteria of the negative reactive attitudes are not satisfied. Of course, justification does this as well, but in a different way. "He realized what he was doing, but it was an emergency." In general, an excuse shows that *one* was not to blame, whereas a justification shows that one was not to *blame*.

Strawson distinguishes a second type of plea. These correspond roughly to standard *exempting* conditions. They show that the agent, temporarily or permanently, globally or locally, is appropriately exempted from the basic demand in the first place. Strawson's examples are being psychotic, being a child, being under great strain, being hypno-tized, being a sociopath ("moral idiot"), and being "unfortunate in for-mative circumstances." His general characterization of pleas of type 2 is that they present the other either as acting uncharacteristically due to extraordinary circumstances, or as psychologically abnormal or morally undeveloped in such a way as to be incapacitated in some or all respects for "ordinary adult interpersonal relationships."

In sum, type-2 pleas bear upon the question of whether the agent is an appropriate "object of that kind of demand for goodwill or regard which is reflected in ordinary reactive attitudes" (p. 51). If so, he or she is seen as a responsible agent, as a potential term in moral relationships, as a member (albeit, perhaps, in less than good standing) of the moral com-munity. Assuming the absence of such exemptions, type-1 pleas bear upon the question of whether the basic demand has been met. These inhibit negative reactive attitudes because they give evidence that their internal criteria are not satisfied. In contrast, type-2 pleas inhibit reactive attitudes because they inhibit the demand those attitudes express (p. 52).

When reactive attitudes are suspended on type-2 grounds, we tend to take what Strawson calls an "objective view." We see individuals not as ones to be resented or esteemed but as ones to be controlled, managed, manipulated, trained.... The objective view does not preclude all emo-tions: "It may include repulsion and fear, it may include pity or even love," though not reciprocal adult love. We have the capacity to adopt an objective view toward capable agents as well; for certain kinds of thera-peutic relationship, or simply to relieve the "strains of involvement," we sometimes call upon this resource.

As we have seen, one of Strawson's concerns is to deny the relevance of any theoretical issue about determinism to moral responsibility. In effect, incompatibilists insist that the truth of determinism would require us to take the objective attitude universally. But in Strawson's view, when we adopt the objective attitude, it is never a result of a theoretical conviction in determinism, but either because one of the exempting pleas is accepted, or for external reasons – fatigue, for example, or relief from the strain of involvement. No coherent thesis of determinism entails that one or more of the pleas is always valid, that disrespect is never meant, or that we are all abnormal or undeveloped in the relevant ways. Holding responsible is an expression of the basic concern and the basic demand, whose "legitimacy" requires neither metaphysical freedom nor efficacy. The practice does not involve a commitment to anything with which determinism could conflict, or which considerations of utility could challenge. This is the basic view as Strawson presents it. For convenience, we may call it the expressive theory of responsibility. [...]

Some Critical Questions

I turn now to certain hard questions for the expressive theory. It accounts nicely for "excusing conditions," pleas of type 1; but exactly – or even roughly – what is its account of type-2 pleas? The "participant" reactive attitudes are said to be "natural human reactions to the good or ill-will or indifference of others as displayed in their attitudes and actions" (p. 53); but this characterization must be incomplete, for some agents who display such attitudes are nevertheless exempted. A child can be malicious, a psychotic can be hostile, a sociopath indifferent, a person under great strain can be rude, a woman or man "unfortunate in formative circumstances" can be cruel.[...]

Following Strawson's idea that type-2 pleas inhibit reactive attitudes *by* inhibiting the basic demand, I propose to construe the exempting conditions as indications of the constraints on intelligible moral demand or, put another way, of the constraints on moral address.[...]

Evil and the Limits of Moral Community

[...]Does morally addressing another make sense unless we suppose that the other can see some reason to take us seriously, to acknowledge our claims? Can we be in a moral community with those who reject the basic terms of moral community? Are the enemies of moral community themselves members? If we suppose that moral address requires moral community, then some forms of evil will be exempting conditions. If holding responsible requires the intelligibility of moral address, and if a condition of such address is that the other be seen as a potential moral interlocutor, then the paradox results that extreme evil disqualifies one for blame.

Consider the case of Robert Harris.

> On the south tier of Death Row, in a section called "Peckerwood Flats" where the white inmates are housed, there will be a small celebration the day Robert Alton Harris dies.
>
> A group of inmates on the row have pledged several dollars for candy, cookies and soda. At the moment they estimate that Harris has been executed, they will eat, drink and toast to his passing.
>
> "The guy's a misery, a total scumbag; we're going to party when he goes," said Richard (Chic) Mroczko, who lived in the cell next to Harris on San Quentin Prison's Death Row for more than a year. "He doesn't care about life, he doesn't care about others, he doesn't care about himself.
>
> "We're not a bunch of Boy Scouts around here, and you might think we're pretty cold-blooded about the whole thing. But then, you just don't know that dude."
>
> San Diego County Assistant Dis. Atty. Richard Huffman, who prosecuted Harris, said, "If a person like Harris can't be executed under California law and federal procedure, then we should be honest and say we're incapable of handling capital punishment."
>
> State Deputy Atty. Gen. Michael D. Wellington asked the court during an appeal hearing for Harris, "If this isn't the kind of defendant that justifies the death penalty, is there ever going to be one?"
>
> What crime did Robert Harris commit to be considered the archetypal candidate for the death penalty? And what kind of man provokes such enmity that even those on Death Row . . . call for his execution?
>
> On July 5, 1978, John Mayeski and Michael Baker had just driven through [a] fast-food restaurant and were sitting in the parking lot eating lunch. Mayeski and Baker . . . lived on the same street and were best friends. They were on their way to a nearby lake for a day of fishing.
>
> At the other end of the parking lot, Robert Harris, 25, and his brother Daniel, 18, were trying to hotwire a [car] when they spotted the two boys. The Harris brothers were planning to rob a bank that afternoon and did not want to use their own car. When Robert Harris could not start the car, he pointed to the [car] where the 16-year-olds were eating and said to Daniel, "We'll take this one."
>
> He pointed a . . . Luger at Mayeski, crawled into the back seat, and told him to drive east . . .
>
> Daniel Harris followed in the Harrises' car. When they reached a canyon area . . . , Robert Harris told the youths he was going to use their car in a bank robbery and assured them that they would not be hurt. Robert Harris yelled to Daniel to get the .22 caliber rifle out of the back seat of their car.

"When I caught up," Daniel said in a recent interview, Robert was telling them about the bank robbery we were going to do. He was telling them that he would leave them some money in the car and all, for us using it. Both of them said that they would wait on top of this little hill until we were gone, and then walk into town and report the car stolen. Robert Harris agreed.

"Michael turned and went through some bushes. John said, 'Good luck,' and turned to leave."

As the two boys walked away, Harris slowly raised the Luger and shot Mayeski in the back, Daniel said. Mayeski yelled: "Oh, God," and slumped to the ground. Harris chased Baker down a hill into a little valley and shot him four times.

Mayeski was still alive when Harris climbed back up the hill, Daniel said. Harris walked over to the boy, knelt down, put the Luger to his head and fired.

"God, everything started to spin," Daniel said. "It was like slow motion. I saw the gun, and then his head exploded like a balloon, . . . I just started running and running. . . . But I heard Robert and turned around.

"He was swinging the rifle and pistol in the air and laughing. God, that laugh made blood and bone freeze in me."

Harris drove [the] car to a friend's house where he and Daniel were staying. Harris walked into the house, carrying the weapons and the bag [containing] the remainder of the slain youths' lunch. Then, about 15 minutes after he had killed the two 16-year-old boys, Harris took the food out of the bag . . . began eating a hamburger. He offered his brother an apple turnover, and Daniel became nauseated and ran to the bathroom. [. . .]

[Later, as they prepared to rob the bank,] Harris pulled out the Luger, noticed blood stains and remnants of flesh on the barrel as a result of the point-blank shot, and said, "I really blew that guy's brains out." And then, again, he started laughing.

. . . Harris was given the death penalty. He has refused all requests for interviews since the conviction.

"He just doesn't see the point of talking," said a sister, . . . who has visited him three times since he has been on Death Row. "He told me that he had his chance, he took the road to hell and there's nothing more to say."

. . . Few of Harris' friends or family were surprised that he ended up on Death row. He had spent seven of the previous 10 years behind bars. Harris, who has an eighth-grade education, was convicted of car theft at 15 and was sentenced to a federal youth center. After being released, he was arrested twice for torturing animals and was convicted of manslaughter for beating a neighbor to death after a dispute.

Barbara Harris, another sister, talked to her brother at a family picnic on July 4, 1978. He had been out of prison less than six months, and his sister had not seen him in several years.

...Barbara Harris noticed his eyes, and she began to shudder...."I thought, 'My God, what have they done to him?' He smiled, but his eyes were so cold, totally flat." [...]

...Harris is a dangerous man on the streets and a dangerous man behind bars, said Mroczko, who spent more than a year in the cell next to Harris'....

"You don't want to deal with him out there," said Mroczko,..."We don't want to deal with him in here."

During his first year on the row, Mroczko said, Harris was involved in several fights on the yard and was caught trying to supply a prisoner in an adjacent yard with a knife. During one fight, Harris was stabbed and the other prisoner was shot by a guard. He grated on people's nerves and one night he kept the whole cell block awake by banging his shoe on a steel water basin and laughing hysterically.

An encounter with Harris always resulted in a confrontation. If an inmate had cigarettes, or something else Harris wanted, and he did not think "you could hold your mud," Mroczko said, he would try to take them.

Harris was a man who just did not know "when to be cool," he said. He was an obnoxious presence in the yard and in his cell, and his behavior precipitated unwanted attention from the guards....

He acted like a man who did not care about anything. His cell was filthy, Mroczko said, and clothes, trash, tobacco and magazines were scattered on the floor....[6]

On the face of it, Harris is an "archetypal candidate" for blame. We respond to his heartlessness and viciousness with moral outrage and loathing. Yet if reactive attitudes were implicitly "invitations to dialogue,"... then Harris would be an inappropriate object of such attitudes. For he is hardly a potential moral interlocutor, "susceptible to the appeal of the principles from the standpoint of which one disapproves."...

However, not all communication is dialogue. Harris refuses dialogue, and this refusal is meant to make a point. It is in effect a repudiation of the moral community.[...]

The roots of evil

I said that Harris is an archetypal candidate for blame – so, at least, we react to him. Does it matter to our reactions how he came to be so? Strawson thinks so, for, among type-2 pleas, he includes "being unfortunate in formative circumstances." We must now investigate the relevance of such historical considerations to the reactive attitudes. As it happens, the case of Robert Harris is again a vivid illustration.[...]

Robert Harris' 29 years...have been dominated by incessant cruelty and profound suffering that he has both experienced and provoked. Violence presaged his birth, and a violent act is expected to end his life.

Harris was born Jan. 15, 1953, several hours after his mother was kicked in the stomach. She was $6\frac{1}{2}$ months pregnant and her husband, an insanely jealous man,...came home drunk and accused her of infidelity. He claimed that the child was not his, threw her down and kicked her. She began hemorrhaging, and he took her to the hospital.

Robert was born that night. His heartbeat stopped at one point...but labor was induced and he was saved. Because of the premature birth, he was a tiny baby; he was kept alive in an incubator and spent months at the hospital.

His father was an alcoholic who was twice convicted of sexually molesting his daughters. He frequently beat his children...and often caused serious injury. Their mother also became an alcoholic and was arrested several times, once for bank robbery.

All of the children had monstrous childhoods. But even in the Harris family,...the abuse Robert was subjected to was unusual.

Before their mother died last year, Barbara Harris said, she talked incessantly about Robert's early years. She felt guilty that she was never able to love him; she felt partly responsible that he ended up on Death Row.

When Robert's father visited his wife in the hospital and saw his son for the first time,...the first thing he said was, "Who is the father of that bastard?" When his mother picked him up from the hospital...she said it was like taking a stranger's baby home.

The pain and permanent injury Robert's mother suffered as a result of the birth,...and the constant abuse she was subjected to by her husband, turned her against her son. Money was tight, she was overworked and he was her fifth child in just a few years. She began to blame all of her problems on Robert, and she grew to hate the child.

"I remember one time we were in the car and Mother was in the back seat with Robbie in her arms. He was crying and my father threw a glass bottle at him, but it hit my mother in the face. The glass shatered and Robbie started screaming. I'll never forget it," she said....

"Her face was all pink, from the mixture of blood and milk. She ended up blaming Robbie for all the hurt, all the things like that. She felt helpless and he was someone to vent her anger on."

...Harris had a learning disability and a speech problem, but there was no money for therapy. When he was at school he felt stupid and classmates teased him, his sister said, and when he was at home he was abused.

"He was the most beautiful of all my mother's children; he was an angel," she said. "He would just break your heart. He wanted love so bad he would beg for any kind of physical contact.

"He'd come up to my mother and just try to rub his little hands on her leg or her arm. He just never got touched at all. She'd just push him away or kick him. One time she bloodied his nose when he was trying to get close to her."

Barbara Harris put her head in her hands and cried softly. "One killer out of nine kids.... The sad thing is he was the most sensitive of all of us. When he was 10 and we all saw 'Bambi,' he cried and cried when Bambi's mother was shot. Everything was pretty to him as a child; he loved animals. But all that changed; it all changed so much."

...All nine children are psychologically crippled as a result of their father, she said, but most have been able to lead useful lives. But Robert was too young, and the abuse lasted too long, she said, for him ever to have had a chance to recover.

[At age 14] Harris was sentenced to a federal youth detention center [for car theft]. He was one of the youngest inmates there, Barbara Harris said, and he grew up "hard and fast."

...Harris was raped several times, his sister said, and he slashed his wrists twice in suicide attempts. He spent more than four years behind bars as a result of an escape, an attempted escape and a parole violation.

The centers were "gladiator schools," Barbara Harris said, and Harris learned to fight and to be mean. By the time he was released from federal prison at 19, all his problems were accentuated. Everyone in the family knew that he needed psychiatric help.

The child who had cried at the movies when Bambi's mother dies had evolved into a man who was arrested several times for abusing animals. He killed cats and dogs, Daniel said, and laughed while torturing them with mop handles, darts and pellet guns. Once he stabbed a prize pig more than 1,000 times.

"The only way he could vent his feelings was to break or kill something," Barbara Harris said. "He took out all the frustrations of his life on animals. He had no feeling for life, no sense of remorse. He reached the point where there wasn't that much left of him."

...Harris' family is ambivalent about his death sentence. [Another sister said that] if she did not know her brother's past so intimately, she would support his execution without hesitation. Barbara has a 16-year-old son; she often imagines the horror of the slain boy's parents.

"If anyone killed my son, I'd try my damnedest, no matter what it took, to have my child revenged," Barbara Harris said. "I know how those parents must suffer every day.

"But Robbie in the gas chamber...." She broke off in mid-sentence and stared out a window. "Well, I still remember the little boy who used to beg for love, for just one pat or word of kindness.... No I can't say I want my brother to die."

...Since Harris has been on Death Row, he has made no demands of time or money on his family. Harris has made only one request; he wants a dignified and serene ceremony after he dies – a ceremony in marked contrast to his life.

He has asked his oldest brother to take his ashes, to drive to the Sierra, hike to a secluded spot and scatter his remains in the trees.[7]

No doubt this history gives pause to the reactive attitudes. Why does it do so? "No wonder Harris is as he is!" we think. What is the relevance of this thought?

Note, to begin with, that the story in no way undermines the judgments that he is brutal, vicious, heartless, mean.[8] Rather, it provides a kind of explanation for his being so. Can the expressive theory explain why the reactive attitudes should be sensitive to such an explanation?

Strawson's general rubric for type-2 pleas (or the subgroup in which this plea is classified) is "being incapacitated for ordinary interpersonal relationships." Does Harris have some independently identifiable incapacity for which his biography provides evidence? Apparently, he *is* incapacitated for such relationships – for example, for friendship, for sympathy, for being affected by moral considerations. To be homicidally hateful and callous in Harris's way is to lack moral concern, and to lack moral concern is to be incapacitated for moral community. However, to exempt Harris on these grounds is problematic. For then everyone who is evil in Harris's way will be exempt, independently of facts about their background. But we had ample evidence about *this* incapacity before we learned of his childhood misfortunes, and that did not affect the reactive attitudes. Those misfortunes affect our responses in a special and non-evidential way. The question is why this should be so.

This would seem to be a hard question for compatibilist views generally. What matters is whether, in one version, the practice of holding responsible can be efficacious as a means of social regulation, or whether, using the expressive theory, the conditions of moral address are met. These questions would seem to be settled by how individuals *are*, not by how they came to be. Facts about background would be, at most, evidence that some other plea is satisfied. In themselves, they would not seem to matter.

A plea of this kind is, on the other hand, grist for the incompatibilists' mill. For they will insist on an essential historical dimension to the concept of responsibility. Harris's history reveals him to be an inevitable product of his formative circumstances. And seeing him as a product is inconsistent with seeing him as a responsible agent. If his cruel attitudes and conduct are the inevitable result of his circumstances, then he is not responsible for them, unless he was responsible for those circumstances. It is this principle that gives the historical dimension of responsibility and of course entails the incompatibility of determinism and responsibility.

In this instance, however, an incompatibilist diagnosis seems doubtful. In the first place, our response to the case is not the simple suspension of reactive attitudes that this diagnosis would lead one to expect, but ambivalence. In the second place, the force of the example does not depend on a belief in the *inevitability* of the upshot. Nothing in the story supports such a belief. The thought is not "It had to be!" but, again, "No wonder!"

Sympathy and Antipathy

How and why, then, does this larger view of Harris's life in fact affect us? It is too simple to say that it leads us to suspend our reactive attitudes. Our response is too complicated and conflicted for that. What appears to happen is that we are unable to command an overall view of his life that permits the reactive attitudes to be sustained without ambivalence. That is because the biography forces us to see him as a *victim*, and so seeing him does not sit well with the reactive attitudes that are so strongly elicited by Harris's character and conduct. Seeing him as a victim does not totally dispel those attitudes. Rather, in light of the "whole" story, conflicting responses are evoked. The sympathy toward the boy he was is at odds with outrage toward the man he is. These responses conflict not in the way that fear dispels anger, but in the way that sympathy is opposed to antipathy. In fact, each of these responses is appropriate, but taken together they do not enable us to respond overall in a coherent way. [...]

Moral luck and moral equality

However, what is arresting about the Harris case is not just the clash between sympathy and antipathy. The case is troubling in a more personal way. The fact that Harris's cruelty is an intelligible response to his circumstances gives a foothold not only for sympathy, but for the thought that if *I* had been subjected to such circumstances, I might well have become as vile. What is unsettling is the thought that one's moral self is such a fragile thing. One tends to think of one's moral sensibilities as going deeper than that (though it is not clear what this means). This thought induces not only an ontological shudder, but a sense of equality with the other: I too am a potential sinner.[9]

This point is merely the obverse of the point about sympathy. Whereas the point about sympathy focuses on our empathetic response to the other, the thought about moral luck turns one's gaze inward. It makes one feel less in a position to cast blame. The fact that my potential for evil has not been nearly so fully actualized is, for all I know, something for which I cannot take credit. The awareness that, in this respect, the others are or may be like oneself clashes with the distancing effect of enmity. [...]

Determinism and Ignorance

Nothing in the foregoing reflections is necessarily inconsistent with the expressive theory. The ways in which reactive attitudes are affected by sympathy and moral luck are intelligible without appealing to any of the conceptions of responsibility that Strawson eschews. Nevertheless, our attitudes remain puzzling in a number of respects. [...]

If determinism is true, then evil is a joint product of nature and nurture. If so, the difference between any evil person and oneself would seem to be a matter of moral luck. For determinism seems to entail that if one had been subjected to the internal and external conditions of some evil person, then one would have been evil as well. If that is so, then the reflections about moral luck seem to entail that the acceptance of determinism should affect our reactive attitudes in the same way as they are affected in Harris's case. In the account we have suggested, then, determinism seems to be relevant to reactive attitudes after all.

Actually, this conclusion does not follow without special metaphysical assumptions. [...] For example, it is widely held that genetic origin is essential to an individual's identity. In that case, the counterfactual, "If I had had Harris's genetic origin and his upbringing, then I would have been as evil as he," will not make sense. Now it might be that Harris's genetic origins are among the determinants of his moral development. Thus, even if this is a deterministic world, there may be no true counterfactual that would support the thought that the difference between Harris and me is a matter of moral luck. There is room for the thought that there is something "in me" by virtue of which I would not have become a vicious person in Harris's circumstances. And if that factor were among my essential properties, so to speak, then that difference between Harris and me would not be a matter of moral luck on my part, but a matter of who we essentially were. That would not, of course, mean that I was essentially good or Harris essentially evil, but that I would not have been corrupted by the same circumstances as those that defeated Harris. To be sure, to suppose that this difference is in itself to my moral credit would be odd. To congratulate me on these grounds would be to congratulate me on being myself. Nevertheless, this difference still might explain what is to my credit, such moral virtues as I may possess. This will seem paradoxical only if we suppose that whatever is a ground of my moral credit must itself be to my credit. But I see no compelling reason to suppose this.

Historical responsibility

Libertarians believe that evil is the product neither of nature nor of nurture, but of free will. Do we understand what this might mean? [...]

This idea is nicely captured by Peter Abelard: "Nothing mars the soul except what is of its own nature, namely consent."[10] The idea is that one cannot simply be caused to be morally bad by the environment. So either Harris's soul is not (morally) marred, or he has been a willing accomplice to the malformation of the self. His evil means that he has consented to what he has become – namely, one who consents to cruelty. Thus, Abelardians try to fill the statistical cracks with the will. The development of the moral self, they will say, is mediated by consent.

We should be struck here by the a priori character of libertarian convictions. How is Harris's consent to be construed, and why *must* it have occurred? What evidence is there that it occurred? Why couldn't Harris just have become that way? What is the difference between his having acquiesced to what he became and his simply having become that way? The libertarian faces the following difficulty: If there is no such difference, then the view is vacuous, for consent was supposed to explain his becoming that way. If there is a difference, what evidence is there that it obtains in a particular case? Isn't there room for considerable doubt about this, and shouldn't libertarians, or we, insofar as we are libertarians, be very doubtful about Harris's responsibility – and indeed, on the Abelardian thesis, even about whether Harris is an evil man, whether his soul is morally marred?... One suspects that the libertarian confidence in their attributions of historical responsibility is rooted in a picture according to which the fact that Harris became that way *proves* that he consented. Then, of course, the appeal to consent is explanatorily vacuous. [...]

Responsibility for the Self

Strawson and others often charge libertarians with a metaphysically dubious conception of the self. The foregoing reflections indicate a basis for this charge. Libertarianism combines the Abelardian view about consent (or something like it) with the principle (or something like it) that to be responsible for anything, one must be responsible for (some of) what produces it. If we think of agents as consenting to this or that *because* they are (or have?) selves of a certain character, then it looks as though they are responsible for so consenting only if they are responsible for the self in which that consent is rooted. To establish this in each case, we have to trace the character of the self to earlier acts of consent. This enterprise seems hopeless, since the trace continues interminably or leads to a self to which the individual did not consent. The libertarian seems committed, then, to bearing the unbearable burden of showing how we can be responsible for ourselves. This burden can seem bearable only in a view of the self as an entity that mysteriously both transcends and intervenes in the "causal nexus," because it is both product and author of its actions and attitudes.

Must libertarians try to bear this burden? Perhaps the idea that they must rests upon a view of the self to which libertarians need not be committed. Perhaps the trouble arises in the first place from viewing the self as a thing standing in causal relation to acts of consent. [...]

The historical dimension of the concept of responsibility results from the principle that one is not responsible for one's conduct if that is necessitated by causes for which one is not responsible. This leads to a problematic requirement that one be responsible for one's self only if one thinks of the self as an entity that causes one's (its) actions and willings. Libertarians can reject this view. What they must affirm is that we are responsible for what we consent to, that consent is not necessitated by causes internal or external to the agent, and that if it were, we could not properly hold the individual responsible for what he or she consents to. These claims are far from self-evident. But they hardly amount to a "panicky metaphysics" (p. 66).[11]

In the end, however, I do not think that libertarianism can be so readily domesticated. The idea that one is responsible for and only for what one consents to is not of course distinctive of libertarianism; that idea has no historical implications. What is distinctive is the further requirement that consent be undetermined. I do not think the idea that consent is undetermined is in itself particularly problematic. The trouble begins only when

we ask why this is *required*. The ground of this requirement is the intuition that unless consent were undetermined, we would not truly be
originators of our deeds. We would be merely products, and not, as it
were, producers. It is this intuition to which the libertarian finds it so
difficult to give content. "Being an originator" does not mean just "consenting to," for that is already covered by the first thesis. Nor is this
notion captured simply by adding the requirement of indeterminism;
that is a merely negative condition. Attempts to specify the condition in
positive terms either cite something that could obtain in a deterministic
world, or something obscurely transcendent.

I suspect, then, that any metaphysically innocuous version of libertarianism must leave its incompatibilist component unmotivated.

Ignorance and Skepticism

I have been exploring some ways in which the expressive theory might
explain the relevance of certain historical considerations. Whatever the
best explanation may be, the remarkable fact is that we are, for the most
part, quite ignorant of these considerations. Why does our ignorance not
give us more pause? If, for whatever reason, reactive attitudes are sensitive to historical considerations, as Strawson acknowledges, and we are
largely ignorant of these matters, then it would seem that most of our
reactive attitudes are hasty, perhaps even benighted, as skeptics have
long maintained. In this respect, our ordinary practices are not as unproblematic as Strawson supposes.

It might be thought that these suspicions about reactive attitudes have
no bearing on responsibility. [...]

With an expressive theory, however, it is not clear that a general
skepticism about the propriety of the reactive attitudes can be separated
from skepticism about responsibility. For the latter concept *is* the concept
of the conditions in which it is appropriate to respond to one another in
reactive ways. In a Strawsonian view, there is no reason for a wedge
between the practices that evince the reactive attitudes and the belief in
responsibility. In a particular case, one may believe another to be responsible without actually responding to him or her in reactive ways (due to
strains of commitment and so on), because one may regard the other as
blameworthy, as an appropriate object of the reactive attitudes by others
in the moral community. But if one thinks that *none* of us mortals is in a
position to blame, then it is doubtful that any sense can be given to the
belief that the other is nonetheless blameworthy. One can still attribute

cowardice, thoughtlessness, cruelty, and so on, to others; but as we have seen, these judgments are not sufficient in a Strawsonian view to characterize the practice of holding responsible. We might try to appeal to the reactive attitudes of a select group of actual or hypothetical judges (here is another job for God to do),[12] but then the connection to reactive attitudes becomes so tenuous or hypothetical that the attitudes lose the central role they are given in "Freedom and Resentment," and the expressive theory loses its distinctive character....

Objectivity and Isolation

It remains unclear to what extent our ordinary practices involve dubious beliefs about ourselves and our histories. To acknowledge the relevance of historical considerations is, on any account, to acknowledge a potential source of skepticism about those practices; moreover, in a Strawsonian account (though not in a libertarian account), such skepticism cannot be readily separated from skepticism about responsibility itself. In this respect, Strawson is inordinately optimistic about our common ways.

However, these practices are vulnerable to a different kind of suspicion. This suspicion is related to Strawson's conception of the place of "retributive" sentiments in those practices, and to his claim that that practice, so conceived, is not something that is optional and open to radical criticism, but rather is part of the "framework" of our conception of human society. One could agree that the expressive theory best gives the basis and content of the practice of holding responsible and still maintain that abandoning this practice is not only conceivable but desirable, for what it expresses is itself destructive of human community. I conclude with some comments on this further issue.

Consider some remarks by Albert Einstein:

> I do not at all believe in human freedom in the philosophical sense. Everybody acts not only under external compulsion but also in accordance with inner necessity. Schopenhauer's saying, "A man can do what he wants, but not want what he wants," has been a very real inspiration to me since my youth; it has been a continual consolation in the face of life's hardships, my own and others', and an unfailing well-spring of tolerance. This realization mercifully mitigates the easily paralysing sense of responsibility and prevents us from taking ourselves and other people all too seriously; it is conducive to a view of life which, in particular, gives humor its due.[13]

Significantly, in the same place Einstein speaks of himself as a "lone traveler," with a "pronounced lack of need for direct contact with other human beings and human communities," who has

> never belonged to my country, my home, my friends, or even my immediate family, with my whole heart; in the face of all these ties, I have never lost a sense of distance and a need for solitude – feelings which increase with the years.

The point that interests me here is not that these remarks confute Strawson's claim that reactive attitudes are never in practice affected by an acceptance of determinism, but that they corroborate his central claim about the alternative to the reactive, participant stance. The "distance" of which Einstein speaks is just an aspect of the "detachment" Strawson thinks characterizes the objective stance. At its extremes, it takes the form of human isolation. What is absent from Einstein's outlook is something that, I suspect, Strawson cherishes: the attachment or commitment to the personal, as it might be called.[14]

Whatever its grounds, Einstein's outlook is not without its appeal. Perhaps part of its appeal can be attributed to a fear of the personal, but it is also appealing precisely on account of its repudiation of the retributive sentiments. In another place, Einstein salutes the person "to whom aggressiveness and resentment are alien."[15] Can such an ideal of the person be pursued only at the cost of the attachment to the personal? Must we choose between isolation and animosity?

Some of Strawson's remarks imply that we must:

> Indignation, disapprobation, like resentment, tend to inhibit or at least to limit our goodwill towards the object of these attitudes, tend to promote at least partial and temporary withdrawal of goodwill ... (These, of course, are not contingent connections.) But these attitudes ... are precisely the correlates of the moral demand in the case where the demand is felt to be disregarded. The making of the demand *is* the proneness to such attitudes. The holding of them does not ... involve ... viewing their object other than as a member of the moral community. The partial withdrawal of goodwill which these attitudes entail, the modification *they* entail of the general demand that another should if possible be spared suffering, is ... the consequence of *continuing* to view him as a member of the moral community; only as one who has offended against its demands. So the preparedness to acquiesce in that infliction of suffering on the offender which is an essential part of punishment is all of a piece with this whole range of attitudes. ... (pp. 62–63)

This passage is troubling. Some have aspired to rid themselves of the readiness to limit goodwill and to acquiesce in the suffering of others not in order to relieve the strains of involvement, nor out of a conviction in determinism, but out of a certain ideal of human relationships, which they see as poisoned by the retributive sentiments. It is an ideal of human fellowship or love which embodies values that are arguably as historically important to our civilization as the notion of moral responsibility itself. The question here is not whether this aspiration is finally commendable, but whether it is compatible with holding one another morally responsible. The passage implies that it is not.

If holding one another responsible involves making the moral demand, and if the making of the demand *is* the proneness to such attitudes, and if such attitudes involve retributive sentiments and hence[16] a limitation of goodwill, then skepticism about retribution is skepticism about responsibility, and holding one another responsible is at odds with one historically important ideal of love.

Many who have this idea, such as Gandhi or King,[17] do not seem to adopt an objective attitude in Strawson's sense. Unlike Einstein's, their lives do not seem characterized by human isolation: They are often intensely involved in the "fray" of interpersonal relations. Nor does it seem plausible to suppose that they do not hold themselves and others morally responsible: They *stand up* for themselves and others against their oppressors; they *confront* their oppressors with the fact of their misconduct, *urging* and even *demanding* consideration for themselves and others; but they manage, or come much closer than others to managing, to do such things without vindictiveness or malice.

Hence, Strawson's claims about the interpenetration of responsibility and the retributive sentiments must not be confused with the expressive theory itself. As these lives suggest, the retributive sentiments can in principle be stripped away from holding responsible and the demands and appeals in which this consists. What is left are various forms of reaction and appeal to others as moral agents. The boundaries of moral responsibility are the boundaries of intelligible moral address. To regard another as morally responsible is to react to him or her as a moral self.[18,19]

Notes

1 Strawson [1962] 1998. Hereafter, page references are given in the text.

2 My interpretation of Strawson's essay will be in many places very conjectural; and I will sometimes signal this fact by speaking of a "Strawsonian" theory.

3   I have learned much from the penetrating exploration of Strawson's essay by Jonathan Bennett: "Accountability," in *Philosophical Subjects*, edited by Zak van Straaten, Oxford: Clarendon Press, 1980, pp. 14–47.

4   Reactive attitudes thus permit a threefold classification. Personal reactive attitudes regarding others' treatment of one (resentment, gratitude, etc.); vicarious analogues of these, regarding others' treatment of others (indignation and approbation); self-reactive attitudes regarding one's own treatment of others (and oneself?) (guilt, shame, moral self-esteem, feeling obligated). Many of the reactive attitudes reflect the basic demand (on oneself and others, for oneself and others), whereas others (for example, gratitude) directly express the basic concern.

   Contrary to some of Strawson's discussion, responsibility does not concern only other-regarding attitudes. You can hold yourself responsible for failing to live up to an ideal that has no particular bearing on the interests or feelings of others. It may be said that others cannot *blame* you for this failure; but that would be a moral claim.

5   Below, this remark is qualified significantly.

6   From Miles Corwin, "Icy Killer's Life Steeped in Violence," *Los Angeles Times*, May 16, 1982. Copyright, 1982, *Los Angeles Times*. Reprinted by permission. For the length of this and the next quotation, I ask for the reader's patience. It is very important here to work with realistic and detailed examples.

7   Miles Corwin, op. cit. Copyright, 1982, *Los Angeles Times*. Reprinted by permission.

8   Although significantly, when his past is in focus, we are less inclined to use certain *reactive* epithets, such as "scumbag." This term is used to express an attitude about the appropriate treatment of the individual (that he is to be thrown in the garbage, flushed down the toilet, etc.). Some other reactive terms are "jerk," "creep," "son of a bitch."

9   In "Determinism and Moral Perspectives," *Philosophy and Phenomenological Research*, September 1960, Elizabeth Beardsley calls attention to the perspective evoked by such cases as Harris, though she links this perspective too closely, in my opinion, to the notion of determinism.

10 From "Intention and Sin," reprinted in Herbert Morris (ed.), *Freedom and Responsibility* (Stanford University Press), 1961 p. 169.

11 For an attempt at libertarianism without metaphysics, see David Wiggins, "Towards a Credible Form of Libertarianism," in T. Honderich (ed.), *Essays on Freedom of Action*, Routledge and Kegan Paul, 1973.

12 Just as Berkeley tried to save the thesis that material objects consist in ideas.

13 Albert Einstein, *Ideas and Opinions*, Crown Publishers, 1982, pp. 8–9.

14 To what extent Einstein lived up to this outlook, I am not prepared to say. Some other writings suggest a different view: "External compulsion can... reduce but never cancel the responsibility of the individual. In the Nuremberg trials, this idea was considered to be self-evident.... Institutions are in a moral sense impotent unless they are supported by the sense of responsibility

of living individuals. An effort to arouse and strengthen this sense of responsibility of the individual is an important service to mankind" (op. cit., p. 27). Is Einstein taking a consequentialist stance here?

15 Ibid.

16 Rather than attempting to separate retribution from responsibility, one might try to harmonize retribution and goodwill. This possibility seems to me worth exploring.

17 For these examples, and the discussion in this section, I am indebted to Lawrence Stern ("Freedom, Blame, and Moral Community," *Journal of Philosophy*, February 14, 1974.

18 We have, of course, seen reasons why these boundaries require further delineation.

19 To Sally Haslanger and Brian Skyrms, I am grateful for discussing bits and pieces of this material with me; to Ferdinand Schoeman, for comments on an earlier draft.

Comments and Questions on Gary Watson "Responsibility and the Limits of Evil: Variations on a Strawsonian Theme"

1. What is it about the reactive attitudes, according to Watson, that makes them so central and important for understanding the idea of moral responsibility? While all theories of moral responsibility recognize some connections between responsibility and the reactive attitudes, says Watson, P. F. Strawson's view is special in the manner in which it makes the reactive attitudes *central* to an adequate theory of moral responsibility. How does Strawson's theory do this? How does he understand moral responsibility? How does Strawson's reactive attitude theory help to solve problems about free will and determinism, according to Watson?
2. What is the distinction drawn by Watson between "excusing" and "exempting" conditions for moral responsibility? Which of these two kinds of conditions is more difficult to account for in Strawson's reactive attitude or expressive theory of responsibility, according to Watson, and why?
3. Watson uses the case of Robert Harris as a test case for the adequacy of Strawson's theory of moral responsibility. Why does he think it is an especially good test case? After reading the details of Harris's story, do you think Harris was morally responsible for his actions? Why or why not? Do you think Harris should have been executed? If so, do you think that information about the past life of criminals of the sort presented by Watson has any bearing on their guilt or innocence, freedom or responsibility?

4. Assess Strawson's theory of freedom and responsibility in the light of your reading of Watson. Do you think Strawson's theory is on the right track or not? Does it show, as Strawson thinks it does, that freedom and responsibility are compatible with determinism?

Suggested Reading

P. F. Strawson's "Freedom and Resentment" is the influential paper in which his reactive attitude theory was first presented. Two other highly recommended critical discussions of Strawson's view are by Susan Wolf, "The Importance of Free Will" (1981) and by Galen Strawson (P. F. Strawson's son), in *Freedom and Belief* (1986, chapter 5). The most developed and original version of a Strawsonian "reactive attitude" theory of moral responsibility in recent philosophy is that of R. Jay Wallace in *Responsibility and the Moral Sentiments* (1994). Anyone wishing to look further into the reactive attitude approach to issues about responsibility and free will should look at Wallace's book.

Part IV:

The Intelligibility Question: Libertarian or Incompatibilist Views of Free Agency and Free Will

12

The Mystery of Metaphysical Freedom

Peter van Inwagen

Editor's Introduction

In the previous reading by van Inwagen, he addressed the compatibility question by arguing (in terms of the consequence argument) that determinism is incompatible with free will. In this reading, van Inwagen addresses a further question, the intelligibility question: can we make sense of a libertarian free will that is incompatible with determinism? Such a free will would seem to require or presuppose indeterminism; and there seem to be as many problems reconciling free will with indeterminism as there are reconciling it with determinism. In the following reading, van Inwagen explores these problems by way of some interesting speculations involving human actions, angels, and God. He shows how difficult it is to make sense of free will if you believe that it is incompatible with determinism and concludes that a libertarian or incompatibilist free will (which he calls "metaphysical freedom") remains a mystery. Yet van Inwagen is also firmly convinced that the consequence argument is sound. So he thinks we must continue to believe in an incompatibilist or metaphysical freedom even if we do not know how to explain it.

[...] Many philosophers have regarded it as evident that we are free, and have accepted something like our argument for the incompatibility of determinism and metaphysical freedom. These philosophers, therefore, have denied that the world is deterministic, have denied that the laws of nature and the past together determine a unique future.

These philosophers (among whom I count myself) face a difficult problem. They assert or postulate that the laws of nature are indeterministic. ... [D]oes postulating or asserting that the laws of nature are indeterministic provide any comfort to those who would like to believe in metaphysical freedom? If the laws are indeterministic, then more than one future is indeed consistent with those laws and the actual past and present – but how can anyone have any choice about which of these futures becomes actual? Isn't it just a matter of chance which becomes actual? If God were to "return" an indeterministic world to precisely its state at some time in the past, and then let the world go forward again, things might indeed happen differently the "second" time. But then, if the world is indeterministic, isn't it just a matter of chance how things *did* happen in the one, actual course of events? And if what we do is just a matter of chance – well, who would want to call that freedom?

It seems, therefore, that, in addition to our argument for the incompatibility of metaphysical freedom and determinism, we have an argument for the incompatibility of metaphysical freedom and *in*determinism. But the world must be either deterministic or indeterministic. It follows that, unless one of the two arguments contains some logical error or proceeds from a false premise, metaphysical freedom must be a contradiction in terms, as much an impossibility as a round square or a liquid wine bottle. We may in fact *define* the problem of metaphysical freedom as the problem of discovering whether either of the two arguments is defective, and (if so) of locating the defect or defects.

The problem of metaphysical freedom, so conceived, is a very *abstract* problem. Although, for historical reasons, it is natural to think of the problem as essentially involving reference to the physical world and its supposedly intransigent laws ("man's life is a line that nature commands him to describe on the surface of the earth ..."), it does not. For suppose that man's life is in fact *not* a line that nature commands him to describe on the surface of the earth. Suppose that nature presents us with two or seventeen or ten thousand lines inscribed on the surface of the earth, and says to us (in effect), "Choose whichever one of them you like." How could it be that we really had any choice about which "line" we followed, when any deliberations we might undertake would themselves have to be segments of the lines that nature has offered us? Imagine that two of the lines that nature offers me diverge at some point – that is, imagine that the lines present the aspect of a fork in a road or a river. The common part of the two lines, the segment that immediately precedes their divergence, represents the course of my deliberations; their divergence from a common origin represents diagrammatically the fact that *either* of two futures is a possible outcome of my deliberations. My deliberations, therefore, do not determine which future I shall choose. But then what *does* determine which future I shall choose? Only chance, it would seem, and if only chance determines which of two paths into the future I follow, then how can it be that I have a choice about which of them I follow?

The problem of metaphysical freedom is so abstract, so very nearly independent of the features of the world in which agents happen to find themselves, that it could – it would; it must – arise in essentially the same form in a world inhabited only by immaterial intelligences, a world whose only inhabitants were, let us say, angels.

Let us consider such a world. It is true that if there were only angels, there would be no physical laws – or at any rate there would be nothing for the laws to apply to, so we might as well say there would be none. But if we assume the angels make choices, we have to assume that time (somehow) exists in this non-physical world, and that the agents are in different "states" at different times. And what is responsible for the way an angel changes its states with the passage of time? One possibility is that it is something structurally analogous to the laws of physics – something that stands to angels as our laws of physics stand to electrons and quarks. (I'm assuming, by the way, that these angels are metaphysical simples, that they are not composed of smaller immaterial things. If they were, we could conduct the argument in terms of the smallest immaterial things, the "elementary particles" of this imaginary immaterial world.) This "something" takes the properties of the angels at any time (and the relations they bear to one another at that time: the analogue, whatever it may be, of spatial relations in a material world) as "input," and delivers as output a sheaf of possible futures and histories of the world. In other words, given the "state of the world" at any time, it tells you what temporal sequences of states could have preceded the world's being in that state at that time, and it tells you what temporal sequences of states could follow the world's being in that state at that time. Maybe it couldn't be written as a set of differential equations (since nothing I have said implies that the properties of and relations among angels are quantifiable) as the laws of our physical world presumably can, but I don't think that affects the point. And the point is: either "the sheaf of possible futures" relative to each moment has only one member or it has more than one. If it has only one, the world of angels is deterministic. And then where is their free will? (Their freedom is the freedom to add to the actual past. And they can only add to the actual past in accordance with the laws that govern the way angels change their properties and their relations to one another with time.) If it has more than one, then the fact that one possible future rather than another, equally possible, future becomes actual seems to be simply a matter of chance. And then where is their free will?

I said above that this way of looking at a postulated "world of angels" was one possibility. But are there really any others? We have to think of the angels as being temporal and as changing their properties with the passage of time if we are to think of them as making choices. And we have to think of them as bearing various relations to one another if we are to think of them as belonging to the same world. And we have to think of them as having natures if we are to think of them as being real things. Every real thing that is in time must have a nature that puts some kinds of constraints on how it can change its states with the passage of time. Or so, at any rate, it seems to me. But if we grant this much, it seems that, insofar as we can imagine a world of non-physical things (angels or any others) we must imagine the inhabitants of this world as being subject to something analogous to the laws of physics. If this "something" is deterministic, then (it seems) we can't think of the inhabitants of our imaginary world as having free will. And if this "something" is *in*deterministic, then (it seems) we can't think of the inhabitants of our imaginary world as having free will. Thus, the "problem of metaphysical freedom" is a problem so abstract and general that it arises in any imaginable world in which there are beings who make choices. The problem, in fact, arises in exactly the same way in relation to God. God, the theologians tell us, although He did in fact create a world, was free not to. (That is, He was *able* not to create a world.) But God has His own nature, which even He cannot violate and cannot change. (He cannot, for example, make Himself less than omnipotent; He cannot break a promise He has made; He cannot command immoral behavior.) And either this nature determines that He shall create a world or it does not. If it does, He was not free not to create. If it does not, then, it would seem, the fact that He *did* create a world was merely a matter of chance. For what, other than chance, could be responsible for the fact that He created a world? His choice or His will? But what determined that he should make *that* choice when the choice not to make a world was also consistent with His nature? What determined that His will should be set on making a world, when a will set on *not* making a world was also consistent with His nature? We should not be surprised that our dilemma concerning metaphysical freedom applies even to God, for the dilemma does not depend on the nature of the agent to whom the concept of metaphysical freedom is applied. The dilemma arises from the concept of metaphysical freedom itself, and its conclusion is that metaphysical freedom is a contradictory concept. And a contradictory concept can no more apply to God than it can apply to anything else.

The concept of metaphysical freedom seems, then, to be contradictory. One way to react to the seeming contradiction in this concept would be to conclude that it was real: metaphysical freedom seems contradictory because it *is* contradictory. (This was the conclusion reached by C. D. Broad.)

But none of us really believes this. A philosopher may argue that consciousness does not exist or that knowledge is impossible or that there is no right or wrong. But no one really believes that he himself is not conscious or that no one knows whether there is such a city as Warsaw; and only interested parties believe that there is nothing morally objectionable about child brothels or slavery or the employment of poison gas against civilians. And everyone really believes in metaphysical freedom, whether or not he would call it by that name. Dr. Johnson famously said, "Sir, we know our will's free, and there's an end on't." Perhaps he was wrong, but he was saying something we all believe. Whether or not we are all, as the existentialists said, condemned to freedom, we are certainly all condemned to *believe in* freedom – and, in fact, condemned to believe that we *know* that we are free. (I am not disputing the sincerity of those philosophers who, like Holbach, have denied in their writings the reality of metaphysical freedom. I am saying rather that their beliefs are contradictory. Perhaps, as they say, they believe that there is no freedom – but, being human beings, they also believe that there is. In my book on freedom, I compared them to the Japanese astronomer who was said to have believed, in the 1930s, that the sun was an astronomically distant ball of hot gas vastly larger than the earth, and also to have believed that the sun was the ancestress of the Japanese imperial dynasty.)

I would ask you to try a simple experiment. Consider some important choice that confronts you. You must, perhaps, decide whether to marry a certain person, or whether to undergo a dangerous but promising course of medical treatment, or whether to report to a superior a colleague you suspect of embezzling money. (Tailor the example to your own life.) Consider the two courses of action that confront you; since I don't know what you have chosen, I'll call them simply A and B. Do you really not believe that you are *able* to do A and *able* to do B? If you do not, then how can it be that you are trying to decide which of them to do? It seems clear to me that when *I* am trying to decide which of two things to do, I commit myself, by the very act of attempting to decide between the two, to the thesis that I am able to do each of them. If I am trying to decide whether to report my colleague, then, by the very act of trying to reach a decision about this matter, I commit myself both to the thesis that I am able to report him and to the thesis that I am able to refrain from reporting him: although I obviously cannot do *both* these things, I can (I believe) do *either*. In sum: whether we are free or not, we believe that we are – and I think we believe, too, that we *know* this. We believe that we know this even if, like Holbach, we *also* believe that we are not free, and, therefore, that we do not know that we are free.

But if we know that we are free – indeed, if we are free and do not know it – there is some defect in one or both of our two arguments. Either there is something wrong with our argument for the conclusion that metaphysical freedom is incompatible with determinism or there is something wrong with our argument for the conclusion that metaphysical freedom is incompatible with *in*determinism – or there is something wrong with both arguments. But which argument is wrong, and why? (Or are they both wrong?) I do not know. I think no one knows. That is why my title is "The *Mystery* of Metaphysical Freedom." I believe I know, as surely as I know anything, that at least one of the two arguments contains a mistake. And yet, having thought very hard about the two arguments for almost thirty years, I confess myself unable to identify even a possible candidate for such a mistake. My *opinion* is that the first argument (the argument for the incompatibility of freedom and determinism) is essentially sound, and that there is, therefore, something wrong with the second argument (the argument for the incompatibility of freedom and indeterminism). But if you ask me *what* it is, I have to say that I am, as current American slang has it, absolutely clueless. Indeed the problem seems to me to be so evidently impossible of solution that I find very attractive a suggestion that has been made by Noam Chomsky (and which was developed by Colin McGinn in his recent book *The Problems of Philosophy*) that there is something about our biology, something about the ways of thinking that are "hardwired" into our brains, that renders it impossible for us human beings to dispel the mystery of metaphysical freedom. However this may be, I am certain that I cannot dispel the mystery, and I am certain that no one else has in fact done so.

Comments and Questions on Peter van Inwagen's "The Mystery of Metaphysical Freedom"

1.   Van Inwagen says that the world must be deterministic or indeterministic? Is he right about this? Is there no third alternative? Why or why not? Granting this, he says that metaphysical freedom (i.e., libertarian

free will) appears to be a "contradictory concept." Why? If you disagree, where do you think his reasoning goes wrong?

2. Someone might think that the reason there is a problem about human free will is because we have bodies and live in a physical universe. So we are subject to physical laws that must be deterministic or indeterministic. They then reason that if we had immaterial or nonphysical minds or souls, we could perhaps escape the problem. This is why van Inwagen introduces angels into the picture. He argues that the same problems about metaphysical freedom would arise for wholly immaterial beings like angels. So it is not just because we have bodies and are physical that there is a problem. Explain his argument on this point and how the appeal to angels enters into it. Do you think he is right, or could the "mystery of metaphysical freedom" be solved by appealing to the idea that we are really disembodied souls who escape the physical laws of nature?

3. Van Inwagen also argues that the mystery of metaphysical freedom also applies to God. Freedom is a central feature of the Judaeo-Christian and other theistic views of God, since God is supposed to have *freely* created the universe. That is, God could have created it or done otherwise (God had a choice about it). Yet van Inwagen argues that the intelligibility problem about indeterminism or chance also applies to God's actions, such as creating the world. Why? Considering this issue from another angle, suppose God is perfectly good, as theists assume, and was faced with choices between good and evil. It seems that God must choose the good and is not free to choose evil. How then can we say that God is *free* (to do otherwise) when it comes to choices between good and evil? God must act out of the necessity of the divine nature. The same is true of saints who are so good they could not even contemplate doing something evil. Do they have free will?

Suggested Reading

Other contemporary philosophers who have discussed the intelligibility problem in a forceful and unique way and argued that libertarian free will is impossible include Galen Strawson, in *Freedom and Belief* (1986, chapter 2) and "The Unhelpfulness of Indeterminism" (2000), also Thomas Nagel, *The View From Nowhere* (1986, chapter 7), Ted Honderich, *How Free Are You?* (1993) and Richard Double (*The Non-reality of Free Will* (1991).

13

The Agent as Cause

Timothy O'Connor

Editor's Introduction

Timothy O'Connor is Associate Professor of Philosophy at Indiana University. The following reading of O'Connor's and the two readings that follow it, by Carl Ginet and Robert Kane, are different attempts to respond to the challenge posed in the previous reading by van Inwagen. They offer different attempts to answer the intelligibility question by giving positive accounts of libertarian free will. O'Connor argues that the only way to dispel what van Inwagen calls the "mystery of metaphysical freedom" is by appealing to a special kind of "personal" or "agent-causation" that is not reducible to causation by events or states of affairs involving agents. In other words, he defends an *agent-causal* account of libertarian free will of the general kind that we first encountered in the earlier reading by Chisholm. O'Connor realizes, however, that agent-causal views, like Chisholm's, have often been criticized for being mysterious themselves. So he attempts to dispel some of the mystery surrounding agent-causal views by developing them further and answering objections to them. He argues that the only way to make sense of libertarian free will is to ascribe to free agents special kinds of causal powers that cannot be fully captured in terms of the event (or "broadly mechanistic") causation that is familiar in the sciences. O'Connor also argues against nonagent-causal accounts of libertarian free will, like those defended in the next two reading selections by Ginet and Kane, which are often called "simple indeterminism" and "causal indeterminism" respectively. He claims that nothing less than a special kind of agent-causation will suffice for libertarian free will.

In the previous essay, Peter van Inwagen argues that "metaphysical freedom" is incompatible with a certain abstract picture of the world (commonly dubbed "determinism"), on which it evolves in strict accordance with physical laws, laws such that the state of the world at any given time ensures a unique outcome at any subsequent moment. I agree that the two are incompatible. But what, in positive terms, does the ordinary understanding of ourselves as intelligent beings who "freely" decide how we shall act require? Where do the "springs of action" lie for beings that truly enjoy "free will"? This is surprisingly difficult to answer with any confidence. A useful way of approaching this question is to consider the various ways we might modify determinism in order to accommodate free will.

The most economical change in the determinist's basic picture is to introduce a causal "loose fit" between those factors influencing my choice (such as my beliefs and desires) and the choice itself. We might suppose, that is, that such factors *cause* my choice in an *in*deterministic way. To say that the causation involved is "indeterministic" is perhaps to say that the laws governing the evolution of the world through time (including that bit of the world which is me) are fundamentally statistical: they allow that (at least at various junctures) a range of alternatives are possible, though they will specify that certain of them are far more likely than others, in accordance with some measure of probability. Applying this general idea to the case of human choices, one might suppose that a free choice requires the following features: I have reasons to act in accordance with each of a range of options. In each case, my having those reasons gives me an objective (probabilistic) tendency to act accordingly. But whatever the relative probabilities of the alternatives, each of them is possible. And whichever of them occurs, the agent's having had a specific reason so to act will have been among the factors that caused it. Let us call this modification of the deterministic picture "causal indeterminism."

Would this be freedom? In my judgment, it would not. It is not enough that any of a range of possible actions are *open* to me to perform. I must have the right sort of *control* over the way the decision goes in a given case. And we may ask of the causal indeterminist, how is it up to me that, on this occasion, this one among two or more causally possible choices was made? I find myself with competing motivations – in my present case, a desire to watch a basketball game, a desire to play a game with my children, and a desire to finish this article – each of a particular "strength." On this occasion, we may suppose, the least probable outcome occurs. On other occasions, more probable outcomes occur. If I am truly acting freely, then presumably I in some way directly control or determine which outcome occurs on a given occasion. But in what does that control consist? The causal indeterminist does not have resources, it seems, to satisfactorily answer this question. Given a sufficiently large number of choices of a large number of people, the pattern of outcomes is likely to conform, more or less, to the statistical character of the underlying laws. There seems nothing more that one can say – in particular, nothing more one can say about the outcome of any particular choice. The indeterministic tendencies arising from my reasons confer a *kind* of control that is too "chancy" to ground significant responsibility. Indeed, it does not differ at all in *kind* from the control that would be had in a deterministic world; it merely introduces an element of "looseness" into its exercise. Given this added looseness, the future *is* open to alternative possibilities. But it remains unclear how I myself could be responsible (in part) for which of those alternatives is realized.

A dilemma is forming. Responsibility for our actions is inconsistent with the deterministic picture of the world. But it is also inconsistent with at least one straightforward kind of indeterministic picture, the kind that most directly carries into the sphere of human action the sort of indeterminism that many theorists believe operates at the level of fundamental physics. Indeed, a good many philosophers suppose that these two pictures (which we have labeled "causal determinism" and "causal indeterminism") exhaust the plausible alternatives. If all this is right, then the conclusion to be drawn is that free will is simply an inconsistent notion. It's not that we just don't happen to have free will; rather, we don't have it because it simply can't be had.

One alternative to this unpalatable conclusion is that entertained by Peter van Inwagen, in his contribution to this volume. Perhaps, van Inwagen writes, "there is something about our biology, something about the ways of thinking that are 'hardwired' into our brains, that renders it impossible for us human beings to dispel the mystery of metaphysical freedom." That is, though the notion of free will isn't truly inconsistent, its nature is "cognitively closed" to us. (After all, we have no reason to be confident that we are able, even "in principle," to grasp *every* difficult notion that, say, God grasps. And the history of philosophical reflection on the idea of freedom of will suggests that it has its subtleties.)

Well, there is certainly no *arguing* against this suggestion, absent the emergence of a stable consensus of opinion on the matter – rather unlikely at this stage of the game. But one may well distrust it on the general grounds that it counsels complacency. (And why stop at the notion of free will? Philosophers disagree over the correct understanding of most significant philosophical concepts.) Furthermore, once a philosopher takes this suggestion seriously, he may well be drawn into a deeper measure of skepticism about the notion of freedom of will than initially intended. Van Inwagen, for example, tells us that he is of the opinion that free will is *in*compatible with determinism. So he supposes that it must be *compatible* with *indeterminism*, even though he fails to see *which* sort of indeterminism will clearly do the trick. But if he and the rest of us are "hardwired" in some manner that precludes our coming to understand adequately the nature of free will, is it likely that we understand it sufficiently to know even *some* of its features? At any rate, the hypothesis ought to automatically undercut one's confidence in any highly *disputed* claims, such as van Inwagen's relative confidence in the thesis that free will is incompatible with determinism. (I note that Colin McGinn, whom van Inwagen cites in this connection, supposes that free will *can* be had under determinism, even though he "can't see how".)

Rather than embrace the despair and skepticism of the "cognitive closure" hypothesis, then let us pick up the argument where we last left it, and see whether a "positive" solution to our problem is in the offing. I argued that, if my decisions to act are simply the indeterministic effects of my beliefs and desires, then they are not up to me. What more do we *want* to say about our decisions, that causal indeterminism leaves out?

Just this, it seems: that I myself freely and directly control the outcome, where "control" here (as everywhere) is evidently a *causal* notion. And the unsatisfactoriness of causal indeterminism suggests that we have to be rather literal about the referent of "I" in this context. If I do something freely, I cannot be thought of as simply an arena in which internal and external factors work together to bring about my action (whether or not these factors are thought to operate in a strictly deterministic fashion). Instead, we want to say with Roderick Chisholm that I am the "end-of-the-line" initiator of the resulting action. What we are after, that is, is a notion of a distinctively personal form of causality (in the parlance of philosophers, "agent causation"), as against the broadly mechanistic form of causality ("event causation") that both the deterministic and causal indeterministic pictures represent as governing *all* forms of activity in nature without exception.

Many philosophers find this notion of "personal" or "agent" causation to be utterly mysterious, or downright incoherent. (Some of those philosophers will agree that it is natural to talk of "agent causation" when trying to articulate an understanding of free will, even though it is an incoherent idea. On their view, the term encapsulates the inconsistent strands in that notion.) Here is a simple reflection that fosters the sense of mystery. We often talk loosely of inanimate objects as causing certain things to happen. An example is the statement that Zimmerman's car knocked down the telephone pole. But it's clear that this does not perspicuously capture the metaphysics of the situation. It is instead simply shorthand for the assertion that the *movement* of Zimmerman's car (a car with a certain mass) caused the pole's falling down. It is, then, this *event* involving Zimmerman's car that brought about the effect, and not simply the car, *qua* enduring object. (No such effects emanate from his car when Zimmerman wisely decides to keep it parked in his garage.) The problem that many see with agent causation is that it rejects any expansion of "loose" talk of agents' causing things to happen into statements asserting that particular events *involving* those agents cause the effects in question. And that can seem mysterious: how can agents cause things to happen without its being true that they do so in virtue of certain features of themselves at the time? The agent is, after all, always an agent; yet he is not always causing some particular effect, such as deciding to complete an article on agent causation. Doesn't this force us to acknowledge that if the agent has decided to complete that article at one particular time, there must have been something *about him* at that time in virtue of which that effect was realized? And isn't that just to say that the *event* of the agent's having those distinguishing features, whatever they were, is what caused the decision?

This simple reflection is perhaps the deepest basis for philosophical suspicion about the notion of agent causation. However, I have come to suspect the suspicion and its various bases. In order to have a clear view of this matter, we need to reflect further on what is involved in our ordinary understanding of causation. Unfortunately, there is precious little agreement among philosophers about these matters. But the brief remarks I will make on this score at least have the advantage of representing a fairly commonsensical view of causation.

On the theory of causation I favor, objects are inherently active or dynamic. That is, they have causal capacities, and these are not "free-floating", but rather are linked to their intrinsic properties – those basic properties whose exact character it is the business of science to investigate.

In the more generally applicable case of *event* (or broadly mechanistic) causation, the *exercise* of such a capacity or tendency proceeds "as a matter of course": a thing's having, in the right circumstances, the capacity-grounding cluster of properties directly generates one of the effects within its range. (For indeterministic capacities, that effect will be but one of a range of *possible* effects; whereas in the deterministic case, there is only one possible outcome.)

The way that agent or personal causation differs from this mechanistic paradigm is in the way the relevant causal capacities are *exercised*. An agent's capacity to freely and directly control the outcome of his deliberation also requires underlying intrinsic properties which ground that capacity. (What sort of properties these might be is an interesting and in certain respects puzzling question, but it is at least partly empirical and not conceptual in nature. In any case, I shall not consider it here.) And no doubt the range of its operation is sharply circumscribed. For what is it, after all, that I directly act on, according to the agency theory? Myself – a complex system regulated by a host of stratified dynamic processes. I don't introduce events *ex nihilo*; (at best) I influence the direction of what is already going on within me. What is going on is a structured, dynamic situation open to some possibilities and not others. So the capacity is also circumscribed by physical and psychological factors at work within the agent while he deliberates. But (and here is the difference from the mechanistic paradigm) having the properties that subserve an *agent*-causal capacity does not suffice to bring about a particular effect (or even the occurrence of some effect or other within a range of possible effects); rather, it *enables* the agent to determine an effect (within the corresponding range). Whether, when, and how such a capacity will be exercised is freely determined by the agent.

That is the core metaphysical difference between the two causal paradigms. But we have yet to discuss how prior desires, intentions, and beliefs (more simply, "reasons") may explain such agent-causal activity. I suggest that we think of the agent's immediate effect as an action-triggering state of *intention* (which endures throughout the action and guides its completion). The content of that intention, in part, is that I act here and now in a particular sort of way. But another aspect of that intention, in my view, is that an action of a specific sort be performed *for certain reasons* the agent had at the time. (After a brief deliberation, I formed the intention to continue to type these words *in order to get the editors of this volume off my back*.) And the basis of the explanatory link lies precisely in this fact that the intention refers to the guiding reason. That is, the caused intention bears its explanation on its sleeve, so to speak. Had the agent generated a different intention, it would have been done (in most cases) for a different reason, to which reason the content of the intention itself would have referred. And if the agent had *several* reasons for performing a particular action, the reason(s) that *actually* moved the agent to act, again, would be reflected in the content of the intention. (None of this is to suggest that determining this content, in retrospect, is always easy. Clearly, I can be mistaken about my own reasons for acting.)

Some say that this account of the explanatory nature of reasons cannot be right: we can simply see that any undetermined instance of agent causation would be random, since by hypothesis nothing causes it. (Even some proponents of agent causation have been worried about this, and have been led to posit infinite hierarchies of agent-causings.) But it is hard to credit this objection. Consider what is being demanded. Agent causation is a form of direct control over one's behavior *par excellence*. But this is held to be insufficient. What is needed, it is argued, is some mechanism by virtue of which the agent controls this controlling. Put thus (though understandably it is not generally put in this way), its absurdity is evident. We needn't control our exercises of control. (For if we did, then wouldn't we also need yet another exercise of control, and so on?) On any coherent conception of human action, there is going to be a *basic* form of activity on which rests all control over less immediate effects. On the agent-causal picture, this basic activity is that of an agent's directly generating an intention to act in accordance with certain reasons.

Others have argued that the suggested account of explanations of free actions by reasons cannot be right, since the reasons to which one points in a given case won't explain why the agent acted as he did *rather than* in one of the other ways that were open to him (alternatives that by hypothesis remained open up to the very moment of choice). But while the issues involved here are subtler, this objection also fails. The objection assumes that adequately explaining an occurrence *ipso facto* involves explaining why that event occurred rather than any imaginable alternative. And this seems too strong a requirement. At bottom, explaining an occurrence involves uncovering the causal factor that generated it. In deterministic cases, where only one outcome is possible, such an explanation will also show why that event occurred rather than any other. But this should not blind us to the fact that the two targets of explanation are distinct: the simple *occurrence* itself and the *contrastive fact* that the outcome occurred rather than any other alternative. We need this distinction not just to understand human free agency, but to understand any indeterministic causal activity, including the apparently indeterministic mechanisms described by physical science. Whether (and in what circumstances) there can *also* be contrastive explanations of such indeterministic outcomes is a difficult question. But whatever we say here, there is little to recommend the claim that an occurrence that has been caused, though not uniquely determined, by some factor is thereby wholly inex-plicable.

More might be said about the "nature of reasons" explanation on the picture just sketched, but I want to turn instead to the complaint that we've swung too far in the direction of freedom. In place of the dimin-ished, freedom-less conception of human action entailed by the deter-ministic picture, we've substituted a rather god-like one: the agent selects from among reasons that are merely passively present before the agent as he deliberates, reasons that do not *move* the agent to act. Though rather implausible on the face of it, such a consequence is embraced by some advocates of agent causation. Chisholm, for example, compares agent causation with divine action:

> If we are responsible, and if what I have been trying to say is true, then we have a prerogative which some would attribute only to God: each of us, when we act, is a prime mover unmoved. In doing what we do, we cause certain events to happen, and nothing – or no one – causes us to cause those events to happen.[1]

But perhaps this is unnecessarily heroic. Though defenders of agent causation have generally insisted on a sharp divide between it and mechanistic causation, we may be able to move tentatively toward greater integration of the two. The goal is not to *reduce* agent causation, in the end, to an all-encompassing mechanistic paradigm, but rather to see how event-causal factors such as the possession of reasons to act may *shape* the distinctively agent-causal capacity. Two things, in particular, seem needed here – if not for all conceivable agents (including God and angels), then at least for human beings as we know them. First, our account should capture the way reasons (in some sense) *move* us to act as we do – and not as external pressures, but as *our* reasons, as our own internal tendencies to act to satisfy certain desires or aims. Secondly, the account should acknowledge that those reasons typically do not have "equal weight," so to speak. It is a truism that, given the structure of my preferences, stable intentions, and so forth, and the situation with which I am faced, I am often far more likely to act in one way rather than in any other. But how might we account for this, if not in terms of a relative tendency, on the part of reasons, to *produce* our actions?

In my view, this is the biggest obstacle to a clear understanding of what free will requires. What we need is a way to modify the traditional notion of a distinctively personal kind of causal capacity and to see it, not as utterly unfettered, but as one that comes "structured", in the sense of having built-in propensities to act (though ones that shift over time in accordance with the agent's changing preferences). But we must do so in such a way that it remains up to me to act on these tendencies or not, so that what I do is not simply the consequence of the vagaries of "chance-like" indeterministic activity, as may be true of microphysical quantum phenomena.

So, the task of harmonizing free and responsible human agency with a world that is fundamentally mechanistic in character remains unfinished. But perhaps we've seen enough to dispel much of the air of profound mystery that some profess to find on considering the very idea of metaphysical freedom.

Notes

1 "Human Freedom and the Self," p. 55–6, this volume.

Comments and Questions on Timothy O'Connor's "The Agent as Cause"

1. Before introducing his agent-causal account of libertarian free will, O'Connor argues that what he calls "causal indeterminist" accounts of libertarian free will are inadequate and won't solve the "mystery of metaphysical freedom." What does he mean by "causal indeterminist" accounts of free will? And why does he think they are inadequate?
2. O'Connor says that an exercise of agent-causation consists of an agent's making a choice or forming an intention to do something *for* certain *reasons* or motives. The reasons or motives, however, do not determine *which* of several different possible choices will be made. The agent has the causal power to make different choices for different reasons and is by hypothesis not caused to make one or the other. O'Connor then considers the following objection. "Some say that this account of the explanatory nature of reasons cannot be right: we can simply see that any undetermined instance of agent causation would be random, since by hypothesis nothing causes it." What is his response to this common objection to agent-causation? Do you think he adequately responds to it? Why or why not?
3. Toward the end of the reading, O'Connor says that some further additions are needed to make the agent-causal view he has defended fully adequate. Among these additions would be an account of the way

that reasons or motives, such as desires, beliefs, and intentions, *move* us to action and how it can be that these reasons or motives do not have "equal weight" – that is, how some reasons or motives "incline" us more or less strongly to one option than others. Another agent-causal theorist, Randolph Clarke, has focused on just these problems in order to criticize O'Connor's theory and offer an alternative agent-causal theory of his own. Clarke argues that the only fully satisfactory way to account for how desires, beliefs and other reasons can *move* us to choose one way or another and how they can incline more or less strongly to different options is to admit that that reasons and motives are indeed partial *causes* of our choices and actions. They are not deterministic causes, but probabilistic causes – they incline the agent in one direction or another without determining the choice. Clarke argues that "traditional" agent-causal theories of free will, like O'Connor's, are deficient because they want to deny altogether that reasons or motives cause choices or actions, either deterministically *or* probabilistically. (One reason they want to deny this is that they fear that free choices cannot be subject to laws, whether deterministic or statistical.) But this, argues Clarke, leaves them without an account of how reasons *move* us to action and do so *to different degrees*. On Clarke's alternative "causal agent-causal view," free actions are not only agent-caused, they are also (indeterministically or probabilistically) event-caused by prior reasons or motives of the agent. Since the causation by reason or motives is only probabilistic, however, Clarke thinks an additional agent-causation is needed anyway. Some extra exercise of agent-causal power is still needed to account for the agent's control over which choice is made. Do you think Clarke's agent-causal view is an improvement over O'Connor's or not? How do you think O'Connor might respond to it?

Suggested Readings

O'Connor's defense of agent-causation is more fully developed in his book *Persons and Causes: The Metaphysics of Free Will* (2000). Clarke's "causal agent-causal view" is more thoroughly defended in his "Agent Causation and Event Causation in the Production of Free Action" (1996). For references to other defenses of agent-causal views, see the suggested further readings at the end of the Chisholm selection in this volume.

14

Freedom, Responsibility and Agency

Carl Ginet

Editor's Introduction

Carl Ginet is Professor Emeritus of Philosophy at Cornell University. In the article reprinted here, he begins by distinguishing three possible views about the nature of libertarian free will – which amount to three different ways in which defenders of libertarian free will might try to answer the intelligibility question. The first of these possible libertarian theories is the *agent-causation view* of O'Connor, Clarke, and others, a version of which was defended by O'Connor in the previous reading. The second possible libertarian view is what Ginet calls the *indeterministic-causation view* and the third – which is the view that Ginet himself defends – is *simple indeterminism*. Ginet argues briefly against the indeterministic-causation view (which he ascribes to Robert Nozick and Robert Kane). But his main concern is to defend his own favored view, *simple indeterminism*, against the *agent-causation* view, especially O'Connor's version of agent-causation. By simple indeterminism, Ginet means the view that a simple mental event (such as a volition to exert force to move one's body) is a free action of the agent when it possesses an "actish phenomenal" quality and in addition the mental action is undetermined by antecedent events. Ginet explains and defends this simple indeterminist view in the reading that follows, offering in the process his own unique view about the nature of action and explanations of action in terms of reasons. He also subjects agent-causation views, like O'Connor's, to critical examination, arguing that his simple indeterminist view is preferable.

Let us say that an action is free if and only if up until the time of the action the agent had it open to her not to perform it: she could then have performed some other action instead or not acted at all. I mean this to be a stipulative definition of free action, not a substantive thesis about it.

There are, however, two substantive, controversial theses about free action, thus defined, that I am going to assume for the purposes of this paper. The problem I want to discuss here arises only for someone (like me) who holds both of these theses. One is the thesis that freedom of action is incompatible with determinism, that free action cannot occur in a completely deterministic universe, a universe where the laws of nature and the state of the world at any given time determine everything that happens after that time. This thesis is usually referred to as incompatibilism.[1] The other thesis is that an agent can be morally responsible for her action only if it is a free action: an agent can merit credit or blame for something she did only if she could have done otherwise. This thesis is commonly referred to as the Principle of Alternative Possibilities, or PAP for short.[2]

It follows from the conjunction of incompatibilism and PAP that an agent is responsible for her action only if that action was not causally determined by antecedent states and events. This consequence may seem – has seemed to many – to present a serious problem. If an action was not causally determined by any antecedent states and events, not even ones in the agent, then how can it be right to say that the agent exercised control over its occurrence, *determined whether* it or something else would occur; and if she did not do that, how can she be responsible for its occurrence? Surely an agent is responsible for her action – or for any other occurrence – only if she made it happen; but how can she, or anything, have made it happen if nothing caused it? But if PAP is right, the agent can be responsible for her action only if she was free to do otherwise, and, if incompatibilism is right, she was free only if her action was not causally necessitated by antecedent events. So it seems that, given the reasonable-sounding principle that an agent is responsible for her action only if she determines whether it happens, the conjunction of PAP and incompatibilism has the consequence that an agent is morally responsible for an action only if the action was both caused and un-caused.

We PAP incompatibilists seem to be stuck with an incoherent account of moral responsibility. We can provide a satisfactory metaphysical foundation for moral agency only if we can dispel that appearance. I believe we can, but at the moment we are not in agreement on how to do it. In what follows I try to explain this disagreement and to defend the way I think is best.

Timothy O'Connor examines three different sorts of response to the problem.[3] The reasoning that raises the problem (the reasoning from the conjunction of PAP and incompatibilism to the unpalatable conclusion that our concept of moral agency is incoherent) relies on an additional premise, namely, the claim that if an action was not determined (in the sense of deterministically caused) by antecedent states and events, then it cannot be that the agent was responsible for it because it cannot be that the agent controlled or determined its occurrence. All three responses deny this additional premise. They all say that they can explain how, despite the action's not being causally necessitated by antecedents, it can nevertheless be right to say that the agent determined or controlled its occurrence. But the three responses differ radically in the accounts they give of what can make it right to say this.

On one view, the agent can be said to have determined or brought about the action if the action has a causal explanation in terms of the reasons for which the agent performed the action. This view holds, as I believe any incompatibilist must hold, that an agent's doing an action for reasons is compatible with the action's not being deterministically caused by the motives that supply her reasons or by any other antecedents. And it holds that a reasons explanation is a kind of *in*deterministic causal explanation, depending on merely probabilistic laws, and it is the fact that an action has this sort of explanation that makes the action something that the *agent* determined. Let us refer to this as the *indeterministic-causation* view.

A second view – which is the view I favor – has it that any attempt to explain an agent's determining of her own action in terms of this or that special sort of cause of it is unnecessary. For an agent to determine whether or not an event, *e*, occurs is for her to make it the case that *e* occurs by performing some suitable free action. If *e* is *not* her own free action then causation must enter into what it is for her to make it the case that *e* occurs: she can do this only by performing some free action that causes *e*. But if *e is* her own free action, then she makes it the case that *e* occurs, not by causing it, but by simply performing it (This latter "by" is logical rather than causal; we have a causal "by" in "I made a C major chord sound by pressing those three keys;" we have a logical "by" in "I made a C major chord sound by making sound simultaneously a C, an E, and a G"). Given that the action is free, the agent determines it, one could say, simply by being its subject, the one whose action it is. That is to say, all free actions are *ipso facto* determined by their subjects. O'Connor dubs this view *simple indeterminism*.

Third, and finally, there is the *agent-causation* view that O'Connor himself favors. This view affirms that the agent controls her action only if there is a direct causal relation between the agent and the action (or some event internal to the action), a causal relation where the relatum on the cause side is not any event in or state of the agent but just the agent herself, that enduring entity. The agent-causation view was put forward in the eighteenth century by Thomas Reid[4] and endorsed in the latter half of the present century by Roderick Chisholm[5] and Richard Taylor.[6] It has been subjected to criticism that many (including me) have thought fatal and has not been widely held in recent decades. But O'Connor has made a challenging attempt to revive it.[7]

O'Connor and I agree in rejecting the indeterministic-causation account of what it is for an agent to determine her action. O'Connor's dissatisfaction with this view arises from his belief that any such account must explain how an agent makes one among the competing motives she faces the efficacious one, and he doesn't see any way that this can be done without resorting to agent-causation. He considers two specific attempts to do it, one by Robert Nozick[8] and one by Robert Kane,[9] and provides illuminating criticism of both.

My reasons for finding the indeterministic-causation account unsatisfactory differ from O'Connor's. One difficulty I see is that there can be free and responsible actions that do not have reasons explanations. An agent can just spontaneously do something for no particular reason and not in order to satisfy any antecedent desire or intention she may have had. (Of course, at the time of an action the agent must always intend to be doing it, or at least the basic action that is its initial phase. But this is a trivial truth about an action, pointing to an intrinsic feature of it that is entailed by its being an action. It cannot provide the sort of *cause* of the action that this account thinks we must have if the agent is to be responsible for her action.) Another problem with the indeterministic causation account is that reasons explanations of actions do not require for their truth the truth of any causal laws (probabilistic or deterministic) connecting the reasons with the actions (a point I will expand on a bit later); and so there can be responsible actions for reasons which are not indeterministically caused by those reasons.

Why we should reject the indeterministic-causation account is, however, not a topic I propose to go further into here. For the rest of this paper I will just assume that that view is out of the running and focus on the issue between my view, simple indeterminism, and O'Connor's agent-causation view. I will look at and respond to O'Connor's objection to my view. And then I will give my objections to his view. In the end I will grudgingly allow that we may speak of agent-causation if we like but we should regard such talk as compatible with my view of what is really there.

But first let me state my view more fully. I will just state it without trying to argue for it, except for those points of contention between O'Connor and me.

Every action, according to me, either is or begins with a causally simple mental action, that is, a mental event that does not consist of one mental event causing others. A simple mental event is an action if and only if it has a certain intrinsic phenomenal quality, which I've dubbed the "act-ish" quality and tried to describe by using agent-causation talk radically qualified by "as if": the simple mental event of my volition to exert force with a part of my body phenomenally seems to me to be intrinsically an event that does not just happen to me, that does not occur unbidden, but it is, rather, as if I make it occur, as if I determine that it will happen just when and as it does (likewise for simple mental acts that are not volitions, such as my mentally saying "Shucks!"). A simple mental event's having this intrinsic actish phenomenal quality is sufficient for its being an *action*. But its having the quality entails nothing either way as to whether it satisfies the incompatibilist requirement for *free* action (which is that it not be causally necessitated by antecedent events).

An action may be causally complex, may consist of a simple mental action plus consequences of it. For example, my action of voluntarily pushing with my arm and hand against a door begins with a volition, a simple mental act of willing to exert a certain force in a certain direction with my arm and hand, and consists further in that volition's causing my arm and hand to exert such a force. My action of opening the door has a still further component of the door's opening being caused by the force exerted against it by my arm and hand.

Now, as I explained earlier, if an event is *not* an action of mine – for example, the door's opening – then I can make that event occur only by causing it, that is, by performing some action that causes it. But I make my own free, simple mental acts occur, not by causing them, but simply by being their subject, by their being my acts. They are *ipso facto* determined or controlled by me, provided they are free, that is, not determined by something else, not causally necessitated by antecedent states and events.

O'Connor readily concedes that there is an actish phenomenal quality to any simple mental action – a quality of its seeming as if I directly bring it about. His difficulty with my account of an agent's determining her own action is that he cannot see how the mere presence or absence of the actish phenomenal quality, without there being also a genuine causal relation to the agent, can make the difference between an event's being one that the agent determines and its being one that the agent does not determine. He says:

> ...how can it plausibly be maintained that the fundamental actions in virtue of which we have control over events within and immediately external to our body may themselves be simply uncaused occurrences; that we may be said to be in control of *these* simply by virtue of their obtaining (undeterminedly)? Perhaps the challenge is most directly posed in these terms: why are volitions *intrinsically* such as to confer control in the absence of determining antecedents?[10]

The issue, O'Connor says, is

> whether or not control over one's actions obtains in virtue of certain purely intrinsic, nonrelational features of those actions together with the negative condition of there being no determining prior causes. I am inclined to think that the onus is clearly on one who affirms this thesis to explain why we should think this to be so.[11]

I confess that I can manage to feel some sympathy for O'Connor's uneasiness here. I am not completely baffled by it. I understand the temptation to say that the actish phenomenal quality alone cannot be enough, the temptation to take literally the impression that the actish quality consists in (the impression that I directly cause my mental action) and treat this impression as an awareness of a real causal relation between me and my action. I appreciate the temptation and I would be more prone than I am to succumb to it were it not that, first, the positing of this special sort of causal relation does not seem to me to solve the problem alleged for my view and, second, there seem to me to be unacceptable difficulties in the very concept of a direct causal relation between the agent as such and a mental event of hers.

The alleged problem with my account could, it seems, be put this way: we feel that an agent's determining or controlling her action – making it occur – must involve something more than just the undetermined occurrence of an event with certain intrinsic properties, whatever those intrinsic properties might be. If that is a fair way of putting the difficulty, then O'Connor's own agent-causation account seems to fail to avoid it.[12] He holds that where an agent causes a simple mental event *e* it is not this event *e* that is her action, but rather it is the whole causally complex event of *her causing e*. He says that "rather than there being a causal relation between agent and action, the relational complex constitutes the action."[13] He tells us that the event the agent directly causes in an action is the coming to be of a state of intention.[14]

On this account it seems that an agent controls her *action* simply in virtue of the action's having a certain intrinsic property (its being the agent's causing something) and its being causally undetermined. About this account one might ask, echoing the question O'Connor asks about my account: Why should an action's being undetermined and having a certain intrinsic property be enough to make it an event that the agent determines or controls? If her action is not caused by anything, not even the agent, then how can we hold the agent responsible for it?

O'Connor recognizes this sort of objection.[15] He tries to rebut it by first arguing that "the very idea of there being sufficient causal conditions for an agent-causal event is unintelligible"[16] and then saying of an agent-causal event:

> Its very nature precludes the possibility of there being a sufficient causal condition for it (as I argued earlier), being an event that is the agent's causing the event internal to it (*e*). Now the event *e* is itself clearly under the control of the agent, since *he* caused it (directly). But would it not, then, be perfectly absurd to raise a doubt concerning whether the agent controlled *his causing e*? Indeed, it seems to me that the question of whether the agent has control over this event is ill framed – it is simply an instance of an agent's exercising direct control over another event.[17]

Here I find myself puzzled. I don't see why it would be absurd to suppose that we are entitled to say that in causing *e* the agent exercised control over *e* only if we are also entitled to say that the agent exercised control over her causing *e*. And I don't see why the question "How is it that the agent controls her causing *e*, given that her causing *e* was not causally determined by anything?" is any more (or less) absurd than the question "How is it that the agent controls her being the subject of an event with the actish phenomenal quality, given that this event was not causally determined by anything?" If the latter question is embarrassing for my account – a question that the account should answer but is unable to answer (as O'Connor thinks it is) – then the former question should be embarrassing for O'Connor's account – not one that it needs to answer – then neither is the latter embarrassing for my account (needless to say, it is the components of this last conditional that I am inclined to affirm: neither question is one that the account it pertains to needs to answer).

That O'Connor thinks otherwise must be because he holds the following about agent-control and causation: (a) if an event is such that it is possible for it to be caused, then an agent's controlling or determining it must be a matter of its being caused in an appropriate way, but (b) if an event is such that it is *not* possible for it to be caused then, of course, an agent's controlling or determining it cannot be a matter of how it is caused. (b) is obvious enough. But (a) is not obvious, and O'Connor has offered no argument for it. My intuition that it is obvious that an event's having the actish phenomenal quality and being causally undetermined makes it one that is controlled and determined by the agent seems to me just as plausible as O'Connor's intuition that it's obvious that an event's being an agent-causal event and therefore one that *could not* be causally determined makes it one that is controlled by the agent.

So my first point is that I don't see why an event's being an agent-causal event and necessarily lacking a sufficient cause makes a better sufficient condition for the event's being one the agent controls than does the event's having the actish phenomenal quality and contingently lacking a sufficient cause. And, I might add, my proposal as to what grounds our saying that an agent directly determines an event has the advantage over O'Connor's of not requiring us to add to our basic posits a special *recherche* sort of causation. [. . .]

It is clear, by the way, why the agent-causation account does not want to allow that any extrinsic condition is needed to give the agent control over her causing *e*. For if it did allow this, then it would be in serious trouble. The only extrinsic condition the agent-causation account has to suggest – the only thing consistent with its idea as to what agent control consists in – is that we posit a further agent-causal relation, this time between the agent and the event of her causing *e*. But the same question can again be raised about the agent's causing of her causing *e*: what gives the agent control of *that*? Thus the account would either fail to give us any ultimate answer to the question of what agent-control consists in or else give us the very implausible answer that it consists in an infinite regress of agent-causings.

Those are my reasons for thinking that positing agent-causation does not solve the alleged problem it is meant to solve. In answer to the question "Why should an action's being undetermined and having a certain intrinsic property be enough to make it an event that the agent determines?" the agent-causationist, as much as the simple indeterminist, has to say, "Well, it just is"; and the property of agent-causation gives no better justification for saying this than does the actish phenomenal quality. In fact, it may give a worse justification, for there are reasons –

two I can think of – to worry about the intelligibility of the notion of agent-causation.

One of my worries on this score is inspired by a question C. D. Broad raised about the coherence of the agent-causation theory. Broad asked:

> How can an event possibly be determined to happen at a certain date if its total cause contained no factor to which the notion of date has any application? And how can the notion of date have any application to anything that is not an event?[18]

On the agent-causation theory, the immediate cause of the occurrence of a particular sort of simple mental event at a particular time is the agent herself, *per se* and not in virtue of any event of which she is the subject. But the agent *per se* cannot *explain* why the event happened precisely when it did rather than at some slightly different time. Only some difference between the agent at the one time and the agent at the other times, some temporally located property, could do that. Nor, it might be added, can the agent *per se* explain why that particular sort of event rather than some other sort happened just then. What sense can it make, then, to say that the agent as such is the *cause* of the occurrence of that particular sort of event rather than some other sort, and is the cause of its occurring at that particular time rather than some other time?

O'Connor confronts this worry and responds by saying:

> An agent-cause does not produce a certain effect by virtue of its very nature, as does an event-cause, but does so at will in the light of considerations accessible to the agent at that time. And so a full explanation of why an agent-caused event occurred will include, among other things, an account of the reasons upon which the agent acted.[19]

O'Connor seems to be suggesting here that when we have an agent-caused event the explanation of the specific nature and timing of the event – that which makes it right to say that the agent determined that just that sort of event rather than some other sort would happen at just that time rather than at some other time – lies in the fact that the agent caused the event for certain reasons she had for bringing about that sort of event at that time.

For this suggestion I see a couple of problems. First, what about cases of spontaneous action where an agent acts in a certain way for no particular reason, at any rate not in order to satisfy any antecedently existing motive? Surely, agent-causation must be involved in such spontaneous actions if it is involved in any.

Second, and more important, it is a fact about reasons explanations[20] that a full explanation in terms of the agent's reasons for acting as she did need not explain why there occurred that particular action *rather than* some other for which she also had reasons. An obvious case of this is where an agent is indifferent between alternative means to the same end – has no reason to prefer one over another – and just arbitrarily chooses one. For example, my reason for picking up the telephone was that I wanted to make a call. But that reason does not explain why I used my left *rather than* my right hand to pick it up, and indeed I need not have had any reason for using one hand rather than the other. Similarly, my reason for picking up the phone does not explain why I picked it up precisely when I did rather than a few seconds earlier or later, and I need not have had any reason for choosing that precise time rather than a slightly earlier or later one. It is possible that there was nothing at all that explains why the one thing was the case rather than any alternative (a possibility that I think O'Connor would not deny). But in that case, it seems natural to infer, there was nothing that *caused* the one rather than any alternative.

But it appears that the agent-causationist cannot make this natural inference. For surely, if agent-causation is involved in the action, it must be that *I caused* it to be my left rather than my right hand that I willed to move and *I caused* the action to happen precisely when it did rather than at a slightly different time. Thus the agent-causation theory is committed to supposing that a *cause* of something can fail to provide any *explanation* of it. If I am the cause of its being my left rather than my right hand that I will to move, but I am not the cause in virtue of any property or change in me at the time – I could in the same circumstances equally well have caused it to be my right hand for the same reasons I caused it to be my left – then there is nothing about this cause of its being my left rather than my right hand that I willed to move – me – that *explains* why it was my left rather than my right hand that I willed to move. If I am the cause of the precise timing of my volition, but it is not the case that I am the cause of this in virtue of any property or change in me at that precise time – I could in the same circumstances equally well have caused it to occur a bit later for the same reasons I caused it when I did – then there is nothing about this cause of its being at that precise time that *explains* its being at that precise time. Broad was, I believe, assuming that it is incoherent to suppose that the cause of something's being the case might fail to explain its being the case, and I am inclined to agree. If X causes it to be the case that Y rather than any alternative then there must be something about X that explains why Y rather than any alternative. I

don't know that I want to go so far as to say that this is self-evident, but
its denial is sufficiently puzzling that we ought not to accept it without
having compelling reason to do so.[21]

My other worry about the concept of agent-causation is that agent-
causation appears to be undetectable. Given that we have a person, *S*,
who is the subject of a simple mental event that has the actish phenomenal quality – a volition, say, or mentally saying a word – and this event is
not causally determined by antecedent events and states, what detectable
difference would it make to the situation whether the agent-causal
relation between *S* and that event was present or not? What independently specifiable difference could distinguish between the case where the
agent causal relation is present and the case where it is not? That is, what
independently specifiable feature could constitute the agent-causal relation? O'Connor does not try to give any account of this and it is hard to
see what account could be given. However the person and her actish
mental event are realized in the ultimate constituents of reality, it is
difficult to imagine what additional thing might be realized there that
would *force* us to describe it as a causal relation between the person
as enduring substance and the event. Whatever independently specifiable difference might be pointed to, we would be free to regard its
coming about as *another event* of which the person is the subject
rather than as a brute causal relation between the subject and the actish
event.

O'Connor does acknowledge that there might be concern about the
detectability of the agent-causal relation.

> . . . it seems that it is impossible in principle, for us ever to know whether
> any events *are* produced in the manner that the agency theory postulates,
> because such an event would be indistinguishable from one which was
> essentially random, not connected by even probabilistic laws to events
> preceding it.[22]

His response to this worry is not to argue that agent-causation *is*
detectable, but rather to claim that, however undetectable it might be,
we are nevertheless forced to posit it in order to give an adequate account
of reasons explanations of action (given that we reject an event-causation
account invoking probabilistic laws). He thinks that my account of
reasons explanations – which invokes neither agent-causation nor probabilistic laws – won't do.

My account of reasons explanations has it that when an action is
correctly explained as one the agent did for a certain reason supplied

by an antecedent motive (a desire or intention), the explanatory connection between the motive and the action is forged, not by causal laws (probabilistic or deterministic) or by agent-causation, but by an *intention* concurrent with the action. The intention has the following content: it refers directly to the current action and to the remembered prior motive and says that this action is to satisfy that motive (or to help to do so). For example, if I push against a door in order to satisfy my antecedent desire to know whether it is locked – my reason for pushing against it is that I desire that information – then it is sufficient for the truth of this explanation that concurrently with my pushing I remember that desire and intend that this pushing will contribute to satisfying it.

But O'Connor thinks that this is not sufficient.

> . . . reasons explanations require a mechanism of control that "hooks up", so to speak, the agent's reasons and consequent decision (and action) . . . On the agency [i.e., agent-causation] theory, an agent's capacity directly to produce a decision in the light of consciously held reasons fills the bill. We cannot *simply* appeal, as, for example, Ginet does, to *internal* (and referential) relations between concurrent intention and prior motives, on the one hand, and that same concurrent intention and the decision (or action), on the other. Without the mediation of a (necessarily causal) "mechanism of control", prior motives cannot *explain* a decision, even though (as it happens) they may coincide with it.[23]

I protest that I simply fail to see why the relation between prior motive and action that I specify does not suffice to guarantee the explanatory connection that we simply when we say the agent did the action in order to satisfy that motive. Why does O'Connor think that we need something further of a causal nature? (The term "causal" could be extended to any sort of explanation, I suppose, on the ground that it is always appropriate to state an explanation using the word "because"; but O'Connor is using the term in a narrower sense).

O'Connor suggests that something causal is needed in order to distinguish "*S* did *A* in order to satisfy her desire" from "*S* did *A* knowing that she would thereby satisfy her desire."[24] I agree that the latter does not entail the former, but my sufficient condition captures the difference. Where it is the case that *S* does *A* believing that she will thereby satisfy her desire but not the case that she does *A* in order to satisfy her desire, my sufficient condition does not obtain: though *S* *believes* of her action that it will satisfy her desire she does not *intend* of it that it will do so (though it is doubtful that one can intend of one's action that it will satisfy one's desire without believing of it at least that it might do so, it is certain that one can believe of one's action that it might satisfy one's desire without intending of it that it do so).

If O'Connor were still to insist that explanation always requires causation, then he would seem to me to be just clinging to a dogma, blind to the possibility that in reasons explanation we have a fundamentally different kind of explanation, a non-causal kind.

Another reason O'Connor has for wanting to posit agent-causation (a reason we all have for being tempted to posit it) is that doing so would allow us to take the actish phenomenal quality seriously. It would allow us to take this its-seeming-as-if-I-directly-cause-it as a literal perception of reality; it is this that makes so prereflectively appealing the idea that what makes a person the agent of an actish event is that she directly causes it. So O'Connor might want to say that, if agent-causation is not independently detectable, then it must *supervene* on the facts that an event with the actish quality occurs in an appropriately complex creature and is not causally determined by its antecedents (and he should add, I think, that it supervenes *only* on such facts: I can't see what alternatives could be plausibly deemed sufficient for the presence of agent-causation). But one who says this has, it seems to me, come over to my view of what is really going on in free and responsible action, retaining only the *language* of agent-causation to describe it. One has, in effect, explicated being agent-caused as having actish quality plus being undetermined by antecedents.

This is agent-causation that I understand better and find more congenial. I might still object that to say that the agent causes the actish event is to stretch the meaning of the term "cause" a bit far, in that this sort of cause would not be any sort of explanation. If the champion of agent-causation replies that this is a small price to pay for the benefits of taking agent-causation talk seriously, then I'm inclined to say: OK, if you insist. I'll give you the agent-causation label as long as you give me my account of the reality it labels.

Notes

1   I have argued for this thesis in Ginet, *On Action* (Cambridge: Cambridge University Press, 1990), Chap. 5.
2   I defend this thesis in Ginet, "In Defense of the Principle of Alternative Possibilities: Why I Don't Find Frankfurt's Argument Convincing," in J. Tomberlin (ed.), *Philosophical Perspectives* 10: Metaphysics (Atascadero, CA: Ridgeview, 1996).
3   See T. O'Connor's instructive paper, "Indeterminism and Free Agency: Three Recent Views," *Philosophy and Phenomenological Research* 53 (1993), pp. 499–526.

4   T. Reid, *Essays on the Active Powers of the Human Mind* (Cambridge: MIT Press, 1969), Essay I.

5   R.M. Chisholm, "Freedom and Action," in K. Lehrer (ed.), *Freedom and Determinism* (New York: Random House, 1966), pp. 11–44.

6   R. Taylor, *Action and Purpose* (Englewood Cliffs, NJ: Prentice-Hall, 1966), Chap. 9.

7   See O'Connor, "Indeterminism and Agency: Three Recent Views," and O'Connor, "Agent Causation," in T. O'Connor (ed.), *Agents, Causes, and Events* (Oxford: Oxford University Press, 1995), pp. 171–200.

8   R. Nozick, *Philosophical Explanations* (Cambridge: Harvard University Press, 1981).

9   R. Kane, *Free Will and Values* (Buffalo: State University of New York Press, 1985).

10   O'Connor, "Indeterminism and Free Agency: Three Recent Views", p. 505.

11   Ibid., pp. 505–506.

12   O'Connor, "Agent Causation."

13   Ibid., p. 182.

14   Ibid., p. 198, note 15.

15   He quotes Chisholm's remark, "If we say this [that the agent's causing *e* was not caused by anything], then we cannot hold *him* responsible for his causing *e* to happen" (Chisholm, "Reflections on Human Agency," *Idealistic Studies* 1 (1970), p. 40).

16   O'Connor, "Agent Causation," p. 185.

17   Ibid., p. 187.

18   C. D. Broad, *Ethics and the History of Philosophy* (London: Routledge & Kegan Paul, 1952), p. 215.

19   O'Connor, "Agent Causation," p. 184.

20   See Reid, *Essays on the Active Powers of the Human Mind*, pp. 285–286.

21   What about indeterministic causation? Might it be causation without explanation? I think not. Let us look at an example. Suppose we have set up the famous two-slit experiment with photon detectors at each slit. A photon detected at slit *A* causes a green light to go on, and one detected at slit *B* causes a red light to go on. A photon is fired toward the screen containing the slits. This event, let us suppose, causes the red light to go on; but it does so indeterministically, since, according to quantum theory, it is compatible with the laws of nature that exactly the same event in exactly the same circumstances should have caused the green light to go on. So, one might be tempted to conclude, the photon's firing caused the red light to go on but does not explain its going on. But this would be wrong. What the firing of the photon caused, but also explains, is (a) the red light's going on *rather than neither light's going on*. What it does not explain is (b) the red light's going on *rather than the green light's going on*. But neither does it cause this. If one asks, "What caused it to be the case that the red light rather than the green light went on?," it would not be correct to answer, "the firing of the photon."

Indeed, the correct answer seems to be that *nothing* is causally responsible for
its being the red rather than the green light that goes on (because nothing is
causally responsible for its being slit *B* rather than slit *A* that the photon goes
through). So we do not have here any state of affairs for which there is a
cause of its obtaining that fails to explain its obtaining.

22   O'Connor, "Agent Causation," p. 195.
23   Ibid., p. 195.
24   Ibid., p. 193.

Comments and Questions on Carl Ginet's "Freedom, Responsibility and Agency"

1.   Anyone who proposes a theory of *free* action must first have a theory
of what an *action* is. What is Ginet's account of what makes something an
action? What, on his account, makes an action a *free* action? Do you find
his accounts of both action and free action plausible? What difficulties do
you see in them, if any?
2.   Ginet considers and responds to an objection made against his simple
indeterminist view by O'Connor. O'Connor does not think Ginet can
account for how agents actually *produce* or cause and how they *control*
their free actions. Why does O'Connor think Ginet's view fails in this
regard? How does Ginet respond to this objection and do you think his
response is adequate? One of Ginet's responses is to say that O'Connor's
view does not do any better at explaining an agent's production and
control of action than Ginet's theory does. Do you think Ginet is right
about this or not?
3.   Ginet then makes several further objections to O'Connor's agent-
causation view. The first of these objections (which he borrows from
C. D. Broad) concerns the timing of actions (when they occur), the second
objection concerns whether agent-causation really explains why an agent
acted as he or she did rather than some other way, and the third concerns
the detectability of agent-causation. Assess these three objections of
Ginet's. Do you think they are valid? How do you think O'Connor or
other agent-causationists might answer them, if they could answer them
at all?

Suggested Reading

Ginet's views about action and free will are spelled out in greater detail in his
book *On Action* (1990). O'Connor's criticisms of Ginet's view are contained in

O'Connor's *Persons and Causes* (2000). Other critical discussions of Ginet's views about action and freedom may be found in Alfred Mele, *Springs of Action* (1992) and Randolph Clarke "Agent-causation and Event Causation in the Production of Free Action" (1996). Other simple indeterminist approaches to free will, similar to Ginet's, but with crucial differences, are defended by Stuart Goetz, "Libertarian Choice" (1997) and Hugh McCann, *The Works of Agency* (1998). For different perspectives on the philosophy of action and the issue of whether reasons for action are causes of action, see *The Philosophy of Action* (1997), edited by Alfred Mele.

15

Free Will: New Directions for an Ancient Problem

Robert Kane

Editor's Introduction

Robert Kane is Professor of Philosophy at the University of Texas at Austin. In the reading that follows he also attempts to give an intelligible account of libertarian free will, but in a way that differs from both traditional agent-causal theories, like those of Chisholm and O'Connor, and from simple indeterminist theories, like Ginet's, both of which he thinks fall short. The third libertarian option defended in this selection is often called causal indeterminism. Kane acknowledges that most libertarian views of the past have been agent-cause theories of one sort or another. But he agrees with Ginet in thinking that agent-cause theories fail to explain what really needs explaining about indeterminist free will; and hence they leave "the mystery of metaphysical freedom" still a mystery. But Kane also argues that we do not have to deny (as Ginet's simple indeterminism does) that explanations of action in terms of reasons or motives are a species of causal explanation in order to make sense of incompatibilist free will. We can allow that reasons or motives cause actions so long as the relevant causal relations are not always deterministic (they may sometimes be nondeterministic or probabilistic). In short, "undetermined" need not always mean "uncaused"; and reasons, like other kinds of causes, may incline without necessitating. Kane argues that a coherent view of libertarian free will can be developed along these lines, one that does a better job of reconciling free will with modern views of human beings in the natural and social sciences than alternative theories do. Kane also argues for a different approach to the compatibility question as well as to the intelligibility question. He thinks that the usual attempts to show the incompatibility of free will and determinism, such as the consequence argument, fall short because they neglect another significant feature of free will besides alternative possibilities (AP), the idea that agents who have free will must be ultimately responsible (UR) for their actions.

The Compatibility Question: AP and UR

In a number of writings over the past two decades, I have sought to answer four questions about free will: (1) Is it compatible (or incompatible) with determinism? (2) Why do we want it? (3) Can we make sense of a free will that is incompatible with determinism? (4) Can such a free will be reconciled with modern images of human beings in the natural and social sciences?[1] On all four questions, I have tried to point current debates about free will in new directions. In this essay, I discuss some of these new directions.

Consider question (1) – the so-called compatibility question – which has received most of the recent attention in free will debates. The first thing we learn from these debates is that if we formulate the compatibility question as in most textbook discussions of free will – "Is freedom compatible with determinism?" – the question is too simple and ill-formed. The reason is that there are many meanings of "freedom" and many of them are compatible with determinism. Even in a determined world, we would want to distinguish persons who are free from such things as physical restraint, addiction or neurosis, coercion, compulsion, covert control or political oppression from persons who are not free from these things; and we could allow that these freedoms would be preferable to their opposites *even in a determined world.*

I think those of us who believe that free will is incompatible with determinism – we incompatibilists and libertarians so-called – should simply concede this point to our compatibilist opponents. Many kinds of freedom worth wanting are indeed compatible with determinism. What we incompatibilists should be insisting upon instead is that there is *at least one* kind of freedom worth wanting that is incompatible with determinism. This significant further freedom, as I see it, is "free *will*," which I define as "the power to be the ultimate creator and sustainer of one's own ends or purposes." To say this further freedom is important is not to deny the importance of everyday compatibilist freedoms from coercion, compulsion, political oppression, and the like; it is only to say that human longings transcend them.

This is one shift in direction for the compatibility question that I insist upon. But there is another of more importance. Most recent and past philosophical debate about the incompatibility of free will and determinism has focused on the question of whether determinism is compatible with "the condition of alternative possibilities" (which I shall call AP) – the requirement that the free agent "could have done otherwise." Most arguments for incompatibilism, such as the "consequence argument" of van Inwagen and others, appeal to AP. Critics of such arguments either deny that AP conflicts with determinism or deny that alternative possibilities are required for moral responsibility or free will in the first place. As I view these contentious debates about AP and incompatibilism, they inevitably tend to stalemate over differing interpretations of "can," "power," "ability," and "could have done otherwise." And I think there are good reasons for these stalemates having to do with the different meanings of freedom just mentioned. In response, I argue that we need to look in new directions. AP alone provides too thin a basis on which to rest the case for incompatibilism: *the compatibility question cannot be resolved by focusing on alternative possibilities alone.*

Fortunately, there is another place to look. In the long history of free will debate one can find another criterion fueling incompatibilist intuitions that is even more important than AP, though comparatively neglected. I call it the condition of ultimate responsibility or UR. The basic idea is this: to be ultimately responsible for an action, an agent must be responsible for anything that is a sufficient reason (condition, cause or motive) for the action's occurring.[2] If, for example, a choice issues from, and can be sufficiently explained by, an agent's character and motives (together with background conditions), then to be *ultimately* responsible for the choice, the agent must be at least in part responsible by virtue of choices or actions voluntarily performed in the past for having the character and motives he or she now has. Compare Aristotle's claim that if a man is responsible for wicked acts that flow from his character, he must at some time in the past have been responsible for forming the wicked character from which these acts flow.

This UR condition accounts for the "ultimate" in the original definition of free will: "the power of agents to be the *ultimate* creators and sustainers of their own ends or purposes." Now UR does not require that we could have done otherwise (AP) for *every* act done of our own free wills – thus vindicating philosophers such as Frankfurt, Fischer, and Dennett, who insist that we can be held morally responsible for many acts even when we could not have done otherwise.[3] But the vindication is only partial. For UR *does* require that we could have done otherwise with respect to *some* acts in our past life histories by which we formed our present characters. I call these "self-forming actions," or SFAs. Consider Dennett's example of Martin Luther. When Luther finally broke with the Church at Rome, he said "Here I stand, I can do no other." Suppose, says Dennett, at that moment Luther was literally right. Given his character and motives, he could not then and there have done otherwise. Does this mean he was not morally responsible, not subject to praise or blame, for his act, or that he was not acting of his own free will? Dennett says "not at all." In saying "I can do no other," Luther was not disowning responsibility for his act, but taking full responsibility for acting of his own free will. So "could have done otherwise," or AP, says Dennett, is not required for moral responsibility or free will.

My response to Dennett is to grant that Luther could have been responsible for this act, even *ultimately* responsible in the sense of UR, though he could not have done otherwise then and there and even if his act was determined. But this would be so to the extent that he was responsible for his present motives and character by virtue of many earlier struggles and self-forming choices (SFAs) that brought him to this point where he could do no other. Those who know Luther's biography know the inner struggles and turmoil he endured getting to that point. Often we act from a will already formed, but it is "our own free will" by virtue of the fact that we formed it by other choices or actions in the past (SFAs) for which we could have done otherwise. If this were not so, there is nothing we could have *ever* done to make ourselves different than we are – a consequence, I believe, that is incompatible with our being (at least to some degree) ultimately responsible for what we are. So SFAs are only a subset of those acts in life for which we are ultimately responsible and which are done "of our own free will." But if none of our acts were self-forming in this way, we would not be *ultimately* responsible for anything we did.

If the case for incompatibility cannot be made on AP alone, it can be made if UR is added; and thus, I suggest, the too-often neglected UR should be moved to center stage in free will debates. If agents must be responsible to some degree for anything that is a sufficient cause or motive for their actions, an impossible infinite regress of past actions would be required unless some actions in the agent's life history (SFAs) did not have either sufficient causes or motives (and hence were undetermined). But this new route to incompatibility raises a host of further questions, including how actions lacking both sufficient causes and motives could themselves be free and responsible actions, and how, if at all, such actions could exist in the natural order where we humans live and have our being. These are versions of questions (3) and (4) listed above, which I call the intelligibility and existence questions for free will, to which I now turn.

The Intelligibility Question

The problem of intelligibility is an ancient one: if free will is not compatible with determinism, it does not seem to be compatible with indeterminism either. The arguments here are familiar and have been made since ancient times. An undetermined or chance event, it is said, occurs spontaneously and is not controlled by anything, hence not controlled by the agent. If, for example, a choice occurred by virtue of a quantum jump or other undetermined event in one's brain it would seem a fluke or accident rather than a responsible choice. Or look at the problem in another way that goes a little deeper. If my choice is really undetermined, that means I could have made a different choice *given exactly the same past* right up to the moment when I did choose. That is what indeterminism and probability mean: exactly the same past, different possible outcomes. Imagine, for example, that I had been deliberating about where to spend my vacation, in Hawaii or Colorado, and after much thought and deliberation had decided I prefered Hawaii and chose it. If the choice was undetermined, then exactly the same deliberation, the same thought processes, the same beliefs, desires, and other motives – not a sliver of difference – that led up to my favoring and choosing Hawaii over Colorado, might by chance have issued in my choosing Colorado instead. That is very strange. If such a thing happened it would seem a fluke or accident, like that quantum jump in the brain just mentioned, not a rational choice. Since I had come to favor Hawaii and was about to choose it, when by chance I chose Colorado, I would wonder what went wrong and perhaps consult a neurologist. For reasons such as these, people have argued through the centuries that undetermined free choices would be "arbitrary," "capricious," "random," "irrational," "uncontrolled," and "inexplicable," not really free and responsible choices at all.

Defenders of an incompatibilist or libertarian free will have a dismal record of answering these familiar charges. Realizing that free will cannot merely be indeterminism or chance, they have appealed to various obscure or mysterious forms of agency or causation to make up the difference. Immanuel Kant said we can't explain free will in scientific and psychological terms, even though we require it for belief in morality.[4] To account for it we have to appeal to the agency of what he called a "noumenal self" outside space and time that could not be studied in scientific terms. Many other respectable philosophers continue to believe that only some sort of appeal to mind/body dualism can make sense of free will. Science might tell us there was indeterminacy or a place for causal gaps in the brain, but a nonmaterial self, or what Nobel physiologist John Eccles calls a "transempirical power center," would have to fill the causal gaps left by physical causes by intervening in the natural order.[5] The most popular appeal among philosophers today is to a special kind of *agent- or immanent causation* that cannot be explained in terms of the ordinary modes of causation in terms of events familiar to the sciences.[6] Free and responsible actions are not determined by prior events, but neither do they occur merely by chance. They are caused by agents in a way that transcends and cannot be explained in terms of ordinary modes of causation by events involving the agents.

I call these familiar libertarian strategies for making sense of free will "extra factor" strategies. The idea behind them is that, since indeterminism leaves it open which way an agent will choose or act, some "extra" kind of causation or agency must be postulated over and above the natural flow of events to account for the agent's going one way or another. Early in my encounters with free will debates, I became disenchanted with all such extra factor strategies. I agree with other libertarian critics, such as Peter van Inwagen and Carl Ginet, that extra factor strategies – including agent-causal theories – do not solve the problems about indeterminism they are suppose to solve and they create further mysteries of their own.[7] If we are going to make progress on the intelligibility and existence questions about incompatibilist free will, I think we have to strike out in new directions, avoiding appeals to extra factor strategies altogether, including special forms of agent-causation. To do this means rethinking issues about indeterminism and responsibility from the ground up, a task to which I now turn.

Indeterminism and Responsibility

The first step is to note that indeterminism does not have to be involved in all acts done "of our own free wills" for which we are ultimately responsible, as argued earlier. Not all such acts have to be undetermined, but only those by which we made ourselves into the kinds of persons we are, namely "self-forming actions" or SFAs. Now I believe these undetermined self-forming actions or SFAs occur at those difficult times of life when we are torn between competing visions of what we should do or become. Perhaps we are torn between doing the moral thing or acting from ambition, or between powerful present desires and long-term goals, or we are faced with difficult tasks for which we have aversions. In all such cases, we are faced with competing motivations and have to make an effort to overcome temptation to do something else we also strongly want. There is tension and uncertainty in our minds about what to do at such times, I suggest, that is reflected in appropriate regions of our brains by movement away from thermodynamic equilibrium – in short, a kind of "stirring up of chaos" in the brain that makes it sensitive to microindeterminacies at the neuronal level. The uncertainty and inner tension we feel at such soul-searching moments of self-formation is thus reflected in the indeterminacy of our neural processes themselves. What is experienced internally as uncertainty then corresponds physically to the opening of a window of opportunity that temporarily screens off complete determination by influences of the past. (By contrast, when we act from predominant motives or settled dispositions, the uncertainty or indeterminacy is muted. If it did play a role in such cases, it *would* be a mere nuisance or fluke, as critics of indeterminism contend.)

When we do decide under such conditions of uncertainty, the outcome is not determined because of the preceding indeterminacy – and yet it can be willed (and hence rational and voluntary) either way owing to the fact that in such self-formation, the agents' prior wills are divided by conflicting motives. Consider a businesswoman who faces such a conflict. She is on her way to an important meeting when she observes an assault taking place in an alley. An inner struggle ensues between her conscience, to stop and call for help, and her career ambitions which tell her she cannot miss this meeting. She has to make an effort of will to overcome the temptation to go on. If she overcomes this temptation, it will be the result of her effort, but if she fails, it will be because she did not *allow* her effort to succeed. And this is due to the fact that, while she willed to overcome temptation, she also willed to fail, for quite different and incommensurable reasons. When we, like the woman, decide in such circumstances, and the indeterminate efforts we are making become determinate choices, we *make* one set of competing reasons or motives prevail over the others then and there *by deciding*.

Now let us add a further piece to the puzzle. Just as indeterminism need not undermine rationality and voluntariness, so indeterminism in and of itself need not undermine control and responsibility. Suppose you are trying to think through a difficult problem, say a mathematical problem, and there is some indeterminacy in your neural processes complicating the task – a kind of chaotic background. It would be like trying to concentrate and solve a problem, say a mathematical problem, with background noise or distraction. Whether you are going to succeed in solving the problem is uncertain and undetermined because of the distracting neural noise. Yet, if you concentrate and solve the problem none the less, we have reason to say you did it and are responsible for it even though it was undetermined whether you would succeed. The indeterministic noise would have been an obstacle that you overcame by your effort.

There are numerous examples supporting this point, where indeterminism functions as an obstacle to success without precluding responsibility. Consider an assassin who is trying to shoot the prime minister, but might miss because of some undetermined events in his nervous system that may lead to a jerking or wavering of his arm. If the assassin does succeed in hitting his target, despite the indeterminism, can he be held responsible? The answer is clearly yes because he intentionally and voluntarily succeeded in doing what he was *trying* to do – kill the prime minister. Yet his action, killing the prime minister, was undetermined. Or, here is another example: a husband, while arguing with his wife, in a fit of rage swings his arm down on her favorite glass-top table intending to break it. Again, we suppose that some indeterminism in his outgoing neural pathways makes the momentum of his arm indeterminate so that it is undetermined whether the table will break right up to the moment when it is struck. Whether the husband breaks the table or not is undetermined and yet he is clearly responsible if he does break it. (It would be a poor excuse for him to say to his wife: "chance did it, not me." Even though indeterminism was involved, chance didn't do it, he did.)

Now these examples – of the mathematical problem, the assassin, and the husband – are not all we want since they do not amount to genuine exercises of (self-forming) free will in SFAs, like the businesswoman's, where the will is divided between conflicting motives. The woman wants to help the victim, but she also wants to go on to her meeting. By contrast, the assassin's will is not equally divided. He wants to kill the prime minister, but does not also want to fail. (If he fails therefore, it will be merely by chance.) Yet these examples of the assassin, the husband, and the like, do provide some clues. To go further, we have to add some new twists.

Imagine in cases of inner conflict characteristic of SFAs, like the businesswoman's, that the indeterministic noise which is providing an obstacle to her overcoming temptation is not coming from an external source, but is coming from her own will, since she also deeply desires to do the opposite. Imagine that two crossing (recurrent) neural networks are involved, each influencing the other, and representing her conflicting motivations. (These are complex networks of interconnected neurons in the brain circulating impulses in feedback loops that are generally involved in higher-level cognitive processing.)[8] The input of one of these neural networks consists in the woman's reasons for acting morally and stopping to help the victim; the input of the other, her ambitious motives for going on to her meeting. The two networks are connected so that the indeterministic noise which is an obstacle to her making one of the choices is coming from her desire to make the other, and vice versa – the indeterminism thus arising from a tension-creating conflict in the will, as we said. In these circumstances, when either of the pathways "wins" (i.e., reaches an activation threshold, which amounts to choice), it will be like your solving the mathematical problem by overcoming the background noise produced by the other. And just as when you solved the mathematical problem by overcoming the distracting noise, one can say you did it and are responsible for it, so one can say this as well, I argue, in the present case, *whichever one is chosen*. The pathway through which the woman succeeds in reaching a choice threshold will have overcome the obstacle in the form of indeterministic noise generated by the other.

Note that, under such conditions, the choices either way will not be "inadvertent," "accidental," "capricious," or "merely random" (as critics of indeterminism say), because they will be *willed* by the agents either way when they are made, and done for *reasons* either way – reasons that the agents then and there *endorse*. But these are the conditions usually required to say something is done "on purpose," rather than accidentally, capriciously or merely by chance. Moreover, these conditions taken together, I argue, rule out each of the reasons we have for saying that agents act, but do not have *control* over their actions (compulsion, coercion, constraint, inadvertence, accident, control by others, etc.).[9] Of course, for undetermined SFAs, agents do not control or determine which choice outcome will occur *before* it occurs; but it does not follow, because one does control or determine which of a set of outcomes is going to occur before it occurs, that one does not control or determine which of them occurs, *when* it occurs. When the above conditions for SFAs are satisfied, agents exercise control over their future lives *then and there* by deciding. Indeed, they have what I call "plural voluntary control" over the options in the following sense: they are able to bring about *whichever* of the options they will, *when* they will to do so, for the reasons they will to do so, on purpose rather than accidentally or by mistake, without being coerced or compelled in doing so or willing to do so, or otherwise controlled in doing or willing to do so by any other agents or mechanisms. Each of these conditions can be satisfied for SFAs as conceived above.[10] The conditions can be summed up by saying, as we sometimes do, that the agents can choose either way, *at will*.

Note also that this account of self-forming choices amounts to a kind of "doubling" of the mathematical problem. It is as if an agent faced with such a choice is *trying* or making an effort to solve *two* cognitive problems at once, or to complete two competing (deliberative) tasks at once – in our example, to make a moral choice and to make a conflicting self-interested choice (corresponding to the two competing neural networks involved). Each task is being thwarted by the indeterminism coming from the other, so it might fail. But if it succeeds, then the agents can be held responsible because, as in the case of solving the mathematical problem, they will have succeeded in doing what they were knowingly and willingly trying to do. Recall the assassin and the husband. Owing to indeterminacies in their neural pathways, the assassin might miss his target or the husband fail to break the table. But if they *succeed*, despite the probability of failure, they are responsible, because they will have succeeded in doing what they were trying to do.

And so it is, I suggest, with self-forming choices, except that in the case of self-forming choices, *whichever way the agents choose* they will have succeeded in doing what they were trying to do because they were simultaneously trying to make both choices, and one is going to succeed. Their failure to do one thing is not a *mere* failure, but a voluntary succeeding in doing the other. Does it make sense to talk about the agent's trying to do two competing things at once in this way, or to solve two cognitive problems at once? Well, we now know that the brain is a parallel processor; it can simultaneously process different kinds of information relevant to tasks such as perception or recognition through different neural pathways. Such a capacity, I believe, is essential to the exercise of free will. In cases of self-formation (SFAs), agents are simultaneously trying to resolve plural and competing cognitive tasks. They are, as we say, of two minds. Yet they are not two separate persons. They are not dissociated from either task. The business woman who wants to go back to help the victim is the same ambitious woman who wants to go to her meeting and make a sale. She is torn inside by different visions of who she is and what she wants to be, as we all are from time to time. But this is the kind of complexity needed for genuine self-formation and free will. And when she succeeds in doing one of the things she is trying to do, she will endorse that as *her* resolution of the conflict in her will, voluntarily and intentionally, not by accident or mistake.

Responsibility, Luck and Chance

You may find all this interesting and yet still find it hard to shake the intuition that if choices are undetermined, they *must* happen merely by chance – and so must be "random," "capricious," "uncontrolled," "irrational," and all the other things usually charged. Such intuitions are deeply ingrained. But if we are ever going to understand free will, I think we will have to break old habits of thought that support such intuitions and learn to think in new ways. The first step in doing this is to question the intuitive connection in most people's minds between "indeterminism's being involved in something" and "its happening merely as a matter of chance or luck." "Chance" and "luck" are terms of ordinary language that carry the connotation of "its being out of my control." So using them already begs certain questions, whereas "indeterminism" is a technical term that merely precludes *deterministic* causation, though not causation altogether. Indeterminism is consistent with nondeterministic or probabilistic causation, where the outcome is not inevitable. It is therefore a mistake (alas, one of the most common in debates about free will) to assume that "undetermined" means "uncaused."

Here is another source of misunderstanding. Since the outcome of the businesswoman's effort (the choice) is undetermined up to the last minute, we may have the image of her first making an effort to overcome the temptation to go on to her meeting and then at the last instant "chance takes over" and decides the issue for her. But this is misleading. On the view I proposed, one cannot separate the indeterminism and the effort of will, so that *first* the effort occurs *followed* by chance or luck (or vice versa). One must think of the effort and the indeterminism as fused; the effort *is* indeterminate and the indeterminism is a property of the effort, not something separate that occurs after or before the effort. The fact that the effort has this property of being indeterminate does not make it any less the woman's *effort*. The complex recurrent neural network that realizes the effort in the brain is circulating impulses in feedback loops and there is some indeterminacy in these circulating impulses. But the whole process is her effort of will and it persists right up to the moment when the choice is made. There is no point at which the effort stops and chance "takes over." She chooses as a result of the effort, even though she might have failed. Similarly, the husband breaks the table as a result of his effort, even though he might have failed because of the indeterminacy. (That is why his excuse, "chance broke the table, not me", is so lame.)

Just as expressions like "she chose *by* chance" can mislead us in such contexts, so can expressions like "she got lucky." Recall that, with the assassin and husband, one might say "they got lucky" in killing the prime minister and breaking the table because their actions were un-determined. Yet they were responsible. So ask yourself this question: why does the inference "he got lucky, *so he was not responsible?*" fail in the cases of the husband and the assassin? The first part of an answer has to do with the point made earlier that "luck," like "chance," has question-begging implications in ordinary language that are not neces-sarily implications of "indeterminism" (which implies only the absence of deterministic causation). The core meaning of "he got lucky" in the assassin and husband cases, which *is* implied by indeterminism, I sug-gest, is that "he succeeded *despite the probability or chance of failure*"; and this core meaning does not imply lack of responsibility, *if he succeeds.*

If "he got lucky" had other meanings in these cases that are often associated with "luck" and "chance" in ordinary usage (for example, the outcome was not his doing, or occurred by *mere* chance, or he was not responsible for it), the inference would not fail for the husband and assassin, as it clearly does. But the point is that these further meanings of "luck" and "chance" do not follow *from the mere presence of indetermin-ism.* The second reason why the inference "he got lucky, so he was not responsible" fails for the assassin and the husband is that *what* they succeeded in doing was what they were *trying* and wanting to do all along (kill the minister and break the table respectively). The third reason is that *when* they succeeded, their reaction was not "oh dear, that was a mistake, an accident – something that *happened* to me, not something I *did.*" Rather they *endorsed* the outcomes as something they were trying and wanting to do all along, that is to say, knowingly and purposefully, not by mistake or accident.

But these conditions are satisfied in the businesswoman's case as well, *either way* she chooses. If she succeeds in choosing to return to help the victim (or in choosing to go on to her meeting) (1) she will have "succeeded *despite the probability or chance of failure,*" (2) she will have succeeded in doing what she was *trying* and *wanting* to do all along (she wanted both outcomes very much, but for different reasons, and was trying to make those reasons prevail in both cases), and (3) when she succeeded (in choosing to return to help) her reaction was not "oh dear, that was a mistake, an accident – something that happened to me, not something I did." Rather she *endorsed* the outcome as something she was trying and wanting to do all along; she recognized it as her resolution of the conflict in her will. And if she had chosen to go on to her meeting she would have endorsed that outcome, recognizing it as her resolution of the conflict in her will.

Perhaps the problem is that we are begging the question by assuming the outcomes of the woman's efforts are *choices* to begin with, if they are undetermined. One might argue this on the grounds that "if an event is undetermined, it must be something that merely *happens* and cannot be somebody's choice or action." But to see how question-begging such a claim would be, one has only to note what it implies: if something is a choice or action, it must be determined – that is, "all choices and actions are determined." Is this supposed to be true of necessity or by definition? If so, the free will issue would be solved by fiat. But beyond that, there is no reason to assume such a claim is true at all. Was the husband's breaking the table not something he *did* simply because the outcome was not determined? Recall that "undetermined" does not mean "uncaused." The breaking of the table was caused by the swing of his arm and, though the outcome was not inevitable, that was good enough for saying he did it and was responsible. Turning to choices, a choice is the formation of an intention or purpose to do something. It resolves uncertainty and indecision in the mind about what to do. Nothing in such a description implies that there could not be some indeterminism in the deliberation and neural processes of an agent preceding choice corresponding to the agent's prior uncertainty about what to do. Recall from preceding arguments that the presence of indeterminism does not mean the outcome happened merely by chance and not by the agent's effort. Self-forming choices are undetermined, but not uncaused. They are caused by the agent's efforts.

Well, perhaps indeterminism does not undermine the idea that something is a *choice* simply, but rather that it is the *agent's* choice. But again, why must it do that? What makes the woman's choice her own on the above account is that it results from her efforts and deliberation which in turn are causally influenced by her reasons and her intentions (for example, her intention to resolve indecision in one way or another). And what makes these efforts, deliberation, reasons, and intentions *hers* is that they are embedded in a larger motivational system realized in her brain in terms of which she defines herself as a practical reasoner and actor.[11] A choice is the agent's when it is produced intentionally by

efforts, deliberation, and reasons that are part of this self-defining motivational system and when, in addition, the agent *endorses* the new intention
or purpose created by the choice into that motivational system as a
further purpose to guide *future* practical reasoning and action.

Well, then, perhaps the issue is not whether the undetermined SFA is a
choice, or even whether it is the *agent's* choice, but rather how much
control she had over it. It may be true, as I argued earlier (in the discussion of plural voluntary control), that the presence of indeterminism need
not eliminate control altogether. But would not the presence of indeterminism at least *diminish* the control persons have over their choices and
other actions? Is it not the case that the assassin's control over whether
the prime minister is killed (his ability to realize his purposes or what he
is trying to do) is lessened by the undetermined impulses in his arm – and
so also for the husband and his breaking the table? And this limitation
seems to be connected with another problem often noted by critics of
libertarian freedom – the problem that indeterminism, wherever it
occurs, seems to be a *hindrance* or *obstacle* to our realizing our purposes and hence an obstacle to (rather than an enhancement of) our
freedom.

There is something to these claims, but I think what is true in them
reveals something important about free will. We should concede that
indeterminism, wherever it occurs, *does* diminish control over what we
are trying to do and *is* a hindrance or obstacle to the realization of our
purposes. But recall that in the case of the businesswoman (and SFAs
generally), the indeterminism that is admittedly diminishing her control
over one thing she is trying to do (the moral act of helping the victim) *is
coming from her own will* – from her desire and effort to do the opposite (go
to her business meeting). And the indeterminism that is diminishing her
control over the other thing she is trying to do (act selfishly and go to her
meeting) is coming from her desire and effort to do the opposite (to be a
moral person and act on moral reasons). So, in each case, the indeterminism *is* functioning as a hindrance or obstacle to her realizing one of her
purposes – a hindrance or obstacle in the form of resistance within her
will which has to be overcome by effort.

If there were no such hindrance – if there were no resistance in her will
– she would indeed in a sense have "complete control" over one of her
options. There would no competing motives that would stand in the way
of her choosing it. But then also she would not be free to rationally and
voluntarily choose the other purpose because she would have no good
competing reasons to do so. Thus, by *being* a hindrance to the realization
of some of our purposes, indeterminism paradoxically opens up the

genuine possibility of pursuing other purposes – of choosing or doing *otherwise* in accordance with, rather than against, our wills (voluntarily) and reasons (rationally). To be genuinely self-forming agents (creators of ourselves) – to have free will – there must at times in life be obstacles and hindrances in our wills of this sort that we must overcome.

Let me conclude with one final objection that is perhaps the most telling and has not yet been discussed. Even if one granted that persons, such as the businesswoman, could make genuine self-forming choices that were undetermined, isn't there something to the charge that such choices would be *arbitrary*? A residual arbitrariness seems to remain in all self-forming choices since the agents cannot in principle have sufficient or overriding *prior* reasons for making one option and one set of reasons prevail over the other. There is some truth to this charge as well, but again I think it is a truth that tells us something important about free will. It tells us that every undetermined self-forming free choice is the initiation of what I have elsewhere called a "value experiment" whose justification lies in the future and is not fully explained by past reasons. In making such a choice we say, in effect, "Let's try this. It is not required by my past, but it is consistent with my past and is one branching pathway my life can now meaningfully take. Whether it is the right choice, only time will tell. Meanwhile, I am willing to take responsibility for it one way or the other."[12]

It is worth noting that the term "arbitrary" comes from the Latin *arbitrium*, which means "judgment" – as in *liberum arbitrium voluntatis*, "free judgment of the will" (the medieval philosophers' designation for free will). Imagine a writer in the middle of a novel. The novel's heroine faces a crisis and the writer has not yet developed her character in sufficient detail to say exactly how she will act. The author makes a "judgment" about this that is not determined by the heroine's already formed past which does not give unique direction. In this sense, the judgment (*arbitrium*) of how she will react is "arbitrary," but not entirely so. It had input from the heroine's fictional past and in turn gave input to her projected future. In a similar way, agents who exercise free will are both authors of and characters in their own stories all at once. By virtue of "self-forming" judgments of the will (*arbitria voluntatis*) (SFAs), they are "arbiters" of their own lives, "making themselves" out of a past that, if they are truly free, does not limit their future pathways to one. Suppose we were to say to such actors, "But look, you didn't have sufficient or *conclusive* prior reasons for choosing as you did since you also had viable reasons for choosing the other way." They might reply, "True enough. But I did have *good* reasons for choosing as I did, which I'm willing to stand by *and take responsibility for*. If they were not sufficient or conclusive reasons, that's because, like the heroine of the novel, I was not a fully formed person before I chose (and still am not, for that matter). Like the author of the novel, I am in the process of writing an unfinished story and forming an unfinished character who, in my case, is myself."

Agent Causation

When I began discussing the intelligibility question several sections ago, I said I would avoid appealing to any "extra factors" to account for libertarian free agency, such as noumenal selves, transempirical power centers, or special forms of agent- or nonevent causation, that libertarians have often appealed to. The preceding account makes no such appeals. It does appeal to the fact that free choices and actions can be caused by efforts, deliberations, beliefs, desires, intentions, and other reasons or motives of agents. But this is causation by events or states of affairs involving agents. It is not the special causation of agent-causal theories that cannot be spelled out in terms of events or states of affairs involving agents, either physical or psychological.[13] Moreover, causation by efforts, beliefs, desires, intentions, and the like is something that even compatibilists appeal to in their accounts of free actions and choices; and it is hard to see how they could give accounts of free agency without doing so. The case is otherwise with such things as noumenal selves, transempirical power centers, or nonevent causation, which are invoked specifically *to salvage libertarian intuitions* about free will and are not needed by non-libertarians.

This is what I mean by not invoking "extra" factors. My account of free will postulates no additional ontological entities or relations that nonlibertarian acounts of free agency do not also need. It does postulate efforts, deliberations, desires, intentions, and the like, and causation of actions by these. But compatibilists must postulate these also if they are going to talk about *free agency*. The only added assumption I have made to account for libertarian free agency is just what you would expect – that some of the mental events or processes involved must be *undetermined*, so that the causation by mental events may be nondeterministic or probabilistic as well as deterministic.

Of course, if any such theory is to succeed, there must be some indeterminism in the brain where undetermined efforts and choices occur. But such a requirement holds for any libertarian theory. If free choices are undetermined, as libertarians suppose, there must be some indeterminacy in the natural world to make room for them; and it is an empirical question whether the indeterminism is there. This is true even if one postulates special kinds of agent-causes or a nonmaterial self to intervene in the brain. The indeterminism must be there to begin with in the brain, if these special forms of agency are to have room to operate. As the ancient Epicurean philosophers said, the atoms must sometimes "swerve" in undetermined ways, if there is to be room in nature for free will.

My suggestion about how indeterminism might enter the picture, if it were available in the physical world, was that conflicts in the wills of agents associated with self-forming choices would "stir up chaos" in the brain, sensitizing it to quantum indeterminacies at the neuronal level, which would then be magnified to effect neural networks as a whole. The brain would thus be stirred up by such conflict for the task of creative problem solving. This is speculative, to be sure. Others have suggested different ways in which indeterminacy might be involved in the brain and free will.[14] But such speculations are not entirely idle either. There is growing evidence that chaos may play a role in human cognitive processing, as it does in many complex physical systems, providing some of the flexibility that the nervous system needs to adapt creatively to an ever-changing environment.[15] Of course, chaotic behavior, though unpredictable, is usually deterministic and does not of itself imply indeterminism. But chaos does involve "sensitivity to initial conditions." Minute differences in the initial conditions of chaotic systems, including living things, may be magnified giving rise to large-scale undetermined effects. If the brain does "make chaos to make sense of the world" (as one recent research paper puts it),[16] its sensitivity to initial conditions may magnify quantum indeterminacies in neural networks whose outputs can depend on minute differences in the timing of firings of individual neurons. The general idea is that some combination of quantum physics and the new sciences of chaos and complexity in self-organizing systems may provide sufficient indeterminacy in nature for free will. But it is only an idea. The question is ultimately an empirical one, to be decided by future research.

What I have tried to do in this paper is answer a different, but equally daunting, question: what could we *do* with the indeterminism to make sense of free will, supposing it were there in the brain? Wouldn't the indeterminism just amount to chance? How could it amount to free will unless one added some "extra factor" in the form of a special kind of agent-causation or transempirical power center to account for agency? As a final test of the answer given to these questions in this essay, it will be instructive to conclude with the following question: what is missing in the account of free will presented in earlier sections that an extra postulate of a special form of nonevent *agent-causation* is supposed to provide? We could ask the same question for other extra factor strategies, such as noumenal selves, transempirical power centers, and the like. But most of these have gone out of favor in recent philosophy, while theories of nonevent agent- (or immanent) causation are still the most commonly discussed and defended libertarian theories today. So I will concentrate on contrasting agent-causal theories with the kind of libertarian theory I defend, which is often called *causal indeterminism*.

Let it be clear first of all that the causal indeterminist theory presented in this essay *does* postulate *agent causation* (though not of the nonevent or nonoccurrent kind). Agents *cause* or bring about their undetermined self-forming choices (SFAs) on this theory by making efforts to do so, voluntarily and intentionally; and agents cause or bring about many other things as well by making efforts to do so, such as deaths of prime ministers, broken tables, messes, accidents, fires, pains, and so on. Whether there is agent causation *in general* is not the issue here. What is at issue is agent-causation (hyphenated) – a *sui generis* form of causation postulated by agent-causal theorists that cannot be spelled out in terms of events and states of affairs involving the agents. It is misleading to frame this debate in such a way that libertarians who are agent-cause theorists believe in agent causation, while nonagent-causal libertarians like myself do not – presumably because we only believe in event causation. The fact is that both sides believe in agent causation. The issue is how it is to be spelled out.

And just as agents can be said to cause their self-forming choices (SFAs) and many other things, on the theory I proposed, so it can be said on this theory that agents *produce* or *bring about* their self-forming choices by making efforts to do so and *produce* many other things by their efforts and other actions. The point is worth making because defenders of agent-causation often claim that what causal indeterminist theories like mine lack – and what (nonevent) agent-causation is supposed to provide – is a conception of agents really *producing* or *bringing about* their undetermined free choices rather than those choices merely occurring by chance. But, as argued earlier, the mere presence of indeterminism does not imply that SFAs and other actions (such as the assassin's or husband's) occur *merely* by chance and not as a result of the agent's voluntary and intentional efforts. Of course, the causation or production in the case of SFAs is nondeterministic or probabilistic, since they are undetermined. But so it is also in the cases of the assassin and the husband who breaks his wife's table. And the burden of my argument was that such nondeterministic causation can support claims that agents really do *produce* what they cause by their voluntary efforts and can be held responsible for doing so.

So we are still looking for what the postulation of nonevent agent-causation is supposed to add to the picture that hasn't been captured. A perceptive recent defender of agent-causation, Timothy O'Connor, provides some further clues about this matter that are worth considering. Speaking to the issue of what causal indeterminist theories like mine lack that nonevent agent-causation is supposed to provide, O'Connor says the following. For causal indeterminist theories, "the agent's internal states [including reasons, motives, etc.] have objective tendencies of some determinate measure to cause certain outcomes. While this provides an *opening* in which the agent might freely select one option from a plurality of real alternatives, it fails to introduce a causal capacity that fills it. And what better here than its being the agent himself that causes the particular action that is to be performed?"[17] The missing element suggested in this quote is the "causal capacity" to "freely select one option from a plurality of real alternatives" that are left open by the (causal) indeterminism of prior events.

Now such a causal capacity is surely important. But why do we have to suppose that agent-causation of a nonevent kind is needed to capture it? The fact is that, on the causal indeterminist view presented, the agent *does* have such a causal capacity. Not only does the businesswoman facing an SFA have a plurality of real alternatives from which to choose, she has the *capacity* to make either choice by making an effort to do so. The conflicting motives in her will and the consequent divisions within her motivational system make it possible for her to choose either way for reasons, voluntarily and intentionally. And this is clearly a *causal* capacity since it is the capacity to *cause* or *produce* either choice outcome (nondeterministically, of course) as a result of her effort against resistance in her will.

This is a remarkable capacity to be sure; and we may assume that it is possessed only by creatures who attain the status of *persons* capable of self-reflection and having the requisite conflicts within their wills. So O'Connor's calling it a form of "*personal* causation" (O'Connor, forthcoming) is altogether apt. But there is no reason to suppose we need to postulate a *nonevent* form of causation to account for it. The *capacity* itself (prior to its exercise) is a complex dispositional *state* of the agent; and its *exercise* is a sequence of *events* or *processes* involving efforts leading to choice and formation of intention, which intention then guides subsequent action (of going back to help the victim or going on to a meeting).

This is a capacity *of* the agent, to be sure, but both the capacity and its exercise are described in terms of properties or states of the agent and in terms of states of affairs, events, and processes involving the agent, as I have done in the preceding paragraph and earlier in the essay.

Is there a residual fear functioning here that the "agent" will somehow disappear from the scene if we describe its capacities and their exercise, including free will, in terms of states and events? Such a fear would be misguided at best. A continuing substance (such as an agent) does not absent the ontological stage because we describe its continuing existence – its *life*, if it is a living thing – including its capacities and their exercise, in terms of states of affairs, events, and processes involving it. One needs more reason than this to think that there are no continuing things or substances, or no agents, but only events, or to think that agents do not cause things, only events cause things. For my part, I should confess that I am a substance ontologist and indeed something of an Aristotelian when it comes to thinking about the nature of living things and the relation of mind to body. Agents are continuing substances with both mental and physical properties. But there is nothing inconsistent in saying this and being a causal indeterminist about free will who thinks that the *lives* of agents, their capacities and the exercise of those capacities, including free will, must be spelled out in terms of states, processes, and events involving them.

Similar remarks are in order about O'Connor's (forthcoming) comments about "emergence" or "emergent properties" of agents (such as emergent causal capacities) in connection with free will. Issues about the existence of emergent properties (like issues about continuing substances) must also be distinguished from issues about nonevent causation. Indeed, I also believe that emergence of a certain kind (now recognized in self-organizing systems) is necessary for free will, even of the causal indeterminist kind that I defend. Once the brain reaches a certain level of complexity, so that there can be conflicts in the will of the kind required for SFAs, the larger motivational system of the brain stirs up chaos and indeterminacy in a part of itself which is the realization of a specific deliberation. In other words, the whole motivational system realized as a comprehensive "self-network" in the brain has the capacity to influence specific parts of itself (processes within it) in novel ways once a certain level of complexity of the whole is attained. This is a kind of emergence of new *capacities* and indeed even a kind of "downwards causation" (novel causal influences of an emergent whole on its parts) such as are now recognized in a number of scientific contexts involving self-organizing and ecological systems (Kuppers 1992; Kauffman 1995; Gilbert and Sarkar 2000).

But this kind of emergence characteristic of self-organizing systems does not, in and of itself, imply causation of a nonoccurrent or nonevent kind, since the wholes and parts involved are states and processes of the organism of various levels of complexity. Of course, O'Connor would like a stronger form of emergence, which would require nonoccurrent causation. But his argument – that some kind of emergence of capacities for holistic or downwards causation of wholes on parts is required for free will – does not prove the need for a *nonevent* kind of causation. Such emergence, which I agree is important for free will, can be accommodated within a theory of the kind I have proposed.

O'Connor (forthcoming) offers yet another argument when he says that what nonagent-causal theories lack and what agent-causation supplies is "the agent's directly controlling the outcome" of an undetermined choice. This is the issue of *control* about which I have said a great deal earlier in this essay. What is it for an agent to have direct *control* at a given time over a set of choice options (e.g., to help the assault victim or go on to a meeting)? The answer given earlier is embodied in the idea of plural voluntary control. Stating it more precisely, agents have plural voluntary control over a set of options at a time when they have the (1) *ability* or *capacity* to (2) *bring about* (3) at that time (4) *whichever* of the options they will or want, (5) for the reasons they will to do so, (6) on purpose or intentionally rather than accidentally, by mistake or merely by chance, hence (7) voluntarily (in accordance with their wills rather than against them), (8) as a result of their efforts, if effort should be required, (9) without being coerced or compelled or (10) otherwise controlled or forced to choose one way or the other by some other agent or mechanism. Agents *exercise* such control *directly* when they voluntarily and intentionally *produce* one of the options (a particular self-forming choice or SFA) *then and there* (at the time in question) under these conditions. I have argued here and in other writings that these conditions can be satisfied for SFAs without appealing to any kind of nonevent agent-causation.[18] Moreover, these conditions of plural voluntary control are the kinds we look for when deciding whether persons are or are not *responsible* for their choices or actions (e.g., when they produce something voluntarily and intentionally as a result of making an effort to do so).

Finally, I want to consider an objection about control made to my theory by another agent-causal theorist, Randolph Clarke. Clarke argues that causal indeterminist theories, like mine, provide "leeway" for choice, but no more control over actions *than compatibilists offer:* and more control than compatibilists offer is needed to account for the genuine libertarian free will and responsibility.[19] I agree that something more in the way of control than compatibilists offer is needed to account for libertarian free will. But I think the "more" control libertarians need is not more of the same *kind* of control compatibilists offer, but rather another kind of control altogether. The kind of control that concerns compatibilists is what might be called "antecedent determining control" – the ability to guarantee or determine *beforehand* which of a number of options is going to occur. If free choices are undetermined, we cannot have antecedent determining control over them, for exercising such control would mean *pre*determining them – determining beforehand just which choice we are going to make. (Even nonevent agent-causation cannot give us that.) What libertarians must require for undetermined SFAs is I think another kind of control altogether (that compatibilists cannot get) – namely, *ultimate* control – the originative control exercised by agents when it is "up to them" which of a set of possible choices or actions will now occur, and up to no one and nothing else over which the agents themselves do not also have control. This is the kind of control required by ultimate responsibility or UR and it is not something that can be captured by compatibilists, since it requires indeterminism. But neither does such ultimate control require nonevent causation, as I have been arguing. What it does require is the ability or capacity to cause or produce any one of a set of possible choices or actions each of which is undetermined (hence nondeterministically) and to do so "at will," that is, rationally (for reasons), voluntarily and intentionally.

Note also that there is a trade-off between this ultimate control and the antecedent determining control that compatibilists want. To have ultimate control over our destinies, we have to give up some antecedent determining control at crucial points in our lives. We have to accept a measure of uncertainty and genuine indeterminacy right up to the moment of decision. Indeterminism does not leave everything unchanged, for it implies "the probability or chance of failure" – though with genuine free will, every failing is also a succeeding, so we are responsible either way. If libertarians were after the same kind of control that compatibilists have to offer – only more of it – then I would agree with Clarke. But I think that what motivates the need for incompatibilism is an interest in a different kind of "control over our lives" altogether – a control which has to do with our being to some degree the ultimate creators or originators of our own purposes or ends and hence ultimate "arbiters" of our own wills. We can't have that in a determined world.

Notes

1 See especially *The Significance of Free Will* (1996), which provides an overview of philosophical debates about all four questions over the past 50 years and further development of many of the ideas of this paper. Also, see an earlier work, *Free Will and Values* (1985) and the articles cited in the suggested reading after this essay and in the bibliography.

2 For a formal statement and defense of this condition, see *The Significance of Free Will*, chapter 3.

3 For defenses of this claim by these authors see the readings in this volume by Dennett, Fischer, and Pereboom.

4 Kant, *The Critique of Practical Reason* (1956), part III.

5 Eccles, *Facing Reality* (1970).

6 For discussion and defense of this view, see the readings in this volume by Chisholm and O'Connor and the suggested reading at the end of each of them.

7 See the preceding essays in this part by van Inwagen and Ginet.

8 Readable and accessible introductions to the role of neural networks (including recurrent networks) in cognitive processing include P. M. Churchland, *The Engine of Reason. The Seat of the Soul* (1996) and Manfred Spitzer, *The Mind Within the Net* (1999).

9 We have to make further assumptions about the case to rule out some of these conditions. For example, we have to assume no one is holding a gun to the woman's head forcing her to go back, or that she is not paralyzed, etc. But the point is that none of these conditions is inconsistent with the case of the woman as we have imagined it. If these other conditions are satisfied, as they can be, and the businesswoman's case is otherwise as I have described it, we have an SFA. I offer the complete argument for this in *The Significance of Free Will*, chapter 8.

10 I show in greater detail that each of these conditions can be satisfied by SFAs in *The Significance of Free Will*, chapter 8.

11 That some such motivational system is necessary to define personhood and agency has been persuasively argued by Fred Dretske (1988), David Velleman (1922) and Owen Flanagan (1992). In *The Significance of Free Will* (pp. 137–42), I call the realization of such a system in the brain the "self-network."

12 *The Significance of Free Will*, pp. 145–6.

13 Mental causation (or causation by mental states such as beliefs and desires) is itself a matter of controversy among philosophers. But I am making only two simple points about it here. First, since mental causation must be assumed by compatibilist accounts of free agency as well as libertarian accounts like my own, whatever problems attach to the idea are not simply problems for libertarian theories or theories like mine. Second, causation by desires,

beliefs, etc. is causation by states or events and does not commit one to nonevent agent-causation. I think both points are defensible. Some libertarians who are simple indeterminists, such as Carl Ginet, would deny the first point (though not the second) since they argue that explanations of actions in terms of beliefs, desires and other mental states are not causal explanations at all. I disagree with this simple indeterminist view, but do not try to argue against it in this essay. See the preceding essay in this volume by Ginet and the suggested reading that follows it.

14 See H. Stapp, *Mind, Matter and Quantum Mechanics* (1993), D. Hodgson, *The Mind Matters* (1991), John Eccles, *How the Self Controls its Brain* (1994), R. Penrose, *Shadows of the Mind* (1994), I. Prigogine and I. Stengers, *Order Out of Chaos* (1984).

15 H. Walter, *Neurophilosophy of Free Will* (2001), summarizes much of this recent research. See also C. Skarda and W. Freeman, "How the Brain Makes Chaos in Order to Make Sense of the World" (1987) and A. Babloyantz and A. Destexhe, "Strange Attractors in the Human Cortex" (1985).

16 Skarda and Freeman. (See note 15.)

17 O'Connor (forthcoming).

18 See *The Significance of Free Will*, chapter 8 and "Responsibility, Luck and Chance: Reflections on Free Will and Indeterminism" (1999).

19 Clarke and others have also posed questions about the (dual) "efforts of will" that precede self-forming choices or SFAs on my theory. The SFAs are nondeterministically caused by these preceding efforts, but are the efforts themselves determined by the agent's prior reasons or motives? My answer is that the efforts agents make in SFA situations are *causally influenced* by their prior reasons or motives, but they are not strictly speaking determined by those reasons because the efforts themselves are indeterminate, which means there is some indeterminism involved in the complex neural processes realizing them in the brain. Thus, the reasons do not determine that an exact amount of effort will be made. This means that indeterminism enters the picture in two stages, first, with the efforts, then with SFAs. One might say that, with the efforts, one opens a "window" of indeterminacy whose upshot is that the choice outcome (the SFA) will not be determined. But the primary locus of indeterminism is in the moment of choice itself, the SFA. The latter is undetermined in a way that allows for robust alternative possibilities (making a moral choice or an ambitious choice). To prepare for this, a measure of indeterminacy enters the picture earlier, in the preceding indeterminate efforts. A related question: do the agents *cause* these efforts? No, not in the way they cause their SFAs, because the efforts are basic actions. Agents *make* the efforts, they do not cause them by doing something else. And what it means to say they make the efforts was spelled out earlier in the account of what it means to say that the businesswoman's choice was *hers*. Finally, are the efforts *freely* made? I distinguish three senses of freedom, all

of which I think are required for a complete account of free action and free will: (1) not being coerced, compelled, controlled etc., (2) acting "of one's own free will" in the sense of a will of one's own making (i.e., satisfying UR) and (3) being an undetermined self-forming action or SFA. Sense (1) is compatibilist (and I think it is necessary for free will, though not sufficient); senses (2) and (3) are incompatibilist. Efforts of will preceding SFAs are free in senses (1) and usually (2) also; SFAs (the full flowering of free will) are true in all three senses.

Comments and Questions on Robert Kane's "Free Will: New Directions for an Ancient Problem"

1.   Kane argues that not all actions done "of our own free wills" have to be undetermined on a libertarian view. Only some crucial actions in our lifetimes which he calls "self-forming actions" (SFAs) have to be undetermined. On what grounds does he argue for these claims? How can one believe that free will is incompatible with determinism and yet allow that something may be done "of our own free will" when it is not undetermined? And what is special about "self-forming actions" (SFAs), as Kane conceives them, that makes them so crucial for free will?

2.   It is natural to think that indeterminism or chance would undermine an agent's *control* and *responsibility* for action. It is also natural to think that indeterminism or chance would make actions merely "accidental" or "random," "capricious" and "irrational." Kane argues that contrary to what we might suppose, none of these claims are true. How does he go about trying to show this? Do you think he succeeds?

3.   A common objection made against all libertarian theories of free will, including the causal indeterminist theory presented in this reading, is called the "luck objection." The objection has been forcefully stated in different ways by Bruce Waller, Alfred Mele, Galen Strawson, Ishtiyaque Haji, Mark Bernstein, Richard Double, Bernard Berofsky, and Peter van Inwagen, among others. It goes like this: if indeterminism is true of choice, then the agent could have made different choices given exactly the same past. Suppose two persons had exactly the same pasts up to the point where they were faced with a choice between lying or telling the truth. One agent lies and the other tells the truth. As Bruce Waller (1990, p. 151) puts the luck objection: if the pasts of these two agents are really identical up to the moment of choice and the difference in their

acts is undetermined, would there be any grounds for distinguishing between them, for saying that one deserves censure for lying and the other praise for telling the truth? Wouldn't it be a matter of luck that they acted one way or the other? Alfred Mele poses the problem in a striking way in terms of one agent in different possible worlds. Suppose in the actual world John lies. If he could have done otherwise given exactly the same past, then we can imagine that in another possible world, which is exactly the same as the actual world up to the moment of choice, John's counterpart in this other possible world, call him John*, tells the truth rather than lying. Mele (1998, p. 582) then argues that "if there is nothing about the agents' powers, capacities, states of mind, moral character and the like that explains this difference in outcome, then the difference is just a matter of luck." It would seem that John* got lucky in his attempt to overcome temptation and do the right thing while John was unlucky. How if at all do you think Kane might respond to this "luck objection"? Do you think it can be successfully be countered by his view? Do you think the other libertarian theories we have considered, such as the agent-causation view or the simple indeterminist view, are subject to this luck objection also? Or would they escape it?

4.   Other causal indeterminist theories of free will different from Kane's have been put forward by Alfred Mele, *Autonomous Agents: From Control to Autonomy* (1995) and Laura Ekstrom, *Free Will* (2000), among others. They differ from Kane in placing the causal indeterminism earlier in the process of deliberation – in the prior coming to mind of thoughts and other considerations relevant to choice or in the prior formation of preferences – rather than in efforts of will and final choices that conclude deliberation, as does Kane. Mele, for example, thinks the luck objection (discussed in the previous question) makes it difficult to say that choices which conclude deliberations can be controlled by the agent if they are undetermined. But indeterminism, he thinks, could enter earlier in deliberation without undermining control. When, for example, I am deliberating about whether to vacation in one place or another, various images, thoughts, memories, may spring to mind that incline me toward favoring one option over the other. These "comings to mind" of relevant thoughts and considerations may very well be undetermined without undermining my control over the subsequent choice. For, what I proceed to *do* with these thoughts and considerations to conclude my deliberation *after* they come to mind need not be undetermined and could be under my control. Assess the pros and cons of this alternative causal indeterminist theory in relation to Kane's. Which do you think is preferable and why? Mele admits that his kind of causal

indeterminist account of freedom does not provide everything in the way of responsibility for choices and actions that libertarians (such as Kane, van Inwagen, Chisholm, Ginet, and O'Connor) might want. But he also thinks that because of the luck objection libertarians cannot *get* everything they want. Mele therefore argues that his modest libertarianism is the best that libertarians can do. Do you agree with him? Explain why or why not.

Suggested Reading

Kane's view is more fully developed in his book *The Significance of Free Will* (1996), which also provides an overview of debates about free will of the past half century. Kane attempts to answer the luck objection (see question 3 above) in "Responsibility, Luck and Chance: Reflections on Free Will and Indeterminism" (1999). He defends his view against critics in "On Free Will: Responses to Clarke, Haji and Mele" (1999a), also in "Responses to Bernard Berofsky, John Martin Fischer and Galen Strawson" (2000) and in "Free Will and Moral Responsibility: Three Recent Views" (with Ishtiyaque Haji and John Martin Fischer) (2000). Other causal indeterminist views, different from Kane's, but also developed as alternatives to agent-causation and simple indeterminism, include Alfred Mele, *Autonomous Agents: From Control to Autonomy* (1995) and Laura Waddell Ekstrom, *Free Will* (2000) (see question 4 above). Still others who have suggested causal indeterminist views include David Wiggins ("Towards a Reasonable Libertarianism," 1973), Richard Sorabji (*Necessity, Cause and Blame: Perspectives on Aristotle's Philosophy*, 1980), and Robert Nozick (*Philosophical Explanations*, 1981). For criticisms of causal indeterminist views, see the previous readings in this volume by O'Connor and Ginet, and also O'Connor's *Persons and Causes* (2000), Randolph Clarke's "Free Choice, Effort and Wanting More" (1999), Ishtiyaque Haji's "Indeterminism and Frankfurt-style Examples" (1999), Alfred Mele's "Ultimate Responsibility and Dumb Luck" (1999) and "Kane, Luck and the Significance of Free Will" (1999a), Bernard Berofsky's "Ultimate Responsibility in a Determined World" (2000), Galen Strawson's "The Impossibility of Moral Responsibility" (1994) and "The Unhelpfulness of Indeterminism" (2000). All three kinds of libertarian theory – agent-causalist, simple indeterminist and causal indeterminist – are discussed in the readings of *Agents, Causes and Events* (1995), edited by O'Connor.

16

Chess, Life and Superlife

David Hodgson

Editor's Introduction

David Hodgson is Chief Justice in Equity and an Additional Judge of Appeal of the Supreme Court of New South Wales, Australia. Although his career has been in the law, he has had a long interest and involvement in philosophy and has published works on science and mind, ethics and free will. In the reading that follows, Hodgson considers the question of how one might conceive an indeterminist account of free choice that is compatible with physical causation as suggested by quantum physics. He is particularly concerned with the question of how the existence of *purpose*, intelligence, and choice can exist in a universe governed by the laws of physics. Hodgson approaches this question in an unusual way by considering analogies provided by different kinds of games. He first considers ordinary games of chess, asking what the relation may be between the physical laws of nature and the rules of chess. He then considers the Game of Life, invented in 1970 by mathematician John Conway, in which systems evolve in accordance with simple rules in unpredictable ways. Finally, Hodgson considers a game of Superlife, which is a more complicated version of Life in an indeterministic universe. He finally asks which universe, the chess, Life, or Superlife universes, is more like our own.

[...] The general shape of an account of choice which is compatible with physical causation as suggested by quantum mechanics can be approached by considering analogies provided by games.

Chess

One early use of that kind of analogy was by Gilbert Ryle in *The Concept of Mind*: he suggested (Ryle 1949, p. 77) that we should not be concerned about what he called "the bogy of mechanism"; and he likened the laws of nature to the rules of the game of chess, pointing out the scope which is left in that game for the exercise of intelligence and choice. However, contrary to the main thesis of Ryle's book, that analogy in fact suggests a kind of *dualism*. If one took the constituents of the physical world to be like a chessboard and chess pieces, the laws of nature to be like the rules of chess, and the development over time of the world to be like the progress of a game of chess, then one would have to postulate something over and above the physical world and the laws of nature – something making choices between alternatives left open by the laws of nature – if one were to explain what goes on in this world; just as one has to postulate players making choices to explain what goes on in a game of chess.

Suppose that some human scientists, to whom the game of chess was unknown, somehow gained access to a universe, distinct from their own, which so far as they could ascertain consisted entirely of what we would understand to be myriad games of chess played competently (with reasonable skill, and no illegal moves) to a finish (no resignations or agreed draws). The space of that universe would be vast numbers of chessboards, the fundamental particles would be various kinds of chess pieces (in two colours); there would be successive discrete time-like steps, and also discrete whole processes corresponding to whole chess games.

The scientists would work out rules governing the movement of the various particles, and rules determining when each process came to an end (and the board in question returned to what they would recognise as an initial configuration). They would work out (1) what moves were possible for particles that we know as pawns, bishops, knights, etc.; (2) that, from the beginning to the end of a process, one particle moves in each time step, and different coloured particles move in successive time steps; (3) how particles can be caused to disappear (can be "captured"); (4) that the particle we know as a king (of either colour), alone of all particles, cannot move to any position where it could be captured by a particle of the other colour; and (5) that a process ends when a king can be captured in the next move by a particle of the other colour and cannot itself move ("checkmate"), or where none of the particles of the colour whose turn it is to move can move ("stalemate"), or where the same configuration of particles occurs three times ("draw by repetition").

They would also detect some further regularities. For example, where it was possible to end a process by "checkmate" in one time step, this would happen in almost all cases; and where it was possible for this to happen in three time steps, irrespective of what happens in the second of those time steps, it would happen in a great but lesser majority of cases. Where it was possible for a process to end in stalemate by one move of a particle of a certain colour, this would happen more often when there were fewer particles of that colour than when there were more. And so on. The scientists could work out quite extensive and elaborate statistics on such matters.

It may be that the scientists would come up with the hypothesis that there were two purposive systems operating in each process, one associated with each colour of the particles; with each system moving its particles with the purpose that the process end in "checkmate" of the king of the other colour, or at worst, in "stalemate" or "draw by repetition". That hypothesis would have the disadvantage that there would need to be much more to the universe in question than the space, the particles, the time-like steps, the mandatory rules, and the statistics: it would require that there also be whatever was necessary to constitute systems having purposes, and having the capabilities necessary to pursue those purposes with some effectiveness. However, the hypothesis would not be excluded by the fact that all observations were substantially in accordance with the statistics which the scientists had worked out; and it would have the advantage that it would make sense of the statistics, which would otherwise be brute facts with no rhyme or reason. If the scientists happened to become aware of the game of chess in their own universe, I think it is likely that they would prefer this "dualistic" hypothesis. (Of course, it could turn out that the purposive systems in fact operated wholly in accordance with deterministic rules other than those of the rules of chess, as do chess-playing computers in our world; but that is another matter – in a chess universe, such systems would still involve a dualism.)

Life

Now suppose that these scientists gain access to a second universe, which so far as they could ascertain consists entirely of what we would understand to be the Game of Life, played on a vast scale. This game was devised in about 1970 by John Conway, a Cambridge mathematician. Its rules can be stated shortly:

> Life occurs on a virtual [and potentially infinite] checkerboard. The squares are called cells. They are in one of two states: alive or dead. Each cell has eight possible neighbours, the cells of which touch its sides or corners.

If a cell on the checkerboard is alive, it will survive in the next time step (or generation) if there are either two or three neighbours also alive. It will die of overcrowding if there are more than three live neighbours, and it will die of exposure if there are fewer than two.

If a cell on the checkerboard is dead, it will remain dead unless exactly three of its eight neighbours are alive. In that case, the cell will be "born" in the next generation (Levy 1993, p. 52).

It is clear that, once an initial configuration of live cells is set up, everything that happens thereafter in this game is entirely determined by these rules. However, given an initial state with sufficient potential, the game unfolds in ways which have some similarities to life in our world. In particular: (1) large-scale events occur, which in many cases unfold in accordance with large-scale rules; (2) minute differences in initial configurations can produce huge differences in outcomes; and (3) accordingly, there is substantial unpredictability as to what will happen when previously unknown large-scale configurations arise.

The space of the Life universe to which our scientists gain access would be a limitless checkerboard, the fundamental particles would be the two possible states of each square or cell ("alive" and "dead"), and there would be successive discrete time-like steps. The scientists would no doubt work out Conway's two rules: if a cell is alive in one time-step, it will be alive in the next time-step if and only if 2 or 3 of the 8 adjoining cells are alive; and if a cell is dead in one time-step, it will be alive in the next time-step if and only if 3 of the 8 adjoining cells are alive. They would hypothesize that everything that happens in this universe is determined by those two rules; and that hypothesis would not be falsified. They would observe interesting larger-scale patterns, and no doubt would work out rules relating to the development of these patterns; but these rules could only indicate the same developments as the two basic rules indicate. The scientists would be unlikely to hypothesise that any purposive systems were operating in this universe.

What about our own universe? Is it more like the chess universe, or the Life universe?

It seems to me fair to say that, after Descartes, a common view among educated Westerners would have been that the physical universe is like the Game of Life everywhere except in parts of the human brain, where (perhaps in the vicinity of the pineal gland) it is like chess. By the end of the nineteenth century, advances in the physical sciences, coupled with Darwin's theory of evolution, had given rise to a strongly competing view among educated Westerners that there is nothing about the human brain to suggest that different rules apply there; and that our universe is like the Game of Life everywhere.

Twentieth-century science has told us a lot more about the details of the laws of nature governing the development of our universe. Obviously, the laws are vastly more complicated than the rules of the Game of Life; but that in itself does not suggest any efficacious purposive systems. In addition, however, it appears that the laws of nature are partly indeterministic – so that they allow for genuine alternatives in the way our universe develops over time. These alternatives, however, seem to occur randomly within statistical parameters; and they generally tend to cancel out at scales much above that of atoms and molecules, so that at those larger scales, we generally seem to have rules which are as deterministic as those of the Game of Life.

One way of putting the issues which I see as dividing the approach to human purpose of people like myself, who contemplate a substantive role for purposive choice and free will, from that of the majority of scientists, who don't, is this: could the indeterminism, which appears to exist at the atomic level, (1) give rise to genuinely open alternatives at the level of human choice and action (like the alternatives open to a chess player); and (2) involve the actual exercise of choice and purpose in selection between those alternatives?

Superlife

Let us now suppose our scientists gain access to a third universe. In this universe, there appears to be a vast and complex game – let us call it Superlife – with regularities which suggest some deterministic and some statistical rules. There also appear in this universe to be many broadly integrated and continuous systems of vast numbers of the particles of this universe, which the scientists call "agents". Each of the states of these systems is unique, being different from all its own earlier states and from all states of all other systems; but contains traces of its own earlier states, which the scientists call "memories". These systems appear to develop over time generally in accordance with the rules of the universe (deterministic and statistical). But unlike the Life universe, the rules of this universe cannot be shown to exclude genuine alternatives in the development of these systems, at a macroscopic scale which the scientists can readily observe; and developments which actually occur tend to suggest that each of the agents is a purposive system, just as was suggested in the case of the systems associated with the different colours in each process in the chess universe.

The scientists come up with two rival hypotheses about this third universe. One is that the development over time of this universe is entirely governed by deterministic and/or statistical rules (and is purely random within the probability parameters indicated by the statistical rules): insofar as purpose appears to be displayed by the systems they call agents, this does not involve genuine choices between available alternatives, and is explained entirely by the history of how these systems were produced, over aeons of time, through countless generations of earlier systems which emerged and dissipated ("evolution"). The other hypothesis is that, while the development over time of the universe does conform to rules, there are leeways left by these rules, and within those leeways the systems called agents really do pursue purposes and really do make choices, between alternatives which the rules really do leave open to them: each choice between such alternatives is a unique efficacious occurrence, determined not by any rules but *by the system itself in its then unique unprecedented state*, with only the alternatives and tendencies being determined by the rules.

The former hypothesis has the advantage of simplicity: there is no need to postulate anything beyond the particles, space, time, and the rules (deterministic and statistical). The latter does require the additional postulate of purpose or choice; but in this universe, unlike the chess universe, there is no necessity to postulate that there is anything more to this universe than the game. Conceivably, it could just be a fact about Superlife that these systems, by virtue of their own properties coupled with the rules and the existence of alternatives, can detect the existence of alternatives and nonconclusive reasons supporting these alternatives, and can make a choice between the alternatives on the basis of those reasons.

Assuming that the scientists can experiment with this Superlife universe, they could try to refute one or other of these hypotheses – but it could be difficult. On the one hand, the scientists could try to show that what appear to be genuine macroscopic alternatives are not really open, or are not relevant to the apparent purposes of the systems. On the other hand, they could try to show that the systems appear to have and give effect to purposes in ways that can't be fully explained by rules and randomness and evolution.

But suppose now that, in the absence of any conclusive or near-conclusive experiment, the scientists notice that the Superlife universe is indistinguishable from their own universe, that the apparently purposive systems are indistinguishable from human beings in their own universe, and that these systems in fact report having experiences and purposes which seem to the scientists to be similar to those which the scientists themselves have. To me, that would make it reasonable for the scientists to treat very seriously indeed the hypothesis that there are real choices and purposes in the Superlife universe – *as indeed in their own.*

Summary

So: I have discussed three types of universe – a chess universe, a Life universe, and a Superlife universe. The chess universe involves outright *dualism*, with purpose provided entirely from outside the particles and rules of the physical universe. The Life universe is a *monistic physicalist* universe, in which everything that happens is just a working out of the behaviour of the particles as required by the rules of the universe. The Superlife universe, our own, appears to have within it both rules and purpose: the mainstream scientific view at present would have it that it is just a more elaborate version of a Life-type universe, with the apparent purposeful conduct being simply the working out of the rules, with or without randomness; whereas I would argue that a very plausible alternative is a strong *dual aspect* view, according to which genuine choice coexists with statistics within a unitary universe, and within certain unitary systems of that universe – with the statistics being apparent to an objective, third-person, physical viewpoint; and choice being apparent to a subjective, first-person, mental viewpoint, and involving real selection between alternatives which the physical viewpoint can only treat as statistical probabilities. In such a universe, there could be compatibility between (apparent) randomness and choice.

Comments and Questions on David Hodgson's "Chess, Life and Superlife"

1.   Hodgson is concerned with the question of how purpose, intelligence, and choice can exist in a world governed by the laws of physics. We normally think of the laws of physics as *mechanistic* and mechanism is the opposite of *purpose*. To counter this fear of mechanism, Gilbert Ryle likened the laws of nature governing the universe to the rules of a game of chess. Though the movements on a chessboard do not violate the laws of physics, nonetheless there is purpose in the movements of the pieces. Hodgson objects that the purpose of a game of chess is not *inside* the

universe of movements happening on the chessboard. The purpose in the movements is coming from outside (from the minds of the players who are moving the pieces). Thus he argues that Ryle's analogy assumes a kind of *dualism* of mind and body – the physical world being entirely mechanistic and the purpose coming from minds outside it. Is this objection of Hodgson's to Ryle's analogy a cogent one in your view? How, if at all, does his analogy of another universe of chessboards studied by human scientists support his objection to Ryle?
2.   Hodgson argues that the Game of Life analogy (that the universe is everywhere like Conway's Game of Life) avoids the "dualism" that infects the chess analogy. Why? He also argues that while, in a Game of Life universe, complex systems may emerge from simple rules, nonetheless in such a universe there is no room for "the actual exercise of choice and purpose in selection between" open alternatives. He argues that this is true even if such a universe is governed by indeterministic laws and thus allows open alternatives. What exactly are his arguments for these claims and do you think they are cogent?
3.   What does Hodgson mean by a Superlife universe and how does it differ from a Game of Life universe? How does he think a Superlife universe might make room for genuine purpose *in* the universe rather than outside it, as in the case of the chess universe?

Suggested Reading

Hodgson's views about physics, mind and freedom are developed further in *The Mind Matters* (1991). Further discussions about how libertarian free will might fit into an indeterministic universe include Storrs McCall, *A Model of the Universe* (1994), and Karl Popper and John Eccles, *The Self and Its Brain* (1977). An interesting collection of essays on physics, neuroscience and free will is B. Libet, A. Freeman, and K. Sutherland (eds.), *The Volitional Brain* (1999).

Part V:

Religion and Free Will: Divine Foreknowledge and Human Freedom

17

Divine Foreknowledge, Evil and the Free Choice of the Will

St. Augustine

Editor's Introduction

St Augustine of Hippo (354–430) was one of the most influential religious thinkers of the Western tradition. He was the last of the early fathers of the Christian Church and the greatest philosopher among them. The following selection is from his treatise, *On the Free Choice of the Will* (391), which was a seminal work for most later discussions of the religious dimensions of the free will problem in Western philosophy. In this work, Augustine poses the question of why there is evil in the world (the so-called "problem of evil"), since God is its creator and is supposed to be perfectly good. Augustine's answer is that God is not the source of the world's evils. Rather God gives creatures, such as humans and angels, free will and the evils of the world arise from the free choices of these creatures. This is the classic "free will defense" for the problem of evil. Free will must be one of the "good things," says Augustine, since God is willing to put up with the possibility of evil, sometimes horrendous evil, in order to give it to creatures. Free will is a good thing because without it there would be no *moral* good or evil among creatures, no genuine responsibility or blameworthiness, and creatures could not choose to love God "of their own free wills" (love being a greater good when it is *freely* given). But if free will is one of the good things and God has indeed given it to us, this raises a further question. How can we have free will, if God has foreknowledge of everything we do and has had such foreknowledge since before we existed? Would that not mean that everything we do was determined long before we were born? At this point the following selection begins. *On the Free Choice of the Will* is written as a dialogue between a student named Euodius and Augustine himself.

Euodius. ...I am deeply troubled by a certain question: how can it be that God has foreknowledge of all future events, and yet that we do not sin by necessity? Anyone who says that an event can happen otherwise than as God has foreknown it is making an insane and malicious attempt to destroy God's foreknowledge. If God, therefore, foreknew that a good man would sin (and you must grant this, if you admit with me that God foreknows all future events) – if this is the case, I do not say that God should not have made the man, for He made him good, and the sin of the man He made cannot hurt God at all (on the contrary, in making him, God showed His goodness, for He showed His justice in punishing the man and His mercy in forgiving him); I do not say that God should not have made the man, but I do say this: since He foreknew that the man would sin, the sin was committed of necessity, because God foreknew that it would happen. How can there be free will where there is such inevitable necessity? [...]

Augustine. How clearly truth cries out from you! For you could not maintain that anything is in our power except actions that are subject to our own will. Therefore, nothing is so completely in our power as the will itself, for it is ready at hand to act immediately, as soon as we will. Thus we are right in saying that we grow old by necessity, not by will; or that we die by necessity, not by will, and so on. Who but a madman would say that we do not will with the will?

Therefore, though God foreknows what we shall will in the future, this does not prove that we do not will anything voluntarily. [...]

Our will [...] is not a will unless it is in our power. And since it is indeed in our power, it is free in us. What we do not, or cannot, have in our power is not free for us. So it follows that we do not deny that God has foreknowledge of all things to be, and yet that we will what we will. For when He has foreknowledge of our will, it is going to be the will that He has foreknown. Therefore, the will is going to be a will because God has foreknowledge of it. Nor can it be a will if it is not in our power. Therefore, God also has knowledge of our power over it. So the power is not taken from me by His foreknowledge; but because of His foreknowledge, the power to will will more certainly be present in me, since God, whose foreknowledge does not err, has foreknown that I shall have the power.[...]

E. ...I do not dare deny any of these points. Yet I still cannot see how God's foreknowledge of our sins can be reconciled with our free choice in sinning. God must, we admit, be just and have foreknowledge. But I would like to know by what justice God punishes sins which must be; or how it is that they do not have to be, when He foreknows that they will be; or why anything which is necessarily done in His creation is not to be attributed to the Creator.

A. Why do you think that our free choice is opposed to God's foreknowledge? Is it simply because it *is* foreknowledge or, rather, because it is God's foreknowledge?

E. Because it is God's.

A. If you foreknew that someone was going to sin, would it not be necessary for him to sin?

E. Yes, he would have to sin, for my foreknowledge would not be genuine unless I foreknew what was certain.

A. Then it is not because it is God's foreknowledge that what He foreknew had to happen, but only because it is foreknowledge. It is not foreknowledge if it does not foreknow what is certain.

E. I agree. But why are you making these points?

A. Because unless I am mistaken, your foreknowledge that a man will sin does not of itself necessitate the sin. Your foreknowledge did not force him to sin even though he was, without doubt, going to sin; otherwise you would not foreknow that which was to be. Thus, these two things are not contradictories. As you, by your foreknowledge, know what someone else is going to do of his own will, so God forces no one to sin; yet He foreknows those who will sin by their own will.

Why cannot He justly punish what He does not force to be done, even though He foreknows it? Your recollection of events in the past does not compel them to occur. In the same way God's foreknowledge of future events does not compel them to take place. As you remember certain things that you have done and yet have not done all the things that you remember, so God foreknows all the things of which He Himself is the Cause, and yet He is not the Cause of all that He foreknows. He is not the evil cause of these acts, though He justly avenges them. You may understand from this, therefore, how justly God punishes sins; for He does not do the things which He knows will happen. Besides, if He ought not to exact punishment from sinners because He foresees that they will sin, He ought not to reward those who act rightly, since in the same way He foresees that they will act rightly. On the contrary, let us acknowledge both that it is proper to His foreknowledge that nothing should escape His notice and that it is proper to His justice that a sin, since it is committed voluntarily, should not go unpunished by His judgement, just as it was not forced to be committed by His foreknowledge.

Comments and Questions on St. Augustine's "Divine Foreknowledge, Evil and the Free Choice of the Will"

1.   Augustine says that our will would not be our will unless it were in our power and because it is in our power we are free. The fact that God foreknows what we will do does not take that power to will away from us, he is saying. We still exercise that power to will when we choose. It is our doing, so we are responsible for it. Is this a satisfactory answer to Euodius's worries about foreknowledge and free will in your view? Why or why not?

2.   It is often said that merely foreknowing that something will happen does not mean that one *makes* it happen. Imagine a team of behavior scientists watching the behavior of humans in a laboratory through a large glass window. They know enough to predict what the behavior of the humans in the laboratory will be, but they never intervene. They forever remain behind the screen while the humans go about their business. It seems that the humans would always be acting on their own – making choices and carrying them out – just as they would if the scientists were not behind the screen. So the presence of the scientists should make no difference to their power and freedom. If they were free in the one scenario without the scientists, they should be equally free with the scientists present since the scientists never actually interefere in their behavior. It seems that Augustine is saying that God's foreknowing our behavior is like this. It does not take away our power. Is this a good argument? Does the mere presence and knowledge of the scientists or God make any difference?

3.   Euodius also seems to be saying that if God has foreknowledge, then our actions would be *necessary* and hence determined. But Augustine in response suggests that this involves a confusion about the meaning of necessity. What is true is that (1) "necessarily, if God foreknows that you will do A, then you will do A" (where the necessity attaches to the whole "if . . . then . . ." statement). But it does not follow from (1) that (2) "necessarily you will do A." To think that (2) follows from (1) is a well-known fallacy of modal logic. Does the fact that going from (1) to (2) is a fallacy suffice to show that God's foreknowledge does not entail that our actions are necessitated?

Suggested Reading

Two informative essays on Augustine's views on freedom and foreknowledge are David Hunt, "On Augustine's Way Out" (1999) and Scott MacDonald, "Primal Sin" (1999). The latter essay is in a collection edited by Gareth Matthews, *The Augustinian Tradition* (1999), which deals with Augustine's philosophy and theology generally. For further modern discussion of the foreknowledge/freedom problem see John Martin Fischer (ed.), *God, Freedom and Foreknowledge* (1989), and W. S. Anglin, *Free Will and the Christian Faith* (1990). Also see the suggested readings after the next reading selection.

18

God, Time, Knowledge and Freedom: The Historical Matrix

William Hasker

Editor's Introduction

William Hasker is Professor of Philosophy at Huntington College in Indiana. The following selection is taken from his book *God, Time and Knowledge* (1989), which is a comprehensive discussion of the problem of divine foreknowledge and human freedom. The reading selection provides a clear account of the history of the problem and the major figures who have contributed to it, including Augustine, Boethius, Thomas Aquinas, William of Ockham, and Luis de Molina. Hasker also examines the major solutions to the problem of foreknowledge and freedom today, including the "eternalist solution," which appeals to God's eternity and timeless knowledge of events, the "Ockhamist solution," which distinguishes between hard and soft facts about the past, and the "Molinist solution," which appeals to God's so-called "middle knowledge," concerning how agents would freely act under certain counterfactual conditions. Hasker explains and critically discusses each of these solutions. He also shows how the problem of foreknowledge and free will is related to a number of other theological concerns about divine *providence* and *prophecy*.

It seems probable that whenever theistic belief encounters or engenders a tradition of philosophical reflection, questions will arise about the relation between divine knowledge and power and human freedom. The Stoics wrestled with such problems, and Cicero framed what may have been the first argument for the incompatibility of foreknowledge and free will, in the form of an argument against divination. The Jewish and Moslem traditions have contributed their share of reflection on these matters. But the fullest and richest development of these questions has occurred in the Christian theological tradition, beginning at least as early as Origen and reaching a climax in the debates of the sixteenth and seventeenth centuries. [...]

Five major figures have been selected for brief treatment here; each played a major role in the development of the tradition, and between them they articulate most of the major alternatives with which we must deal.[1]

Augustine

Augustine of Hippo (354–430) has the distinction of having occupied, and perhaps created, three distinct positions that are relevant to our topic. In the early book *On Free Will* he discusses the classical problem of foreknowledge and free will, and offers some answers that still resonate today:

> *Euodius.* . . . I still do not see why these two things – God's foreknowledge of our sins, and our free choice in sinning – are not opposed to one another. . . .
> *Augustine.* Why then do you think that our free choice is opposed to God's foreknowledge? Is it because it is foreknowledge, or because it is God's foreknowledge?
> E. Rather because it is God's.
> A. Well, if you foreknew that someone was going to sin, would it not be necessary that he should sin?
> E. Surely it would be necessary that he should sin, for it would not be foreknowledge, if I did not foreknow a certainty.
> A. Therefore, it is necessary that what God foreknows must happen, not because it is God's foreknowledge, but simply because it is foreknowledge; for if what He foreknew were not certain it would be no foreknowledge.
> E. I agree: but why are you making these points?
> A. Because if I am not mistaken you would not necessarily compel a man to sin who you foreknow was going to sin; although without doubt he will sin, for otherwise you would not foreknow that it will be so. And so, just as these two are not opposed, that you know by your foreknowledge what another is going to do of his own will: so God, while compelling no one to sin, nevertheless foresees those who will sin of their own volition.[2]

Here Augustine deploys two of the classical arguments for the compatibility of foreknowledge and free will – or, as we shall say henceforth, for compatibilism: Knowledge as such does not compel, and human beings are able to foreknow the free actions of others without removing their freedom. Nevertheless, there remains the implication, accepted by both Euodius and Augustine, that if a person's sin is foreknown, whether by God or by another person, it is necessary that the person should sin;[3] the necessity involved here, however, is held not to be incompatible with free will.

The second major position occupied – and in this case, we can say confidently, created – by Augustine, is the doctrine that God is timelessly eternal and has timeless knowledge of temporal events.[4] In his famous words from the *Confessions*:

> Nor dost Thou by time, precede time: else shouldest Thou not precede all times. But Thou precedest all things past, by the sublimity of an ever-present eternity; and surpassest all future because they are future, and when they come, they shall be past; but Thou art the Same, and Thy years fail not. Thy years neither come nor go; whereas ours both come and go, that they all may come. Thy years stand together, because they do stand; nor are departing thrust out by coming years, for they pass not away; but ours shall all be, when they shall no more be. Thy years are one day; and Thy day is not daily, but To-day, seeing Thy To-day gives not place unto tomorrow, for neither doth it replace yesterday. Thy To-day, is Eternity.[5]

What may puzzle us is that this conception, destined to play such a momentous role in the controversy over divine foreknowledge, was so far as we can tell never employed to this end by Augustine himself. It may be that Augustine was fully satisfied with the answers he had given in *On Free Will* and thus felt no need for further illumination on this topic. And on the other hand it is possible that the connection between divine eternity and the foreknowledge problem, which seems so evident since it was made by Boethius, is in itself neither evident nor inevitable. My favorite solution to the puzzle, however, goes in another direction: I surmise that by the time Augustine wrote the *Confessions* his commitment to belief in free will in anything approaching the libertarian sense[6] had been sufficiently weakened that he was no longer disposed to feel the foreknowledge problem as a pressing one. It is acknowledged that Augustine reached a turning point in his thought about grace and free will in the first of his two books *To Simplician – On Various Questions*.[7] Of this book he said in his *Retractions*, "In answering this question [concerning Romans 9:10–29] I have tried hard to maintain the free choice of the human will, but the grace of God prevailed."[8] Evidence for the effect of this change on Augustine's thinking about foreknowledge will be drawn from a passage in *The City of God* in which he once again addresses that topic. The occasion is an argument of Cicero's against foreknowledge,[9] which Augustine summarizes as follows:

> What is it, then, that Cicero feared in the prescience of future things? Doubtless it was this – that if all future things have been foreknown, they will happen in the order in which they have been foreknown; and if they come to pass in this order, there is a certain order of things foreknown by God; and if a certain order of things, then a certain order of causes, for nothing can happen which is not preceded by some efficient cause. But if there is a certain order of causes according to which everything happens which does happen, then by fate, says he, all things happen which do happen. But if this be so, then is there nothing in our own power, and there is no such thing as freedom of will; and if we grant that, says he, the whole economy of human life is subverted.[10]

Augustine replies:

> We assert both that God knows all things before they come to pass, and that we do by our free will whatsoever we know and feel to be done by us only because we will it.... But it does not follow that, though there is for God a certain order of all causes, there must therefore be nothing depending on the free exercise of our own wills, for our wills themselves are included in that order of causes which is certain to God, and is embraced by His foreknowledge, for human wills are also causes of human actions; and He who foreknew all the causes of things would certainly among those causes not have been ignorant of our wills.[11]

Note Augustine's assertion that "we do by our free will whatsoever we know and feel to be done by us only because we will it"; no concern is evinced here about prior, determining *psychological* causes, and the statement is strongly suggestive of what would now be termed a "soft determinist"[12] conception of free will. Even more revealing, however, is Augustine's response to Cicero's charge that, given foreknowledge, there is "a certain order of causes according to which everything happens which does happen." In responding to this claim, with its powerful evocation of determinism, Augustine does not say, as a modern libertarian would say, that the free will functions as an uncaused or undetermined cause and that the "order of causes" is thus not deterministic. Nor does he object to Cicero's assumption that it is only through such a deterministic order that God could foreknow the future. What he says, rather, is that the will is *included in* the order of causes. But a "free will" that can be part of a deterministic order of causes is surely a soft determinist free will, not one that is free in the libertarian sense. Augustine's answer to Cicero is a rather clear statement of theological determinism.

Boethius

Augustine's influence on subsequent theology and philosophy was immense, but his deterministic position on grace and free will did not become normative in any branch of the church until the Reformation. So the problem of foreknowledge and free will remained on the agenda, and Boethius (480–524) took the important step of viewing, and indeed resolving, the issue in terms of Augustine's conception of divine eternity. For the definition of eternity, we turn to *The Consolation of Philosophy*:

> Now, eternity is the complete possession of an endless life enjoyed as one simultaneous whole; this will appear clearer from a comparison with temporal things. For whatever is living in time proceeds in the present from times past to times future; and nothing existing in time is so constituted as to embrace the whole span of its life at once, but it has not yet grasped tomorrow, while it has already lost yesterday. In this life of today you are living in no more than a fleeting, transitory moment. . . . What is rightly called eternal is that which grasps and possesses simultaneously the entire fullness of an unending life, a life which lacks nothing of the future and has lost nothing of the fleeting past. Such a being must necessarily always be its whole self, unchangingly present to itself, and the infinity of changing time must be as one present before him.[13]

He states the implications for God's knowledge:

> Since, then, every judgment comprehends the objects of its thought according to its own nature, and since God has an ever present and eternal state, His knowledge also, surpassing every temporal movement, remains in the simplicity of its own present and, embracing infinite lengths of past and future, views with its own simple comprehension all things as if they were taking place in the present. If you will weigh the foresight with which God discerns all things, you will rightly esteem it to be the knowledge of a never fading instant rather than a foreknowledge of the "future." It should therefore rather be called *provision* than *prevision* because, placed high above all lowly things, it looks out over all as from the loftiest mountain top.[14]

Boethius also addresses the "necessity" that, according to Augustine, attaches to anything that is foreknown, either by God or by human beings. He distinguishes two kinds of necessity:

> One is simple: for instance, it is necessary that all men are mortal. The other is conditional: for instance, if you really know that a man is walking, he must be walking. For what a man really knows cannot be otherwise than it is known to be. But the conditional kind of necessity by no means implies the simple kind.... Therefore free acts, when referred to the divine intuition, become necessary in the conditional sense because God's knowledge provides that condition; on the other hand, viewed by themselves, they do not lose the perfect freedom of their nature. Without doubt, then, all things which God foreknows do come to pass, but certain of them proceed from free will.[15]

The point, I take it, is this: Once we have distinguished conditional necessity from simple necessity (what Aquinas was to call "absolute" necessity), it is evident that only the latter is inconsistent with free will. It is clear, furthermore, from our own case, that *present* knowledge does not imply simple necessity: If I know that you are walking, this does not imply that your walking is necessary. It might, however, be thought that *fore*knowledge implies simple necessity – for instance, because (as Cicero and the late Augustine agree) foreknowledge requires a "certain order of causes." But given divine timelessness, *fore*knowledge is precisely what we do not have.

Aquinas

Thomas Aquinas (1225–1274), as is well known, embraced the Boethian doctrine of divine timelessness, and by doing so he contributed greatly to its continued popularity down to the present. He is noted here, however, rather for his statement of one of the *objections* to God's knowledge of future contingent things: By a more penetrating statement of the argument for incompatibilism, he also brought about new insight into the character of the answer provided by the doctrine of timelessness. To set the stage for this, we return briefly to Euodius's statement of the argument for incompatibilism, a statement that is typical of many others: "But I would like to know ... how it is that [sins] do not have to be, when He foreknows that they will be."[16] Now this argument is not completely stated, but it may seem reasonable to suppose that it is an instance of the form:

Necessarily, if God knows that *P*, then *P*.
God knows that *P*.
Therefore, necessarily *P*.

But of course, this argument is invalid, which may lead us to suppose that Augustine could, and should, have dealt with it even more summarily than he actually did. Now, I am by no means certain that the argument is correctly and perspicuously represented by the form suggested above, though it does undeniably leave itself open to this interpretation . . .

If you do doubt this, then you are ready for Thomas's formulation of the argument, which is as an objection to his claim that God knows future contingent things:

> Every conditional proposition of which the antecedent is absolutely necessary, must have an absolutely necessary consequent. For the antecedent is to the consequent as principles are to the conclusion: and from necessary principles only a necessary conclusion can follow, as is proved in *Poster.* i. But this is a true conditional proposition, *If God knew that this thing will be, it will be*, for the knowledge of God is only of true things. Now the antecedent of this is absolutely necessary, because it is eternal, and because it is signified as past. Therefore the consequent is also absolutely necessary. Therefore, whatever God knows, is necessary; and so the knowledge of God is not of contingent things.[17]

Here the missing ingredient for Euodius's argument is supplied, namely, the fact that God's knowledge is itself absolutely (or simply) necessary, "because it is eternal, and because it is signified as past." Given this, the form of the argument becomes:

Necessarily, if God has known that *P*, then *P*.
Necessarily, God has known that *P*.
Therefore, necessarily *P*.

Thomas has thereby formulated a really powerful argument for incompatibilism, one that tests his mettle to the limit.[18]

In responding to this objection Thomas first mentions and then sets aside several unsatisfactory answers, but he finally replies:

> When the antecedent contains anything belonging to an act of the soul, the consequent must be taken not as it is in itself, but as it is in the soul: for the existence of a thing in itself is different from the existence of a thing in the soul. For example, when I say, *What the soul understands is immaterial;* this is to

be understood that it is immaterial as it is in the intellect, not as it is in itself. Likewise if I say, *If God knew anything, it will be,* the consequent must be understood as it is subject to the divine knowledge, that is, as it is in its presentiality. And thus it is necessary, as also is the antecedent: *for everything that is, while it is, must necessarily be,* as the Philosopher says in *Periherm.* i.[19]

Further light is shed by his answer to the next objection:

> Things reduced to act in time, are known by us successively in time, but by God (are known) in eternity, which is above time. Whence to us they cannot be certain, forasmuch as we know future contingent things as such; but (they are certain) to God alone, whose understanding is in eternity above time. Just as he who goes along the road, does not see those who come after him; whereas he who sees the whole road from a height, sees at once all travelling by the way. Hence what is known by us must be necessary even as it is in itself; for what is future contingent in itself, cannot be known by us. Whereas what is known by God must be necessary according to the mode in which they are subject to the divine knowledge, as already stated, but not absolutely as considered in their own causes.[20]

The answer, then, goes something like this: What God knows *is* necessary, simply and absolutely necessary, *as it is known by God*; for it is known by God *as present,* and *everything* that is present is necessary – by the time something *is,* it is then *too late* for it not to be! But this, of course, does not remove either the freedom of a free action or the contingency of a contingent event. What *would* interfere with freedom and contingency would be a necessity of the action or event *as they are coming to be* – or, as Thomas says, "in their own causes." Now, certain and infallible foreknowledge on *our* part *would* imply such a prior necessity of an occurrence, and so Thomas, unlike Augustine, denies that we ever do have advance knowledge of what is truly contingent.

Whether Thomas's position on this matter is coherent and correct remains, of course, a debatable question... What can be said at this point, however, is that Thomas has raised both the argument for incompatibilism and the response in terms of divine eternity to new heights of precision and penetration.

Before leaving Thomas, it may be of interest to consider briefly one of his rejected answers to the objection discussed above. He writes:

> Some say that this antecedent, *God knew this contingent to be future,* is not necessary, but contingent; because although it is past, still it imports relation to the future. This however does not remove necessity from it; for

whatever has had relation to the future, must have had it, although the future sometimes does not follow.[21]

It would be most interesting to know *who* said this[22] because it is not difficult to see in this reply an anticipation of the Ockhamist solution to the foreknowledge problem, a solution that will occupy us in the next section... God's knowledge does indeed lie in the past, the reply states, but it does not partake of the necessity that attaches to the past in general, because "it imports relation to the future." As we have learned to say, facts about God's past knowledge are "soft facts" about the past and not "hard facts." Unfortunately, Thomas's reason for rejecting this reply is not as clearly stated as the reply itself.[23] But it is, I think, of considerable interest to note that Thomas was aware of this solution, and had considered and rejected it.

Ockham

William of Ockham (*c.* 1285–1349) may have given more sustained attention, and almost certainly devoted more literary effort, to the problem of free will and foreknowledge than any of the earlier thinkers we have considered.[24] Yet in the view of many contemporary philosophers his important contribution to the topic is focused in a single idea, or perhaps in a pair of closely related ideas. To set the stage for this contribution, recall for a moment the powerful objection to God's knowledge of future contingents which was formulated by Aquinas and discussed in the last section. By introducing the notion that the past, as such, is necessary, Thomas transformed what might have appeared to be a trivially fallacious argument into a formidable objection to his position. Thomas is able finally to rebut the objection only by appealing to his doctrine that God, and God's knowledge, are timelessly eternal.

Now, Thomas's argument was if anything even more formidable for William of Ockham than for Thomas himself, because Ockham rejected the notion of divine timelessness. He did not, however, reject the notion of the past as being necessary; rather, he distinguished a special sort of necessity that pertains to the past, called by him necessity *per accidens*, "accidental necessity."[25] But given this, it looks as though the argument

Necessarily, if God has known that *P*, then *P*.
Necessarily, God has known that *P*.
Therefore, necessarily *P*.

is going to be, not only valid, but also sound. And if so, then incompatibilism is triumphant and the divine foreknowledge of future contingents is impossible.

Ockham's reply is both ingenious and subtle. He writes:

> Some propositions are about the present as regards both their wording and their subject matter (*secundum vocem et secundum rem*). Where such [propositions] are concerned, it is universally true that every true proposition about the present has [corresponding to it] a necessary one about the past – e.g., "Socrates is seated," "Socrates is walking," "Socrates is just," and the like.
>
> Other propositions are about the present as regards their wording only and are equivalently about the future, since their truth depends on the truth of propositions about the future. Where such [propositions] are concerned, the rule that every true proposition about the present has [corresponding to it] a necessary one about the past is not true.[26]

The idea that a "true proposition about the present has corresponding to it a necessary one about the past" is further clarified when Ockham says, "If 'Socrates is seated' is true at some time, 'Socrates was seated' will be necessary ever afterwards."[27] The necessity of the latter proposition is of course necessity *per accidens*, accidental necessity.[28] But, and this is the important point, not all present-tense propositions generate or correspond to accidentally necessary propositions about the past. Consider, for instance, the following proposition: "The bride-to-be is trying on her wedding dress." This proposition, though grammatically present tense, is at least in part of the sort Ockham would describe as "equivalently about the future"; since it implies that the young woman in question will in fact become a bride, its truth "depends on the truth of a future [proposition]," and thus "it is not required that a necessary proposition about the past correspond to the true proposition about the present."[29] So the proposition "The bride-to-be was trying on her wedding dress" will *not* be necessary *per accidens* beginning from the time of the trying on.[30]

But now that we have this apparatus in place, the application to the foreknowledge problem is straightforward. In the case where "*P*" is a future contingent proposition, "God knows that *P*" is a proposition whose truth "depends on the truth of a future proposition," namely, "*P*" itself, so the proposition "God has known that *P*" is not accidentally necessary, and the argument taken from Aquinas, though valid, is unsound. Propositions about God's past knowledge of future events do n partake of the necessity of the past.

Ockham believed that this argument was successful in removing any incompatibility between foreknowledge and free will. Nevertheless, he admitted to great difficulty in understanding *how* God could foreknow free actions. In order to appreciate his difficulty, it will be helpful to have before us his definition of free will, which is a rather exact (and exacting) libertarian definition: Freedom is "that power whereby I can do diverse things indifferently and contingently, such that I can cause, or not cause, the same effect, when all conditions other than this power are the same."[31]

We have already noted his rejection of Boethian timelessness, but he also objected to the teaching of Duns Scotus according to which God knows future contingent propositions by knowing his own will. He writes:

> I ask whether or not the determination of a created will necessarily follows the determination of the divine will. If it does, then the will necessarily acts [as it does], just as fire does, and so merit and demerit are done away with. If it does not, then the determination of a created will is required for knowing determinately one or the other part of a contradiction regarding those [future things that depend absolutely on a created will]. For the determination of the uncreated will does not suffice, because a created will can oppose the determination [of the uncreated will]. Therefore, since the determination of the [created] will was not from eternity, God did not have certain cognition of the things that remained [for a created will to determine].[32]

In the end, Ockham is forced to a rather unsatisfactory conclusion: "I maintain that it is impossible to express clearly the way in which God knows future contingents. Nevertheless it must be held that He does so, but contingently."[33]

Molina

In a sense, Luis de Molina (1535–1600) began his investigation at the point at which Ockham ended his. Like Ockham, he was persuaded that there was no logical inconsistency between divine foreknowledge and human freedom[34] but he sought to understand the *way* in which God is able to know future free actions. Like Ockham, he rejected the Boethian-Thomistic solution in terms of timeless knowledge, and he also rejected as inconsistent with free will the view of contemporary Thomists, such as Báñez, according to which "God knows the future free acts of men, even conditional future free acts, in virtue of His predetermining decrees, by which He decides to give the "physical premotion" which is necessary for any human act."[35] (It will be noted that this is quite similar to the view of Scotus that was rejected by Ockham.)

Molina's solution to the problem was formulated in terms of divine *scientia media* or "middle knowledge." This type of divine knowledge is so called, because it is, as it were, intermediate between God's "natural knowledge" by which he knows antecedently all possibilities, and his "free knowledge" by which *"after* the free act of His will, God knew *absolutely and determinately, without any condition or hypothesis*, which ones from among all the contingent states of affairs were *in fact* going to obtain and, likewise, which ones were not going to obtain."[36] In addition to these two types, there is according to Molina yet another: "Finally, the third type is *middle* knowledge, by which, in virtue of the most profound and inscrutable comprehension of each free will, He saw in His own essence what each such will would do with its innate freedom were it to be placed in this or in that or, indeed, in infinitely many orders of things – even though it would really be able, if it so willed, to do the opposite."[37]

It is easy to see how middle knowledge enables God to know future free actions. He knows by middle knowledge what each possible free creature *would* do if placed in any possible situation; then he decides which possible creatures to make actual, and which situations they shall be placed in; and, in virtue of his having decided this, his middle knowledge again informs him concerning what the *actual* free creatures will *in fact* do. [...]

On casual consideration, middle knowledge may appear to be simply an obvious implication of divine omniscience: If God knows everything, how could he fail to know *this*? And by the same token, it may seem relatively innocuous. Both impressions, however, are mistaken. Middle knowledge is not a straightforward implication of omniscience, because it is not evident that the truths postulated by this theory exist to be known. In ordinary foreknowledge, it may be argued, what God knows is the agent's *actual decision* to do one thing or another. But with regard to a situation that never in fact arises, no decision is ever made, and none exists for God to know. And if the decision in question is supposed to be a *free* decision, then all of the circumstances of the case (including the agent's character and prior inclinations) are consistent with any of the possible choices that might be made. Lacking the agent's *actual* making of the choice, then, there is nothing that disambiguates the situation and makes it true that some one of the options is the one that *would be* selected. This line of argument indicates the single most important objection that the proponent of middle knowledge must seek to answer.

But the very same feature that makes middle knowledge problematic (viz., that God can know the outcome of choices that are never actually made) also makes it extraordinarily useful for theological purposes. Consider the following counterfactual: "If A were in circumstances C, she would do X." According to middle knowledge, God knows the truth of this *whether or not* A ever actually *is* placed in circumstances C; indeed, God knows this whether or not A even exists, so that his knowledge about this is entirely independent of any of *God's own decisions* about creation and providence. But this, of course, makes such knowledge ideal for God to use in *deciding* whether or not to create A, and, if he does create her, whether or not to place her in circumstances C. As Molina says:

> God in his eternity knew by natural knowledge all the things that he could do: that he could create this world and infinitely many other worlds . . . [and] given his complete comprehension and penetrating insight concerning all things and causes, he saw what would be the case if he chose to produce this order or a different order; how each person, left to his own free will, would make use of his liberty with such-and-such an amount of divine assistance, given such and such opportunities, temptations and other circumstances, and what he would freely do, retaining all the time the ability to do the opposite in the same opportunities temptations and other circumstances.[38]

Another way to look at the matter is this: It is evident that, if God had created a thoroughly deterministic world, his creative plan would have involved no risks whatsoever; all of the causal antecedents of such a world would be set up to produce exactly the results God intended. But it seems extremely plausible that in a world involving libertarian free choice, some risks are inevitable: God in creating such a world makes it possible for us to freely bring about great good, but also great evil – and which we in fact choose is up to us, not to God. Thus, the frequently heard statement that God "limits his power" by choosing to create free creatures. But according to the theory of middle knowledge, this is not quite correct. To be sure, it is still the creatures, not God, who determine their own free responses to various situations. But God, in choosing to create them and place them in those situations, knew exactly what their responses would be; he views the future, not as a risk taker seeking to optimize probable outcomes, but as a planner who knowingly accepts and incorporates into his plan exactly those outcomes that in fact occur –

though, to be sure, some of them may not be the outcomes he would most prefer. The element of risk is entirely eliminated.

As we have already seen, the chief difficulty that the proponent of middle knowledge must confront is the contention that the truths God is alleged to know, commonly called "counterfactuals of freedom," do not exist to be known. Most of the arguments *for* counterfactuals of freedom seem to depend on general considerations of philosophical plausibility, but in the medieval controversy there were also arguments based on Scripture. A favorite text for this purpose is found in I Samuel 23, which recounts an incident in the troubled relationship of David with King Saul.[39] David, currently in occupation of the city of Keilah, consults Yahweh by means of the ephod about the rumors that Saul intends to attack the city:

> "Will Saul come down, as thy servant has heard? O LORD, the God of Israel, I beseech thee, tell thy servant." And the LORD said, "He will come down." Then said David, "Will the men of Keilah surrender me and my men into the hand of Saul?" And the LORD said, "They will surrender you." (I Samuel 23: 11–12, RSV)

The advocates of middle knowledge took this passage as evidence that God knew the following two propositions to be true:

(1) If David stayed in Keilah, Saul would besiege the city.
(2) If David stayed in Keilah and Saul besieged the city, the men of Keilah would surrender David to Saul.

But (given the assumption that Saul and the men of Keilah would act freely in performing the specified actions), these two propositions are counterfactuals of freedom, and the incident as a whole is a dramatic demonstration of the existence and practical efficacy of middle knowledge.

But this argument is hardly compelling. As Anthony Kenny points out, the ephod seems to have been a yes–no device hardly possessing the subtlety required to distinguish between various possible conditionals that might have been asserted in answer to David's questions. Kenny, indeed, suggests that we may understand material conditionals here[40] but that seems hardly likely, since on that construal both conditionals would be true simply in virtue of the fact that their antecedents are false. Much more plausible candidates are given by Robert Adams:

(3)   If David stayed in Keilah, Saul would *probably* besiege the city.
(4)   If David stayed in Keilah and Saul besieged the city, the men of Keilah would *probably* surrender David to Saul.

As Adams points out, "(3) and (4) are enough for David to act on, if he is prudent, but they will not satisfy the partisans of middle knowledge."[41] The prospects for a scriptural proof of middle knowledge, therefore, do not seem promising.

But of course, the argument just given shows only that the responses to David's questions *need not* be taken as asserting counterfactuals of freedom, not that they *cannot* be so understood. And there are not lacking situations in everyday life in which it seems plausible that we are taking counterfactuals of freedom to be true. Plantinga, for example, says he believes that "If Bob Adams were to offer to take me climbing at Tahquitz Rock the next time I come to California, I would gladly (and freely) accept."[42] And Adams notes that "there does not normally seem to be any uncertainty at all about what a butcher, for example, would have done if I had asked him to sell me a pound of ground beef, although we suppose he would have had free will in the matter."[43]

So the discussion of examples seems to end in a stand-off. Still, the proponent of middle knowledge needs to address the question mentioned earlier: How is it possible for counterfactuals of freedom to be *true*? What is the truth maker for these propositions? At this point the advocate of middle knowledge is presented with an attractive opportunity, but one that it is imperative for her to resist. The opportunity is simply to claim that counterfactuals of freedom are true in virtue of the *character and psychological tendencies* of the agents named in them. The attractiveness of this is evident in that in nearly all of the cases where we are disposed to accept such counterfactuals as true, the epistemic grounds for our acceptance would be found precisely in our knowledge of such psychological facts – Saul besieging Keilah, Adams's compliant butcher, and Plantinga climbing Tahquitz Rock are all cases in point. But the weakness of the suggestion becomes apparent when the following question is asked: Are the psychological facts about the agent, together with a description of the situation, plus relevant psychological laws, supposed to *entail* that the agent would respond as indicated? If the answer is yes, then the counterfactual may be *true* but it is not a counterfactual of *freedom*; the agent is not then free in the relevant (libertarian) sense.[44] If on the other hand the answer is no, then how can those psychological facts provide good grounds for the assertion that the agent *definitely would* (as opposed, say, to *very probably would*) respond in that way?

Probably the best line for the proponent of middle knowledge to take here is the one suggested by Suárez: When a counterfactual of freedom is true, it is simply an ultimate fact about the free agent in question that, if placed in the indicated circumstances, she would act as the counterfactual states; this fact requires no analysis or metaphysical grounding in terms of further, noncounterfactual states of affairs. (Or, if the agent in question does not actually exist, it is a fact about a particular *essence* that, if it were instantiated and its instantiation were placed in such circumstances, the instantiation would act as stated.) Adams, commenting on this, says, "I do not think I have any conception . . . of the sort of . . . property that Suárez ascribes to possible agents with respect to their acts under possible conditions. Nor do I think that I have any other primitive understanding of what it would be for the relevant subjunctive conditionals to be true." Nevertheless, he admits that Suárez's view on this is of the "least clearly unsatisfactory type," because "It is very difficult to refute someone who claims to have a primitive understanding which I seem not to have."[45]

Notes

1   An excellent survey of the later medieval developments is given in Calvin Normore, "Future Contingents," in *The Cambridge History of Later Medieval Philosophy*, ed. N. Kretzmann et al. (Cambridge: Cambridge University Press, 1982), pp. 358–81.
2   *St. Augustine on Free Will*, trans. Caroll Mason Sparrow (Charlottesville, Va.: University of Virginia Press, 1947), bk. 3, chap. 4, pp. 93–94.
3   Since Augustine accepts the classical view that knowledge as such must be certain in order to be knowledge, he does not distinguish between human knowledge and God's with regard to their certainty.
4   Several of the Greek philosophers had what might be described as a doctrine of divine timelessness. But in their view contingent temporal events are so lacking in inherent dignity as to be beneath God's notice. The combination of divine timelessness with comprehensive divine knowledge of temporal events constitutes Augustine's distinctive contribution.
5   *The Confessions of St. Augustine*, trans. Edward B. Pusey (New York: Random House, 1949), bk. 11, pp. 252–53.
6   We must of course be wary of reading modern definitions of various philosophical positions into ancient texts. Nevertheless, it is abundantly clear that Augustine's early thoughts on free will were closer to what is now termed "libertarianism" than were those he entertained later in life.
7   In *Augustine: Earlier Writings*, trans. John H. S. Burleigh (Philadelphia: Westminster Press, 1953), pp. 370–406.

8   Ibid., p. 370.

9   Cicero's argument is found in *De divinat.*, bks. 2 and 3.

10   *The City of God by Saint Augustine*, trans. Marcus Dods (New York: Random House, 1950), bk. 5, chap. 9, p. 153.

11   Ibid., p. 154.

12   Or, "compatibilist" – but we are reserving *that* term for a position on the foreknowledge controversy.

13   Boethius, *The Consolation of Philosophy*, ed. James J. Buchanan (New York: Frederick Ungar, 1957), bk. 5, prose 6, pp. 62–63.

14   Ibid., p. 64.

15   Ibid., pp. 65–66.

16   *Augustine on Free Will*, bk. 3, chap. 4, p. 93.

17   Thomas Aquinas, *Summa Theologica*, trans. Fathers of the English Dominican Province, 2d ed. (London: Burnes Oates & Washbourne, 1920), I, 14, 13, Obj. 2.

18   For an excellent discussion of this objection, see A. N. Prior, "The Formalities of Omniscience," in *Papers on Time and Tense* (Oxford: Oxford University Press, 1968), pp. 31–38.

19   Ibid., I, 14, 13, Reply Obj. 2.

20   Ibid., I, 14, 13, Reply Obj. 3.

21   Ibid., I, 14, 13, Reply Obj. 2.

22   Calvin Normore cites Robert Grosseteste and Peter Lombard as having held views similar to this, so it is possible that Aquinas had either or both of them in mind ("Future Contingents," p. 370).

23   I hazard as a conjecture the following interpretation of the claim "Whatever has had relation to the future, must have had it, although the future sometimes does not follow." I take "whatever has had relation to the future" to be an intentional attitude of some sort – say, expectation, or belief, or hope, or fear, or knowledge. If the occurrence of the intentional attitude is now past, then it is *now* necessary that that attitude was directed to the anticipated future, even though the future may actually turn out differently than expected. (In the fall of every year, it is still true that Ernie Banks hoped that spring that the Cubs would win the pennant – the truth of *that* lies in the past, and is thus immutable and necessary, regardless of whether the Cubs do or don't fulfill Ernie's hopes.) To be sure, when the intentional attitude in question is one of *knowledge*, whether divine or human, then the failure of the future to correspond cannot occur. But Aquinas strengthens his point by considering the more general case.

24   See William Ockham, *Predestination, God's Foreknowledge, and Future Contingents*, trans. Marilyn McCord Adams and Norman Kretzmann (New York: Appleton-Century-Crofts, 1969).

25   An excellent recent discussion of this notion is found in Alfred J. Freddoso, "Accidental Necessity and Logical Determinisim," *Journal of Philosophy* 80 (1983): 257–78.

26 Ockham, *Predestination*, pp. 46–47.
27 Ibid., p. 92.
28 The necessity is "accidental" because, unlike the necessity of the truths of logic, it is not essential to the proposition that possesses it; it is something a proposition has at one time but not at another.
29 Ibid., p. 92.
30 It will, however, be thus necessary *after the wedding*.
31 *Quod.* I, q. 16, cited by Ernest A. Moody, "William of Ockham," *Encyclopedia of Philosophy*, 8: 315.
32 Ockham, *Predestination*, p. 49.
33 Ibid., p. 50.
34 His reasons for affirming consistency, however, are not the same as Ockham's.
35 Frederick Copleston, S. J., *A History of Philosophy*, vol. III: *Ockham to Suarez* (London: Burns and Oates, 1968), p. 343.
36 Luis de Molina, *On Divine Foreknowledge (Part IV of the Concordia)*, trans. Alfred J. Freddoso (Ithaca, N. Y.: Cornell University Press, 1988), Disputation 52, par. 9 (emphasis in original). My thanks to Professor Freddoso for allowing me to use a manuscript copy of his forthcoming translation.
37 Ibid.
38 L. Molina, "De Scientia Dei," quoted by Anthony Kenny, *The God of the Philosophers* (Oxford: Oxford University Press, 1979), pp. 62–63.
39 For my discussion of this passage I rely chiefly on R. M. Adams, "Middle Knowledge and the Problem of Evil," *American Philosophical Quarterly* 14 (1977): 109–117. See also Kenny, *The God of the Philosophers*, pp. 63–64.
40 Kenny, *The God of the Philosophers*, p. 64.
41 Adams, "Middle Knowledge," p. 111.
42 "Reply to Robert M. Adams," in Tomberlin and van Inwagen, eds., *Alvin Plantinga* (Dordrecht: D. Reidel, 1985), p. 373.
43 Adams, "Middle Knowledge," p. 115.
44 There are complexities in our use of such expressions as "acting freely" that are not always sufficiently taken note of. For example, it may happen that an action is "psychologically inevitable" for a person, based on that person's character and dispositions, yet we say that the person acts "freely" *if the character and dispositions are thought to be the result of previous freely chosen actions of the person*. Thus, it is said of the redeemed in heaven both that they freely serve and worship God, and that they are not able to sin; this happy inability is the result of their own free choices and is not typically seen as a diminution of freedom. But acts of this sort are *not* free in the very strict sense required by libertarianism. If we are exacting in our *definition* of "free" but lax in *applying* the term, trouble is inevitable.
45 Adams, "Middle Knowledge," p. 112.

Comments and Questions on William Hasker's "God, Time, Knowledge and Freedom: The Historical Matrix"

1. One way of trying to solve the dilemma of divine foreknowledge and human freedom is by appealing to the "eternity" of God (as do Augustine, Boethius, and Aquinas) and to the fact that God knows all things timelessly, or in a eternal present. If this is so, then strictly speaking God does not *fore*know any actions, so free actions are presumably not *predestined* by God. Do you think this "eternalist" solution presented in Hasker's discussions of Boethius and Aquinas resolves the conflict between divine omniscience and human freedom? Why or why not?

2. The "Ockhamist" solution to the foreknowledge/freedom problem (originated by William of Ockham) relies on the distinction between hard and soft facts about the past. Explain this distinction. What were Ockham's reasons for saying that God's foreknowledge is a soft fact about the past; and how would its being a soft fact solve the freedom/foreknowledge problem? Do you think the Ockhamist solution works? Why or why not?

3. What exactly is "middle knowledge" and how is God's possession of middle knowledge suppose to resolve the conflict between divine foreknowledge and human freedom? Molinists, or defenders of the middle knowledge solution to the foreknowledge problem, often argue that their view of middle knowledge helps to explain divine prophecies and God's providence. This is illustrated in the reading in terms of the story from the Bible of God's prophesying that if Saul besieged the city, the men of Keilah would surrender David to Saul. Does this story show that middle knowledge can account for prophecy without eliminating free will? Why or why not?

Suggested Reading

Hasker's *God, Time and Knowledge* (1989), from which this selection is taken, is a comprehensive discussion of the freedom/foreknowledge issue. Another excellent survey of modern debates about this issue is Linda Zagzebski's *The Dilemma of Freedom and Foreknowledge* (1991). An earlier work that is also highly informative is Anthony Kenny's *The God of the Philosophers* (1979). An "eternalist" solution is defended by Eleonore Stump and Norman Kretzmann, "Prophecy, Past Truth, and Eternity" (1991) and Brian Leftow, *Time and Eternity* (1991). A Molinist solution is defended by Thomas Flint, *Divine Providence: The Molinist Account* (1998) and is discussed by Alfredo Freddoso in his introduction to his translation of Molina's *On Divine Foreknowledge* (1988). The Ockhamist solution is discussed in Alvin Plantinga's "On Ockham's Way Out" (1986) and by Marilyn Adams, *William Ockham* (1987). Also see the suggested readings at the end of the preceding selection from Augustine.

Glossary with Commentary on Key Terms and References to the Readings

agent-causation (or **immanent causation**): a special kind of causation of an action (or specifically of a free action) by an agent or person that cannot be reduced to or fully explained by causation of that action by events, processes, and states of affairs involving the agent. (It is common to hyphenate the expression "agent-causation" to signify that such a special kind of causal relation between an agent and an action is meant.) Roderick Chisholm calls this special kind of agent-causation "immanent causation" and distinguishes it from "transeunt causation" – the usual form of causation of events and states of affairs by other events and states of affairs. Many libertarians appeal to this idea in the attempt to make sense of an indeterminist free will. It is defended in this volume by Chisholm and O'Connor. It is criticized by van Inwagen (second selection), Ginet, and Kane. See **causes** or **causation, incompatibilism, libertarianism**.

alternative possibilities (for choice or action): an agent has alternative possibilities – for example, to choose or do A or B – at a time t just in case the agent has the power or ability (at t) to choose or do A and the power or ability (at t) to choose or do B. If the agent has chosen one of the options, the presence of alternative possibilities means that the agent could have chosen the other, or "could have done otherwise." The relation of alternative possibilities to free will, responsibility, and determinism is the subject of several readings, especially those of Nielsen, van Inwagen, Dennett, Fischer, and Pereboom.

causal determinism: the view that all events and states of affairs are *determined* by antecedent causes and laws of nature. See **determinism, causes** or **causation**.

causal indeterminism: the view that free choices and actions are caused by the agents' reasons and motives, intentions and efforts, but indeterministically, not deterministically. Causal indeterminism is a libertarian theory of free will because it rejects the idea that all free choices and actions are caused deterministically. It is an alternative to other libertarian theories, such as the theory of agent-causation or simple indeterminism, since it avoids appeals to any special forms of agent or immanent causation that cannot be spelled out in terms of causation by events or states of affairs and it does not deny (as simple indeterminists do) that explanations in terms of reasons and motives, intentions and efforts are a species of causal explanation. Causal indeterminism is defended in the reading of this volume by Kane. It is criticized by Ginet and O'Connor. (Ginet calls it "the indeterministic-causation view." It is also sometimes called "event-causal libertarianism.")

causes or **causation**: in ordinary usage, to cause something is to produce it or bring it about. Things or substances, whether animate or inanimate, can be causes in this ordinary sense. Thus, the rock caused the window to break or the cat caused the lamp to fall. Being more precise, however, we would say it was the-rock's-striking-the-window that caused it to break and the-cat's-jumping-on-the-table that caused it to fall; and these are *events* involving the objects. Thus, many philosophers are inclined to think that causes are normally events that produce or bring about other events (their effects). Events in this context also include states or states of affairs, which can also be cited as causes. (For example, a structural defect in the bridge caused it to collapse.) One of the controversies about free will is whether all causation (including causation by agents or substances) can be spelled out or interpreted in terms of causation between events and states of affairs, as is commonly assumed, or whether free will requires a special kind of ("agent-" or "immanent") causation that cannot be reduced to causation in terms of events and states of affairs involving the agents. See **agent-causation**. Another issue about causation related to free will concerns causation and *determinism*. Causes need not always determine their effects. There are nondeterministic or probabilistic causes which sometimes bring about their effects, but do not do so always or inevitably. One must be careful therefore not to identify "caused" with "determined" or to define determinism as the view that "every event is caused" without noting that, if determinism is true, all causes must be such that, given them, their effects are inevitable. Such issues are discussed in the readings by Dennett, Kane, and Hodgson. See **determinism**.

classical compatibilism: the view that to be "free" means (1) to have the power (i.e., capacity plus opportunity) to do what you will or want to do, which in turn means (2) that there is an absence of *constraints* or *impediments* (physical restraint, coercion, paralysis, etc.) preventing you from doing what you will or want to do. Classical compatibilists also usually defend (3) a *conditional* or *hypothetical* analysis of "could have done otherwise," according to which it means "you *would* have done otherwise, *if* you had willed or wanted to do otherwise" (as does Nielsen in his selection in this volume). And they argue that if *freedom* is defined in terms of (1)–(3), it is compatible with determinism. The reading by Nielsen in this volume defends a classical compatibilist position. A number of contributors to this volume, such as Dennett, Frankfurt, Wolf, and Watson are compatibilists, but think the classical compatibilist account of freedom is not sufficient and try to improve upon it. See **compatibilism**.

coercion: forcing someone to do something they would not otherwise want to do. A standard case is the thief with a gun to your head who coerces you to turn over your money. In one sense you do it willingly because the alternative of losing your life is worse. But in another sense you do it against your will, since you do not want to hand over the money. Coercion is a standard kind of *constraint* against the will that compatibilists have in mind when they define freedom as the absence of constraints. See **constraints, classical compatibilism**.

compatibilism: the view that freedom and responsibility in every significant sense worth wanting (including free will) are compatible with determinism. Thus, there is no conflict between determinism and free will. See **classical compatibilism**.

compulsion: conditions such as addiction or alcoholism in which there are certain desires that agents cannot help acting upon. Compulsion along with coercion is considered a standard kind of *constraint* against the will that compatibilists have in mind when they define freedom as an absence of constraints. See the reading by Frankfurt for a "hierarchical" account of compulsion and addiction. Some philosophers discussing free will (such as Nielsen in this volume) use the terms "compulsion" and "being compelled" in a general sense to mean being "forced" to do something against one's will, so that it includes cases of coercion as well as compulsion as it is defined here. See **coercion, constraints, classical compatibilism**.

consequence argument: the most widely discussed contemporary argument for the incompatibilism of free will and determinism. This argument is discussed in the first selection by van Inwagen in this volume.

constraints (freedom defined as the absence of): conditions such as physical restaint, coercion, compulsions, or oppression that prevent us from doing what we will or want. Compatibilists usually define freedom as an "absence of constraints." See **classical compatibilism**.

deep self views: compatibilist views of free will and responsibility which distinguish between desires and other motives that represent an agent's deep or true or authentic self versus desires or motives that are foreign or alien to one's self in the sense that one does not identify with them as representing one's true or authentic self. Free and responsible agents according to such views are those whose wills are within the control of their deep or true or authentic selves. Deep Self Views are discussed in the reading by Susan Wolf. She considers three kinds of Deep Self view, those of Harry Frankfurt, Gary Watson, and Charles Taylor. Her own view she calls a Sane Deep Self View.

determinism: the view that every event and state of affairs is determined in the following sense. An event or state of affairs E is determined just in case there are conditions (such as the decrees of fate, the foreordaining acts of God, or antecedent physical causes plus laws of nature), such that it *must* be the case that *if* those conditions obtain, then E occurs. In brief, E is *inevitable* (could not but occur), given the determining conditions. There are different forms of determinism – fatalistic, logical, theological, physical, biological, psychological, social, etc. – depending on the nature of the conditions thought to be determining (acts of God, laws of logic, laws of nature, strongest motives, etc.). See **logical fatalism** or **logical determinism, theological determinism, causal determinism, physical determinism, psychological determinism, social** or **cultural determinism**.

Frankfurt-style examples: examples of a kind first put forward by Harry Frankfurt designed to refute the so-called "principle of alternative possibilities" (PAP): an action is morally responsible only if the agent could have done otherwise than perform it. In Frankfurt-style examples, there is a controller or mechanism that can prevent an agent from doing otherwise. But the controller or mechanism will not intervene unless the agent is about to do otherwise. When the agent does on his or her own what the controller or mechanism wants, the controller or mechanism does not intervene. In cases where the controller or mechanism does not intervene, Frankfurt argues, the agents can be morally responsible (because they acted on their own) even though they could not have done otherwise. Frankfurt-style examples (or cases or scenarios) are discussed in the readings by Fischer and Pereboom. See **alternative possibilities, responsibility**.

free will (in the traditional sense): the power or ability (1) to choose and to act upon an array of alternative possibilities, so that we could have chosen or acted otherwise and (2) to choose and act in such manner that the origins or sources of our choices or actions are in us and not in something else over which we have no control. Incompatibilists believe that determinism would rule out a power satisfying these conditions. Compatibilists argue either that determinism would not rule out such a power or that these features are not really required for free will. See **free will (in the hierarchical sense)**.

free will (in the hierarchical sense): (in Harry Frankfurt's terms) "having the will you want to have," which means that your first-order desires are in conformity with your second-order volitions (i.e., desires that your first-order desires be effective in action). That is, you have the "will" (first-order desires) you "want" or "will" (second-order desires or volitions) to have. Hierarchical theorists such as Frankfurt believe that free will in this sense (the correct sense, according to them) is compatible with determinism. See **hierarchical motivation**.

hard determinism: the view that (1) determinism is true and (2) free will (in the traditional sense) is incompatible with determinism, so that (3) free will in the traditional sense does not exist. See **determinism, free will (in the traditional sense), incompatibilism, libertarianism, soft determinism**.

hierarchical motivation: a notion introduced by Harry Frankfurt (see his reading in this volume) according to which agents can be moved to choose and act, not only by first-order desires but also by second- and higher-order desires about what first-order desires they want to be effective in action. Second-order desires about what first-order desires an agent wants to be effective in action are called by Frankfurt *second-order volitions*. Frankfurt defines free will in hierarchical terms. See **free will (in the hierarchical sense), reasons** or **motives, deep self views**.

immanent causation: See **agent-causation**.

incompatibilism: the view that free will in the traditional sense is incompatible with determinism. See **free will (in the traditional sense), determinism**.

indeterministic-causation view: another name for the view usually called "causal indeterminism." See **causal indeterminism**.

indeterminists: those who deny that all events and states of affairs are determined, i.e., that determinism is true. See **determinism**.

libertarianism (concerning free will): (from the Latin *liber*, meaning "free"), the view that (1) free will in the traditional sense is incompatible with determinism and that (2) humans do possess such an incompatibilist free will, so that determinism is false. Libertarians are both incompatibilists and indeterminists. See **incompatibilism, free will (in the traditional sense), determinism**.

logical fatalism or **logical determinism**: the view first put forward by ancient Greek schools of thought, such as the Megarian and Stoic philosophers, that all events (including human actions) are fated or determined by the laws of logic. If every proposition must be true or false (as the logical "principle of bivalence" requires) and if this is true of future-tensed propositions as well, such as (X) "a sea-fight will occur tomorrow," then it seems that whatever occurs, must occur. For if proposition X is true today, the sea-fight cannot but occur tomorrow, and if X is false today, a sea-fight cannot occur tomorrow. See **determinism**.

metaphysical freedom: the name used by van Inwagen for incompatibilist or libertarian free will. See **libertarianism**.

middle knowledge: the knowledge of future human free actions ascribed to God by Luis de Molina (and those who share his view, called *Molinists*). It is God's foreknowledge of what each free creature *would* in fact do, *if* that creature were placed in any circumstances he or she might be placed in. Molina held that God has such foreknowledge even of free human acts that are causally undetermined. It is called "middle" knowledge because it is something between God's knowledge of all things that are merely *possible* and God's knowledge of all things that *actually* occur. Middle knowledge is knowledge of what agents would actually do, but under various hypothetical circumstances. It is discussed in the reading by Hasker. See **theological determinism**.

moral responsibility: See **responsibility**.

physical determinism: the view that all events and states of affairs are determined by antecedent physical causes and the laws of physics. See **determinism**.

predestinationism: See **theological determinism**.

principle of alternative possibilities (PAP): See **Frankfurt-style examples**.

psychological determinism: the view that all choices and actions are determined by the strongest prior motives or reasons of the agent. See **determinism, reasons or motives**.

reactive attitudes: attitudes such as resentment, admiration, indignation, blame, guilt, and others by which we react to ourselves and others as morally responsible agents. According to the theory of P.F. Strawson, to be morally responsible amounts to being a fit subject of such attitudes. It is to be enmeshed in a form of life or moral community in which such attitudes play a constitutive role. Strawson's view is discussed in the reading by Watson. See **responsibility**.

reasons or **motives** for action: psychological attitudes such as beliefs, desires, wants, intentions, preferences, and the like, which may be cited in answer to the question "Why did you (he, she, etc.) do that?" (Why did you telephone Mary?

Because I *wanted* to learn the answer to question 5 on the test and I *believed* she knew.) Citing reasons or motives thus provides *explanations* for actions. One of the issues in free will debates is whether reasons or motives which *explain* actions also *cause* the actions they explain. Some philosophers say yes (reasons cause actions), some say no. "Reason" and "motive" are ambiguous as between the psychological attitude (I wanted to know the answer) and the *content* or *object* of that psychological attitude (to know the answer) – what the attitude is *about*. For we can cite either one when asked "why did you do that (e.g., call Mary)?" – "because I wanted to learn the answer," or just "to learn the answer." Usually in free will debates, as in this volume, when authors talk about reasons and motives, they mean the psychological atitudes (wants, beliefs, etc.), but sometimes they mean the contents of these attitudes or what the attitudes are about. Also in such debates, "reasons" and "motives" are usually used interchangeably. The literal difference is that reasons "explain" actions, while motives "move" us to action. But if motives move us to action then they help to explain action; and reasons explain action when they move us to action. A crucial debate regarding free will is whether explanations of actions in terms of reasons or motives are *causal* explanations. This issue is discussed in the readings by O'Connor, Ginet, and Kane. See **causes and causation**.

reasons-explanations (of actions): explanations of actions which cite the agents' reasons or motives. See **reasons** or **motives**.

responsibility: accountability for one's actions, liability for praise or blame, praiseworthiness or blameworthiness. Legal responsibility is accountability before the law and hence liability to legal reward or punishment. Moral responsibility is accountability for one's moral character and for the rightness or wrongness of one's actions.

sane deep self view: See **deep self views**.

semicompatibilism: the view that freedom is incompatible with determinism because it requires alternative possibilities, or the power to do otherwise, but moral responsibility is compatible with determinism because it does not require alternative possibilities. See **compatibilism, determinism, alternative possibilities**.

simple indeterminism: another incompatibilist or libertarian view of free will, according to which free actions can be explained by reasons or motives without being caused or determined by those reasons or motives. Simple indeterminists rely on the idea that explanations in terms of reasons are not causal explanations. If reasons do not cause actions, they do not determine actions. Simple indeterminism is an alternative to both agent-causation and causal indeterminism as possible libertarian accounts of free will. A simple indeterminist view is defended in the reading by Ginet. See **agent-causation, causal indeterminism, libertarianism, incompatibilism, reasons** or **motives**.

social or **cultural determinism**: the view that all human choices and actions are determined by social and cultural learning or conditioning (given background biological and physical facts). See **determinism**.

soft determinism: the view that (1) determinism is true, but that (2) freedom and responsibility in every significant sense (including free will) are both compatible with determinism. Soft determinists are compatibilists and determinists. See **compatibilism, determinism, hard determinism**.

successor views (to hard determinism): contemporary views that share two assumptions with hard determinism, namely, (1) that free will is incompatible with determinism and (2) that an incompatibilist or libertarian free will cannot exist. Successor views remain noncommittal, however, about the third thesis of hard determinism, (3) that determinism is true. Such views often hold (2) – that libertarian free will cannot exist – because they believe (3') that free will is not compatible with determinism and not compatible with indeterminism either. See **hard determinism, libertarianism**.

theological determinism: the view that all human choices or actions are determined as a result either of being foreordained or foreknown by God, or both. More popularly known as **predestinationism**. See **determinism**.

ultimate responsibility (UR): the kind of responsibility we have when we are the ultimate sources or originators of at least some important features of our wills, or characters and motives (including our purposes). "Ultimate" means that no one or nothing which we do not have control over can be the total source of our characters, motives, and purposes. This notion is discussed in the reading by Kane. See **responsibility**.

wanton: as defined by Harry Frankfurt, wantons are those who do not care about their will. Their first-order desires move them to do certain things, but they have no second-order desires about which first-order desires they prefer or want to be moved by. The class of wantons for Frankfurt includes nonhuman animals and very small children. They lack free will, according to Frankfurt, because they are incapable of reflective self-evaluation about their desires and of being moved by higher-order desires. See **hierarchical motivation**.

Bibliography

Adams, Marilyn. 1987. *William Ockham*. Notre Dame, IN: Notre Dame University Press.

Adams, Robert Merrihew. 1977. "Middle Knowledge and the Problem of Evil." *American Philosophical Quarterly* 14: 1–12.

Anglin, W. S. 1990. *Free Will and the Christian Faith*. Oxford: Oxford University Press.

Aquinas, St. Thomas. 1945. *Basic Writings of St. Thomas Aquinas*, vol. I. ed. A. Pegis. New York: Random House.

Aristotle. 1915. *Nichomachean Ethics*. Vol. 9 of *The Works of Aristotle*, ed. W. D. Ross. London: Oxford University Press.

Augustine, St. 1964. *On the Free Choice of the Will*. Indianapolis, IN: Bobbs-Merrill.

Austin, J. L. 1961. "Ifs and Cans." In J. O. Urmson and G. J. Warnock, eds. *Philosophical Papers*. Oxford: Clarendon Press: 205–32.

Ayer, A. J. 1954. "Freedom and Necessity." In *Philosophical Essays*. New York: St. Martin's Press: 3–20.

Babloyantz, A. and A. Destexhe. 1985. "Strange Attractors in the Human Cortex." In L. Rensing et al., eds. *Temporal Disorder in Human Oscillatory Systems*. New York: Springer-Verlag: 132–43.

Balaguer, Mark. 1999. "Libertarianism as a Scientifically Reputable View." *Philosophical Studies* 93: 189–211.

Basinger, David. 1986. "Middle Knowledge and Classical Christian Thought." *Religious Studies* 22: 407–22.

Bennett, Jonathan. 1980. "Accountability." In Z. van Straaten, ed., *Philosophical Subjects*. Oxford: Clarendon Press: 86–103.

Benson, Paul. 1987. "Freedom and Value." *Journal of Philosophy* 84: 465–87.

Berlin, Isaiah. 1969. *Four Essays on Liberty*. Oxford: Oxford University Press.

Bernstein, Mark. 1983. "Socialization and Autonomy." *Mind* 93: 120–3.

Berofsky, Bernard. 1987. *Freedom From Necessity*. London: Routledge & Kegan Paul.

Berofsky, Bernard. 2000. "Ultimate Responsibility in a Determined World." *Philosophy and Phenomenological Research* 60: 135–40.

Bishop, John. 1989. *Natural Agency*. Cambridge, UK: Cambridge University Press.

Bishop, Robert C. and Frederick K. Kronz. 1999. "Is Chaos Indeterministic?" In Maria Luisa Dalla Chiara, et al., eds. *Language, Quantum, Music: Selected Papers of the Tenth International Congress of Logic, Methodology & Philosophy of Science*. London: Kluwer Academic Publishers: 129–41.

Blumenfeld, David. 1971. "The Principle of Alternative Possibilities." *Journal of Philosophy* 68: 339–45.

Bok, Hilary. 1998. *Freedom and Responsibility*. Princeton, NJ: Princeton University Press.

Brant, Dale Eric. 1997. "On Plantinga's Way Out." *Faith and Philosophy* 14: 378–87.

Bratman, Michael. 1996. "Identification, Decision and Treating as a Reason." *Philosophical Topics* 24: 1–18.

Broad, C. D. 1952. "Determinism, Indeterminism and Libertarianism." In B. Berofsky, ed., 1966. *Free Will and Determinism*. New York: Harper and Row: 135–59.

Buss, Sarah and Lee Overton, eds., 2001. *The Contours of Agency: Essays in Honor of Harry Frankfurt*. Cambridge, MA: MIT Press.

Campbell, C. A. 1951. "Is Free Will a Pseudo-problem?" *Mind* 60: 446–65. In B. Berofsky, ed., 1966. *Free Will and Determinism*. New York: Harper and Row: 112–35.

Chisholm, R. M. 1982. "Human Freedom and the Self." In G. Watson, ed., *Free Will*. Oxford: Oxford University Press 24–35. Reprinted in P. van Inwagen and D. Zimmerman, eds., 1998. *Metaphysics: The Big Questions*. Oxford: Blackwell.

Churchland, Paul M. 1996. *The Engine of Reason. The Seat of the Soul*. Cambridge, MA: MIT Press.

Clarke, Randolph. 1996. "Agent Causation and Event Causation in the Production of Free Action." *Philosophical Topics* 24: 19–48.

Clarke, Randolph. 1999. "Free Choice, Effort and Wanting More." *Philosophical Explorations* 2: 20–41.

Copp, David. 1997. "Defending the Principle of Alternative Possibilities: Blameworthiness and Moral Responsibility." *Nous* 31: 441–56.

Cover, Jan and John O'Leary-Hawthorne. 1996. "Free Agency and Materialism." In D. Howard-Snyder and J. Jordan, eds. *Faith, Freedom and Rationality*. Lanham, MD: Rowman and Littlefield: 47–71.

Davidson, Donald. 1963. "Actions, Reasons and Causes." In D. Davidson, 1980. *Essays on Actions and Events*. Oxford: Clarendon Press: 5–20.

Dekker, Eef. 2000. *Middle Knowledge*. Leuven: Peeters.

Dennett, Daniel. 1984. *Elbow Room: The Varieties of Free Will Worth Wanting*. Cambridge, MA: MIT Press.

Dilman, Ilham. 1999. *Free Will: An Historical and Philosophical Introduction*. London: Routledge.

Double, Richard. 1991. *The Non-reality of Free Will*. Oxford: Oxford University Press.

Double, Richard. 1996. *Metaphilosophy and Free Will*. Oxford: Oxford University Press.

Dretske, Fred. 1988. *Explaining Behavior: Reasons in a World of Causes*. Cambridge, MA: MIT Press.

Earman, John. 1986. *A Primer on Determinism*. Dordrecht: Reidel.

Eccles, John. 1970. *Facing Reality*. New York: Springer-Verlag.

Eccles, John. 1994. *How the Self Controls its Brain*. Berlin: Springer.

Eccles, John and Karl Popper. 1977. *The Self and its Brain*. New York: Springer-Verlag.

Ekstrom, Laura Waddell. 2000. *Free Will: A Philosophical Study*. Boulder, CO: Westview Press.

Felt, James, S. J. 1994. *Making Sense of Your Freedom*. Ithaca, NY: Cornell University Press.

Fischer, John Martin. ed., 1986. *Moral Responsibility*. Ithaca, NY: Cornell University Press.

Fischer, John Martin. ed., 1989. *God, Freedom and Foreknowledge*. Stanford, CA: Stanford University Press.

Fischer, John Martin. 1994. *The Metaphysics of Free Will: A Study of Control*. Oxford: Blackwell.

Fischer, John Martin and Mark Ravizza, eds., 1993. *Perspectives on Moral Responsibility*. Ithaca, NY: Cornell University Press.

Fischer, John Martin. 1995. "Libertarianism and Avoidability: A Reply to Widerker." *Faith and Philosophy* 12: 119–25.

Fischer, John Martin. 1999a. "Recent Work on Moral Responsibility." *Ethics* 110: 91–139.

Fischer, John Martin. 1999b. "Responsibility and Self-Expression." *Journal of Ethics* 3: 277–97.

Fischer, John Martin. 2000. "*The Significance of Free Will* by Robert Kane." *Philosophy and Phenomenological Research* 60: 141–8.

Fischer, John Martin and Mark Ravizza. 1998. *Responsibility and Control: A Theory of Moral Responsibility*. Cambridge, UK: Cambridge University Press.

Flanagan, Owen. 1992. *Consciousness Reconsidered*. Cambridge, MA: MIT Press.

Flew, Antony and Godfrey Vesey. 1987. *Agency and Necessity*. Oxford: Blackwell.

Flint, Thomas. 1987. "Compatibilism and the Argument from Unavoidability." *Journal of Philosophy* 84: 423–40.

Flint, Thomas. 1998. *Divine Providence: The Molinist Account*. Ithaca, NY: Cornell University Press.

Foster, John. 1991. *The Immaterial Self*. London: Routledge.

Frankfurt, Harry. 1969. "Alternate Possibilities and Moral Responsibility." *Journal of Philosophy* 66: 829–39.

Frankfurt, Harry. 1971. "Freedom of the Will and the Concept of a Person." *Journal of Philosophy* 68: 5–20.

Frankfurt, Harry. 1988. *The Importance of What We Care About*. New York: Cambridge University Press.

Frankfurt, Harry. 1999. "Responses." *Journal of Ethics* 3: 367–72.

Freddoso, Alfred. 1983. "Accidental Necessity and Logical Determinism." *Journal of Philosophy* 80: 257–78.

Freddoso, Alfred. 1988. Trans. and introduction to Luis de Molina, *On Divine Foreknowledge*. Part IV of *Concordia*. Ithaca, NY: Cornell University Press.

Gallois, Andre. 1977. "Van Inwagen on Free Will and Determinism." *Philosophical Studies* 32: 99–105.

Gilbert, Scott F. and Sahotra Sarkar. 2000. "Embracing Complexity: Organicism for the Twenty-first Century." *Developmental Dynamics* 219: 1–9.

Ginet, Carl. 1966. "Might We Have No Choice?" In K. Lehrer, ed., *Freedom and Determinism*. New York: Random House: 87–104.

Ginet, Carl. 1990. *On Action*. Cambridge, UK: Cambridge University Press.

Ginet, Carl. 1996. "In Defense of the Principle of Alternative Possibilities: Why I Don't Find Frankfurt's Argument Convincing." *Philosophical Perspectives* 10: 403–17.

Goetz, Stewart C. 1997. "Libertarian Choice." *Faith and Philosophy* 14: 195–211.

Goetz, Stewart C. 1999. "Stumping for Widerker." *Faith and Philosophy* 16: 83–9.

Goetz, Stewart C. forthcoming. "Stump on Libertarianism and Alternative Possibilities." *Faith and Philosophy*.

Gomberg, Paul. 1975. "Free Will as Ultimate Responsibility." *American Philosophical Quarterly* 15: 205–12.

Haji, Ishtiyaque. 1998. *Moral Appraisability*. New York: Oxford University Press.

Haji, Ishtiyaque. 1999. "Indeterminism and Frankfurt-style Examples." *Philosophical Explorations* 2: 42–58.

Hasker, William. 1989. *God, Time and Knowledge*. Ithaca, NY: Cornell University Press.

Heil, John and Alfred Mele, eds., 1993. *Mental Causation*. Oxford: Oxford University Press.

Hill, Christopher. 1992. "Van Inwagen on the Consequence Argument." *Analysis* 52: 49–55.

Hobbes, Thomas. 1962. *The English Works of Thomas Hobbes*. Vol 5. Ed. by W. Molesworth. London: Scientia Aalen.

Hodgson, David. 1999. "Hume's Mistake." In B. Libet, A. Freeman and K. Sutherland, eds. *The Volitional Brain: Towards a Neuroscience of Free Will*. Thorverten, UK: Imprint Academic: 201–24.

Hodgson, David. 1991. *The Mind Matters*. Oxford: Clarendon Press.

Honderich, Ted, ed., 1973. *Essays on Freedom of Action*. London: Routledge & Kegan Paul.

Honderich, Ted, 1988. *A Theory of Determinism*. 2 Vols. Oxford: Clarendon Press.

Honderich, Ted. 1993. *How Free Are You?* Oxford: Oxford University Press.

Hook, Sidney, ed., 1958. *Determinism and Freedom in the Age of Modern Science*. New York: Collier-Macmillan.

Horgan, Terence. 1985. "Compatibilism and the Consequence Argument." *Philosophical Studies* 47: 339–56.

Howard-Snyder, Daniel and Jeff Jordan, eds., 1996. *Faith, Freedom and Rationality*. Lanham, MD: Rowman and Littlefield.

Hume, David. 1955. *An Enquiry Concerning Human Understanding*. Ed. by L. A. Selby-Bigge. Oxford: Clarendon Press.

Hume, David. 1967. *A Treatise of Human Nature*. Ed. by L. A. Selby-Bigge. Oxford: Clarendon Press.

Hunt, David. 1996. "Frankfurt Counterexamples: Some Comments on the Widerker–Fischer Debate." *Faith and Philosophy* 13: 395–401.

Hunt, David. 1999. "On Augustine's Way Out." *Faith and Philosophy* 16: 3–26.

Hunt, David. 2000. "Moral Responsibility and Avoidable Action." *Philosophical Studies* 97: 195–227.

Huxley, Aldous. [1932] 1989. *Brave New World*. San Francisco: Harper-Collins.

James, William. 1956. *The Will to Believe and Other Essays*. New York: Dover.

Kane, Robert. 1985. *Free Will and Values*. Albany, NY: State University of New York Press.

Kane, Robert. 1996. *The Significance of Free Will*. Oxford: Oxford University Press.

Kane, Robert. 1999. "Responsibility, Luck and Chance: Reflections on Free Will and Indeterminism." *The Journal of Philosophy* 96(5): 217–40.

Kane, Robert. 1999a. "On Free Will, Responsibility and Indeterminism: Responses to Clarke, Haji and Mele." *Philosophical Explorations: An International Journal for the Philosophy of Mind and Action* 2: 105–21.

Kane, Robert (ed.) 2000. "Responses to Bernard Berofsky, John Martin Fischer and Galen Strawson." *Philosophy and Phenomenological Research* 60: 129–34; 157–67.

Kane, Robert. 2000a. "The Dual Regress of Free Will and the Role of Alternative Possibilities." *Philosophical Perspectives* 14: 57–79.

Kane, Robert, Ishtiyaque Haji and John Martin Fischer. 2000. "Free Will and Moral Responsibility: Three Recent Views." *The Journal of Ethics* 4(4): 1–91.

Kant, Immanuel. 1956. *Critique of Practical Reason*. Trans. by L. W. Beck. Indianapolis, IN: Bobbs-Merrill.

Kant, Immanuel. 1958. *Critique of Pure Reason*. Trans. by N. K. Smith. London: Macmillan.

Kapitan, Tomis. 1989. "Doxastic Freedom: A Compatibilist Alternative". *American Philosophical Quarterly* 26: 31–41.

Kapitan, Tomis. 1996. "Modal Principles in the Metaphysics of Free Will". *Philosophical Perspectives* 10: 419–45.

Kauffman, Stuart. 1995. *At Home in the Universe*. New York: Oxford University Press.

Kenny, Anthony. 1978. *Free Will and Responsibility*. London: Routledge & Kegan Paul.

Kenny, Anthony. 1979. *The God of the Philosophers*. Oxford: Oxford University Press.

Klein, Martha. 1990. *Determinism, Blameworthiness and Deprivation*. Oxford: Oxford University Press.

Koons, Robert. 2000. *Realism Regained: An Exact Theory of Causation, Teleology and Mind*. Oxford: University of Oxford Press.

Kuppers, Bernd-Olaf. 1992. "Understanding Complexity". In A. Beckermann, H. Flohr and J. Kim, eds. *Emergence or Reduction*? Berlin: Walter de Gruyter: 241–56.

Lamb, James. 1977. "On a Proof of Incompatibilism". *The Philosophical Review* 86: 20–35.

Laplace, P. S. 1951. *A Philosophical Essay on Probabilities*. New York: Dover Publications.

Leftow, Brian. 1991. *Time and Eternity*. Ithaca, NY: Cornell University Press.

Lehrer, Keith, ed., 1966. *Freedom and Determinism*. New York: Random House.

Lehrer, Keith. 1968. "Can's Without 'If's.'" *Analysis* 29: 29–32.

Lehrer, Keith. 1997. *Self-Trust: A Study of Reason, Knowledge and Autonomy*. Oxford: Clarendon Press.

Levy, S. 1993. *Artificial Life*. Harmondsworth, UK: Penguin.

Lewis, David. 1981. "Are We Free to Break the Laws?" *Theoria* 47: 113–21. Reprinted in Lewis, 1986, *Philosophical Papers*. Oxford: Oxford University Press, Vol. II: 291–8.

Libet, B., Anthony Freeman and Keith Sutherland, eds., 1999. *The Volitional Brain: Towards a Neuroscience of Free Will*. Thorverten, UK: Imprint Academic.

Lucas, J. R. 1970. *The Freedom of the Will*. Oxford: Oxford University Press.

MacDonald, Scott. 1999. "Primal Sin." In G. Matthews (ed.) *The Augustinian Tradition*. Berkeley, CA: University of California Press: 110–39.

MacDonald, Scott and Eleonore Stump. 1998. *Aquinas's Moral Theory*. Ithaca, NY: Cornell University Press.

Magill, Kevin. 1997. *Experience and Freedom: Self-determination Without Illusions*. London: Macmillan.

Mates, Benson. 1961. *Stoic Logic*. Berkeley: University of California Press.

McCall, Storrs. 1999. "Deliberation Reasons and Explanation Reasons." In R. Jackendoff et al., eds. *Language. Logic and Concepts*. Cambridge MA: MIT Press: 97–108.

McCall, Storrs. 1994. *A Model of the Universe*. Oxford: Clarendon Press.

McCann, Hugh. 1998. *The Works of Agency: On Human Action, Will and Freedom*. Ithaca, NY: Cornell University Press.

McKay, Thomas and David Johnson. 1996. "A Reconsideration of an Argument Against Compatibilism." *Philosophical Topics* 24: 113–22.

McKenna, Michael. 1997. "Alternative Possibilities and the Failure of the Counter-example Strategy". *Journal of Social Philosophy* 28: 71–85.

McKenna, Michael. 1998. "Does Strong Compatibilism Survive Frankfurt-style Examples?" *Philosophical Studies* 91: 259–64.

McKenna, Michael. 1998a. "The Limits of Evil and the Role of Address." *Journal of Ethics* 2: 123–42.

Mele, Alfred. 1992. *Springs of Action: Understanding Intentional Behavior*. Oxford: Oxford University Press.

Mele, Alfred. 1995. *Autonomous Agents: From Self-Control to Autonomy*. New York: Oxford University Press.

Mele, Alfred. 1996. "Soft Libertarianism and Frankfurt-style Scenarios." *Philosophical Topics* 24: 123–41.

Mele, Alfred, ed., 1997. *The Philosophy of Action*. Oxford: Oxford University Press

Mele, Alfred. 1998. "Review of Robert Kane's *The Significance of Free Will*." *Journal of Philosophy* 95: 581–4.

Mele, Alfred. 1999. "Ultimate Responsibility and Dumb Luck." *Social Philosophy and Policy* 16: 274–93.

Mele, Alfred. 1999a. "Kane, Luck and the Significance of Free Will." *Philosophical Explorations* 2: 96–104.

Mele, Alfred and David Robb. 1998. "Rescuing Frankfurt-style Cases." *The Philosophical Review* 107: 97–112.

Mill, J. S. 1874. "From an Examination of Sir William Hamilton's Philosophy." In S. Morgenbesser and J. H. Walsh, eds. 1962. *Free Will*. Englewood Cliffs, NJ: Prentice Hall: 57–69.

Milton, John. (1955). *Paradise Lost*. London: Methuen.

Moore, G. E. 1912. "Free Will." In *Ethics*. Oxford: Oxford University Press: 291–8.

Morgenbesser, Sidney and J. H. Walsh, eds., 1962. *Free Will*. Englewood Cliffs, NJ: Prentice Hall.

Nagel, Thomas. 1986. *The View From Nowhere*. New York: Oxford University Press.

Narveson, Jan. 1977. "Compatibilism Defended." *Philosophical Studies* 32: 83–8.

Nathan, Nicholas. 1992. *Will and World*. Oxford: Oxford University Press.

Naylor, Margery Bedford. 1984. "Frankfurt on the Principle of Alternative Possibilities." *Philosophical Studies* 46: 249–58.

Nielsen, Kai. 1971. *Reason and Practice*. New York: Harper and Row.

Neely, Wright. 1974. "Freedom and Desire." *The Philosophical Review* 83: 32–54.

Nozick, Robert. 1981. *Philosophical Explanations*. Cambridge, MA: Harvard University Press.

Ockham, William. 1983. *Predestination, Foreknowledge, and Future Contingents*, 2nd edn. Trans. by Marilyn McCord Adams and Norman Kretzmann. Indianapolis, IN: Hackett.

O'Connor, Timothy. 1993. "Indeterminism and Free Agency: Three Recent Views." *Philosophy and Phenomenological Research* 53: 499–526.

O'Connor, Timothy. 1993a. "On the Transfer of Necessity." *Nous* 27: 204–18.

O'Connor, Timothy, ed., 1995. *Agents, Causes and Events: Essays on Free Will and Indeterminism*. Oxford: Oxford University Press.

O'Connor, Timothy. 2000. *Persons and Causes: The Metaphysics of Free Will*. New York: Oxford University Press.

O'Connor, Timothy. Forthcoming. "Libertarian Views: Dualist and Agent-Causal Theories." In Robert Kane, ed. *The Oxford Handbook on Free Will*. New York and Oxford: Oxford University Press.

Orwell, George, 1949. *1984*. London: Secker and Warburg.

O'Shaughnessy, Brian. 1980. *The Will*, 2 Vols. Cambridge, UK: Cambridge University Press.

Peacocke, Christopher. 1999. *Being Known*. Oxford: Clarendon Press.

Penrose, Roger. 1994. *Shadows of the Mind*. Oxford: Oxford University Press.

Penrose, Roger. 1989. *The Emperor's New Mind*. Oxford: Oxford University Press.

Pereboom, Derk. 2000. "Alternative Possibilities and Causal Histories." *Philosophical Perspectives* 14: 119–37.

Pereboom, Derk. 2001. *Living Without Free Will*. Cambridge, UK: Cambridge University Press.

Pettit, Phillip and Michael Smith. 1996. "Freedom In Belief and Desire." *Journal of Philosophy* 9: 429–49.

Pike, Nelson. 1965. "Divine Omniscience and Voluntary Action." *The Philosophical Review* 74: 27–46.

Pink, T. L. 1996. *The Psychology of Freedom*. Cambridge, UK: Cambridge University Press.

Plantinga, Alvin. 1986. "On Ockham's Way Out." *Faith and Philosophy* 3: 235–69.

Prigogine, I. and Stengers, I. 1984. *Order Out of Chaos*. New York: Bantam.

Reid, Thomas. 1969. *Essay on the Active Powers of the Human Mind*. Cambridge, MA: MIT Press.

Reid, Thomas. 1983. *The Works of Thomas Reid*. Ed. by W. Hamilton. Hildeshein: George Ulm Verlag.

Rowe, William. 1987. "Two Concepts of Freedom." Presidential Address. *Proceedings of the American Philosophical Association* 62: 43–64. Reprinted in T. O'Connor, ed., 1995. *Agents, Causes and Events*. Oxford: Oxford University Press: 151–72.

Rowe, William. 1991. *Thomas Reid On Freedom and Morality*. Ithaca, NY: Cornell University Press.

Rumi, Jalalu'ddin. 1956. *Rumi, Poet and Mystic*. Trans. and ed. by R. A Nicholson. London: George Allen & Unwin.

Russell, Paul. 1995. *Freedom and Moral Sentiment*. New York: Oxford University Press.

Ryle, Gilbert. 1949. *Concept of Mind*. London: Hutchinson.

Schlick, Moritz. 1966. "When is a Man Responsible?" In B. Berofsky, ed. *Free Will and Determinism*. New York: Harper and Row: 54–62.

Schoeman, F., ed., 1987. *Responsibility, Character and Emotions*. Cambridge, UK: Cambridge University Press.

Scott, George P., ed., 1991. *Time, Rhythms and Chaos in the New Dialogue With Nature*. Ames, IA: Iowa State University Press.

Scott, George P., and Michael McMillen, eds., 1980. *Dissipative Structures and Spatiotemporal Organization Studies in Biomedical Research*. Ames, IA: Iowa State University Press.

Shatz, David. 1985. "Free Will and the Structure of Motivation." *Midwest Studies in Philosophy* 10: 451–82.

Shatz, David. 1988. "Compatibilism, Values and 'Could Have Done Otherwise.'" *Philosophical Topics* 16: 151–200.

Skarda, C. and W. Freeman. 1987. "How the Brain Makes Chaos in Order to Make Sense of the World." *Behavioral and Brain Sciences* 10: 161–95.

Skinner, B. F. [1948] 1962. *Walden Two*. New York: Macmillan.

Skinner, B. F. 1971. *Beyond Freedom and Dignity*. New York: Vintage Books.

Slote, Michael. 1980. "Understanding Free Will." *Journal of Philosophy* 77: 136–51.

Slote, Michael. 1982. "Selective Necessity and the Free Will Problem." *Journal of Philosophy* 79: 5–24.

Smilansky, Saul. 2000. *Free Will and Illusion*. Oxford: Clarendon Press.

Sobel, Jordan Howard. 1998. *Puzzles for the Will*. Toronto: University of Toronto Press.

Sorabji, Richard. 1980. *Necessity, Cause and Blame: Perspectives on Aristotle's Philosophy*. Ithaca, NY: Cornell University Press.

Speak, Daniel. 1999. "Fischer and Avoidability: A Reply to Widerker and Katzoff." *Faith and Philosophy* 16: 239–47.

Spitzer, Manfred. 1999. *The Mind Within the Net*. Cambridge, MA: MIT Press.

Stapp, Henry P. 1993. *Mind, Matter and Quantum Mechanics*. New York: Springer Verlag.

Strawson, Galen. 1986. *Freedom and Belief*. Oxford: Oxford University Press.

Strawson, Galen. 1994. "The Impossibility of Moral Responsibility." *Philosophical Studies* 75: 5–24.

Strawson, Galen. 2000. "The Unhelpfulness of Indeterminism." *Philosophy and Phenomenological Research* 60: 149–56.

Strawson, Peter F. 1959. *Individuals: An Essay in Descriptive Metaphysics*. London: Methuen.

Strawson, Peter F. 1962. "Freedom and Resentment." *Proceedings of the British Academy* 48: 1–25. Reprinted in J. M. Fischer and M. Ravizza, eds., 1998. *Perspectives on Moral Responsibility*. Ithaca, NY: Cornell University Press: 45–66.

Stump, Eleonore. 1990. "Intellect, Will, and the Principle of Alternative Possibilities." In M. Beaty, ed. *Christian Theism and the Problems of Philosophy*. Notre Dame, IN: Notre Dame University Press: 254–85.

Stump, Eleonore. 1996. "Libertarian Freedom and the Principle of Alternative Possibilities." In D. Howard-Snyder and J. Jordan, eds. *Faith, Freedom, and Rationality*. Lanham, MD: Rowman and Littlefield: 73–88.

Stump, Eleonore. 1999a. "Alternative Possibilities and Moral Responsibility: The Flicker of Freedom." *Journal of Ethics* 3: 299–324.

Stump, Eleonore. 1999b. "Dust, Determinism and Frankfurt: A Reply to Goetz." *Faith and Philosophy* 16: 413–22.

Stump, Eleonore and Norman Kretzmann. 1991. "Prophecy, Past Truth, and Eternity." *Philosophical Perspectives* 5: 395–424.

Swanton, Christine. 1992. *Freedom: A Coherence Theory*. Indianapolis, IN: Hackett.

Swinburne, Richard. 1986. *The Evolution of the Soul*. Oxford: Clarendon Press.
Swinburne, Richard. 1989. *Responsibility and Atonement*. Oxford: Clarendon Press.
Talbott, Thomas. 1988. "On Free Agency and the Concept of Power." *Pacific Philosophical Quarterly* 69: 241–54.
Talbott, Thomas. 1993. "Theological Fatalism and Modal Confusion." *International Journal for Philosophy of Religion* 33: 65–88.
Taylor, Charles. 1982. "Responsibility for Self." In G. Watson, ed. *Free Will*. Oxford: Oxford University Press: 111–26.
Taylor, Richard. 1966. *Action and Purpose*. Englewood Cliffs, NJ: Prentice Hall.
Thornton, Mark. 1990. *Do We Have Free Will?* New York: St. Martin's Press.
Thorp, John. 1980. *Free Will: A Defense Against Neurophysiological Determinism*. London: Routledge & Kegan Paul.
Trusted, Jennifer. 1984. *Free Will and Responsibility*. Oxford: Oxford University Press.
van Inwagen, Peter. 1975. "The Incompatibility of Free Will and Determinism." *Philosophical Studies* 27: 185–99.
van Inwagen, Peter. 1983. *An Essay on Free Will*. Oxford: Clarendon Press.
Velleman, J. David. 1992. "What Happens when Someone Acts?" *Mind* 101: 461–81.
Vivhelin, Kadri. 1988. "The Modal Argument for Incompatibilism." *Philosophical Studies* 53: 227–44.
Wallace, R. Jay. 1994. *Responsibility and the Moral Sentiments*. Cambridge, MA: Harvard University Press.
Waller, Bruce. 1990. *Freedom Without Responsibility*. Philadelphia: Temple University Press.
Walter, Henrik. 2001. *Neurophilosophy of Free Will*. Cambridge, MA: MIT Press.
Warfield, Ted. 1996. "Determinism and Moral Responsibility are Incompatible." *Philosophical Topics* 24: 215–26.
Watson, Gary. 1975. "Free Agency." *Journal of Philosophy* 72: 205–20. Reprinted in and cited from Watson, ed., 1982. *Free Will*. Oxford: Oxford University Press: 96–110.
Watson, Gary, ed. 1982. *Free Will*. Oxford: Oxford University Press.
Watson, Gary. 1987. "Responsibility and the Limits of Evil: Variations on a Strawsonian Theme." In F. Schoeman, ed. *Responsibility, Character and Emotions*. Cambridge, UK: Cambridge University Press: 256–88.
Weatherford, Roy. 1991. *The Implications of Determinism*. London: Routledge.
Widerker, David. 1987. "On an Argument for Incompatibilism." *Analysis* 47: 37–41.
Widerker, David. 1995a. "Libertarianism and Frankfurt's Attack on the Principle of Alternative Possibilities." *The Philosophical Review* 104: 247–61.
Widerker, David. 1995b. "Libertarian Freedom and the Avoidability of Decisions." *Faith and Philosophy* 12: 113–18.
Widerker, David. 2000. "Frankfurt's Attack on the Principle of Alternative Possibilities: A Further Look." *Philosophical Perspectives* 14: 181–202.

Widerker, David and Charlotte Katzoff. 1996. "Avoidability and Libertarianism: A Response to Fischer." *Faith and Philosophy* 13: 415–21.

Widerker, David and Michael McKenna, eds., 2002. *Freedom, Responsibility and Agency: Essays on the Importance of Alternative Possibilities.* Aldershot, UK: Ashgate Press.

Wiggins, David. 1973. "Towards a Reasonable Libertarianism." In T. Honderich, ed. *Essays on Freedom of Action.* London: Routledge & Kegan Paul: 31–61.

Williams, Clifford. 1980. *Free Will and Determinism.* Indianapolis, IN: Hackett.

Wolf, Susan. 1981. "The Importance of Free Will." *Mind* 90: 386–405.

Wolf, Susan. 1987. "Sanity and the Metaphysics of Responsibility." In F. Schoeman, ed. *Responsibility, Character and Emotions.* Cambridge, UK: Cambridge University Press: 45–64.

Wolf, Susan. 1990. *Freedom Within Reason.* Oxford: Oxford University Press.

Woody, J. Melvin. 1998. *Freedom's Embrace.* University Park, PA: University of Pennsylvania Press.

Wyma, Keith. 1997. "Moral Responsibility and the Leeway for Action." *American Philosophical Quarterly* 34: 57–70.

Zagzebski, Linda T. 1991. *The Dilemma of Freedom and Foreknowledge.* Oxford: Oxford University Press.

Zimmerman, David. 1981. "Hierarchical Motivation and the Freedom of the Will." *Pacific Philosophical Quarterly* 62: 354–68.

Zimmerman, Michael. 1989. *An Essay on Moral Responsibility.* Totowa, NJ: Rowman and Littlefield.

Index

CPSIA information can be obtained at www.ICGtesting.com
Printed in the USA
LVOW06s1328160713

342999LV00012B/265/P